The SLOW MEDITERRANEAN KITCHEN

The SLOW MEDITERRANEAN KITCHEN

Recipes for the Passionate Cook

PAULA WOLFERT

WILEY

John Wiley & Sons, Inc.

Portions of this book have appeared in somewhat different form in *Food & Wine* magazine, *Metropolitan Home, Gourmet, Saveur, Cooking, Fine Cooking,* and the *New York Times*. Pork and Orange-Flavored Beans is from Aglaia Kremezi's *The Foods of the Greeks Islands* (New York: Houghton Mifflin Company, 2000). Printed with permission. Oven-Baked Polenta first appeared as No-Stir Polenta in Paula Wolfert's *Mediterranean Grains & Greens* (New York: HarperCollins, 1998).

This book is printed on acid-free paper. ∞

Published by John Wiley & Sons, Inc., Hoboken, New Jersey
Published simultaneously in Canada

For general information on our other products and services or for technical support, please contact our Customer Care Department within the United States at (800) 762-2974, outside the United States at (317) 572-3993 or fax (317) 572-4002.

Wiley also publishes its books in a variety of electronic formats. Some content that appears in print may not be available in electronic books. For more information about Wiley products, visit our web site at www.wiley.com.

Photographs by Christopher Hirsheimer

Interior design by Joel Avirom and Jason Snyder

Library of Congress Cataloging-in-Publication Data:

Wolfert, Paula.
 The slow Mediterranean kitchen : recipes for the passionate cook /
Paula Wolfert.
   p. cm.
 ISBN 0-471-26288-9 (Cloth)
 I. Cookery, Mediterranean. I. Title.
 TX725.M35 W6434 2003
 641.59′1822--dc21

                      2002153265

Printed in the United States of America

10 9 8 7 6 5 4 3 2 1

To the Memory of Catherine Brandel
(1943–1999)

Her food was marvelous, always cooked with love,
and she had the kindest and most generous smile
I have ever seen on a human face.

CONTENTS

ACKNOWLEDGMENTS

One of my favorite things to do when I finish a book is to think back on all the wonderful people who have helped me. I consider myself very lucky to have met so many people who were willing to share their time and expertise, and I hope every one of them will find his or her name in the various lists below, arranged within each region.

The following people have helped me in major ways:

My husband, Bill Bayer—my best friend, resident taster, editor, and critic.

Chef Haouari Abderrazak, who shared his vast knowledge and insights regarding North African cooking.

Clara Maria de Amezua, who gave me invaluable guidance on Spanish cooking.

Aglaia Kremezi for her boundless enthusiam while sharing her love for and knowledge of Greek cooking.

Ayfer Unsal for her thoughtful assistance in teaching me so much about Turkish cooking.

Alice Waters for leading the way.

A special thank you to my editor at *Food & Wine* magazine, Tina Uljaki, for being so patient and encouraging. Thanks also to Editor-in-Chief Dana Cowin, for being so gracious, and to Marcia Kiesel and Grace Parisi for their careful testing and good advice.

I am sincerely grateful to my friends Dun Gifford and Sara Baer Sinnott of Oldways Preservation and Trust for opening the door to new ways to look at the world of food, and for providing valuable assistance and inspiration.

Thanks to Dr. Mazhar Unsal, Filiz Hösukoğlu, Yuksel Unal, Engin Akin, Dr. Ayşe Baysal, Hidayet Sahin, Arif Develi, Zeliha Güngören, Maviye Kayakiran, Surpuhi Karfun, and Bahriye Unal for their help on Turkish and Armenian cooking.

Thanks to Anne-Marie Weiss Armush, chef Greg Malouf, Samira Yago Cholagh, Nora George, and Susan Torgeson for their help on Middle Eastern cooking. Thanks to Janet Mendel, Lourdes March, Lola Massieu, Jose Guerra, Steve Winston, chefs Carlos Posadas, Alejandro Fernandez Gavilan and his wife, Nati, Bertha Gilberta Ivañez, Norberto Jorge, Jose Carrasco Jurado, Josep Lladonosa i Giro, Maria-Dolores Mejias, Carlos Oyabide, and Richard Stephens for their help on Spanish cooking.

Thanks to Diane Kochilas, Mirsini Lampraki, Lefteris Menegos, and the Music Dance Group of the Island of Paros, Niki Moquist, and chefs Stefanos Kovas and Lefteris Lazarou for their help on Greek and Cypriot Cooking. Also, special thanks to Dimitri and Cristina Pantemolitis for their hospitality, notes, and recipes.

Thanks to Faith Willinger, David Downie, Alison Harris, Fred Plotkin, Dario Cecchini, Luca Pusceddu, Puccio Fischetti, Franco Rossi, chefs Maria Luisa Fischetti, Patrizio Cirri, and Adolfo di'Martino for their help on Italian cooking.

Thanks to chefs Daniel Antoine, Jean-Charles Baron, Michel Bras, Francis Garcia, Alain Lorca, Laurent Manrique, the late Jean-Louis Palladin, Lucien Vanel, and Jean-Pierre Xiradakis for their help on French cooking.

Thanks to Rafih Benjelloun, Taieb Dridi, Fatima Hal, Houda Mokadmi, Mourad Lalhou, Zor Ouazzani, and Barbara Temsamani for their help on North African cooking.

I have been variously helped by the advice of the following listed here alphabetically: Jon and Barbara Beckmann, Eleanor Bertino, Diane Harris Brown, Daphne Derven, Dr. Adam Drewnowski, Aliza Green, Gael Greene, Barbara Haber, Suzanne Hamlin, Dana Jacobi, Niloufer King, Peggy Knickerbocker, Wendy Lane, Fran McCullough, Harold

McGee, Shelley Meneged, Sue Moore, Jim Poris, Hervé This, Patti Unterman, James Villas, Donna Warner, Robert Wolke, and Marilynne Wright.

My thanks also to the following chefs: Mary Canales, Jim Dodge, Kevin Gibson, Mark Gordon, Russell Moore, Jim Neal, Judy Rodgers, Joe Simone, and Ana Sortun.

I owe a particular debt to my agent, Susan Lescher, for her strength and steadfastness, and to her assistant Carolyn Larson, for her constant support.

I lift a glass to Susan Wyler for her fine editing, determination, and friendship in making this book what it is.

I offer special thanks to designers Joel Avirom and Jason Snyder, senior production editor Andrea Johnson, and copyeditor Virginia McRae. I am sincerely grateful to photographer Christopher Hirsheimer and to food stylist Julia Lee for enhancing these pages with such beautiful photographs.

INTRODUCTION

I take great pleasure in preparing food from scratch. There's just *something* about slowly cooked food—meats turning tender and succulent, fruits and vegetables flavorful and satiny—that appeals to me. In this frantic cyber-age, when everything happens so fast and events occur at blinding speeds, the slow approach to food preparation helps me to ground myself. Not only does such food taste delicious, it is also relaxing and pleasurable to make.

I have written six books about Mediterranean cooking as a way of experiencing the Mediterranean lifestyle. Mediterranean lands have changed over the years. Today the friendly but voluptuous eating experiences I have extolled in book after book are not always that easy to find. Yet I continue to seek them out because they represent the Mediterranean of my dreams, the Mediterranean I cherish, the Mediterranean I have mythologized.

> *Perfection is attained by slow degrees;*
> *it requires the hand of time.*
> —VOLTAIRE

The Slow Mediterranean Kitchen is my attempt to recapture the feeling of that lifestyle, offering recipes to the home cook whereby she or he may find a measure of contentment in preparing a fine dish, then serving it to family and friends. Some may apply the terms "comfort food" and "homey food" to my recipes for the North African *tagine,* French *ragout,* Spanish *estofado,* Italian *brasato,* and eastern Mediterranean *guvech.* I just think of these stews as "slow-cooked" for the way they allow me to enjoy the process of creating them, the sensuality of my results, and the revitalization that occurs when I take deep pleasure in my cooking.

Yes, fast cooking can be exciting, but it is also stressful and exacting. A few seconds off, and you can ruin a dish. Slow-cooking is relaxing and also more forgiving, since there's usually a decent margin of error. Of course we must pay attention when doing any type of cooking, but with slow-cooking we needn't constantly check the clock.

Slow-cooking is ancient, the way food was prepared when humans first began to cook. I find something very earthy and "connecting" when I execute slow-cooked dishes—a connection to the grand tradition of cookery, to hundreds of generations of cooks from the past, perhaps even resonating to some aspect of the cosmic process that envelops us in our hurried contemporary world.

Please think for a moment about the word *slow.* There is more to it in regard to cooking than may at first be apparent. For example, the simple act of salting meat, then leaving it overnight to age a little and develop flavor is "slow." Combining ingredients the day before so that their flavors will blend is "slow." Brining and marinating are "slow." Pickling and curing are "slow." Allowing a roast or a whole fish to rest after being cooked so the juices can work themselves through the meat is slow cooking, too. Even the simple act of leaving bread out on the counter to turn stale for use in cooking is "slow."

The ancient Greek philosopher Heraclitus famously proclaimed, *"panta rei"*—"everything flows." The most common interpretation goes something like: "You can't stick your foot into the same river twice." In regard to cooking, you can think of this phrase as meaning that no matter what you do, every time you cook a dish, it will come out a little differently. Usually the differences are inadvertent, due to such things as quality of ingredients and temperament of the cook.

But for me, *panta rei* has a deeper meaning when applied to the kitchen. I hope you will think of my recipes here as "flowing" recipes—the slow transformation of taste over time. For example, in my Stop-and-Go Braised Oxtails with Oyster Mushrooms, I employ multiple timed reductions while deglazing the bottom of the pan with vinegar and mushroom-soaking water to develop a rich complex sauce. In my Fall-Apart Lamb Shanks with Almond-Chocolate Picada, the long, lazy cooking transforms the rather ordinary shanks into meat that is plump

THE SLOW FOOD MOVEMENT

This book was not sponsored by the official Slow Food movement, but we share much in common, and, in fact, I am a member and juror of Slow Food USA (see membership information below).

Much has been written about the Slow Food movement. For those who have missed the articles, here is a brief summary: Slow Food was founded in 1986 by Italian journalist Carlo Petrini in reaction to a plan to build a McDonald's on the Spanish Steps in Rome. Thus from the start there was a tinge of antiglobalization to the project. But Slow Food soon became far more than a response to an American fast food chain outlet. It quickly encompassed a host of other issues having to do with food and the frantic pace of modern life. Slow food champions biodiversity and ecology, homemade and handmade food products, regionalism in food production, slow careful cooking and slow eating, the conviviality of the table, taking pleasure in living as well as eating, taking time, in the proverbial phrase, to smell the roses.

It also stands against everything contrary to the above: genetically modified food products, standardization of food and food products, loss of regionalism, environmental degradation, eating too fast, living too fast, and the loss of the table as meeting place for family and friends. In short, I humbly believe that the principles behind Slow Food could be the manifesto for this book.

If you feel sympathy with these principles, then I urge you to join Slow Food. There are numerous local chapters (called *convivia*) in the United States, so there is probably one near where you live. Membership includes a subscription to the magazine *Slow* and access to dinners and numerous other activities. Visit www.slowfood.com on the Internet for further information.

and delicious. In my Braised Veal Stuffed with Green Olives, slow gentle cooking in a small amount of liquid develops intense flavor with a minimum amount of handwork.

With slow-cooking, food products slowly mutate, flowing from one form into another. Quick grilling and sautéing also transform products, but the transformation is rapid. With slow cooking we can feel it happening, as wonderful aromas start floating through the house, exciting our appetites and creating a mood preparatory to our sitting down together to enjoy a meal.

To sum up, let me say that this is a book for people who truly enjoy cooking. It's for those days when you really feel like being in the kitchen, want to handcraft a dish without feeling rushed, want to enjoy the sensuality of food preparation and the special joy of serving dishes that will give pleasure to others.

THE RECIPES

Some of the recipes here are super simple, others are user-friendly, and a few are fairly demanding. Think of these harder recipes as adventures, jigsaw puzzles, if you will. You may not want to make them every day, but hopefully you will enjoy completing the "puzzle." And please note that I am careful before I offer a recipe that requires serious work, wanting to be certain that the cook's hard labor will be well paid off. By the same token, if a recipe calls for relatively unusual ingredients that may require special ordering or be difficult to find, I again make a special point of assuring myself the effort will be worth it.

When people ask me to name my favorites among the many recipes I have written, I counter with a question of my own: "How much time do you have?" If you are in a hurry, there's a whole range of recipes I recommend. But if you want to enjoy the process of cooking, then I recommend the kind of recipes I offer here.

There are many slow recipes in my other books, but this is the first time I have fastened upon "slow" as a theme. If you don't find versions of some of your favorites here, please look at my other books where there are hundreds more.

You won't actually save time preparing these dishes. Meats still must be browned, vegetables peeled, sauces thickened. And, no, you can't abandon your high standards just because your cooking will be slow. But part of slow-cooking means cooking at your convenience. You do the prep work in advance, then put the pot in a slow oven and let the magic do its work. Your joy comes from the process and also from the results.

All the recipes here are from my fieldwork. Many come from Mediterranean home cooks, city and village women who have welcomed me into their kitchens. Others come from professional chefs or from colleagues, fellow researchers.

You may find recipes that you know in other quicker versions, and may wonder why I have chosen to present them here in slow form. Often the reason has to do with special details I learned on my travels, such as soaking dried porcini with a pinch of sugar for several hours in order to build intensity of flavor.

Slow-cooking doesn't necessarily mean putting a lot of stuff together in an electric slow-cooker, then leaving it to cook for hours. Often I ask you to add ingredients at different times along the way, so that everything comes together at the end. Occasionally I ask you to start your cooking cold (*cuisson à froid,* as the French say)—in cold rather than heated oil so that the aromatics flavor the oil without searing the food, which allows the oil, in turn, to transfer its tastes to the other ingredients. In one recipe I even suggest that you start cooking a chicken in a cold oven so that the flesh will slowly dry out while it soaks in the flavorings as the oven warms, resulting in a particularly rich-flavored dish.

With slow cooking the size, age, and quality of a vegetable, bird, or a piece of meat will have much to do with the cooking time. Of course I offer timings with each recipe, but I have also made an effort in my notes to help you see or smell when a dish is done.

There are just a few extra items of equipment you may need if you are serious about cooking slow. One is a good probe thermometer. Another is a sturdy heavy-bottomed pot. Earthenware and heavy iron pots are perfect for slow-cooked Mediterranean recipes.

Every Mediterranean country has great dishes. But with food as with other things, life isn't fair—some countries offer many more than others. My choices in this regard are always personal. In my travels I search out dishes that I love, then try to work out ways of reproducing them at home. Some, I find, simply can't be reproduced, or turn out not to be as good as I

KITCHEN PERFORMANCE ANXIETY

One extra benefit of slow-cooking is the way it can help us deal with "kitchen performance anxiety."

What is KPA? British food writer Terri Judd defines it as the severe stress felt by a home cook who feels she or he cannot possibly perform to the exacting standards of television cooking personalities who create fast gorgeous meals on TV. Judd goes on to say that as a result of KPA, the dinner party "is becoming a declining pastime with fewer Brits choosing to take on the pressures of entertaining." She cites a poll in which 61 percent of those interviewed considered hosting a dinner party a more anxious experience than attending a job interview or going out on a first date. She further cites a study by David Warbutron, professor of psychology at the University of Reading, who reported symptoms of KPA ranging from freezing up to rapid heartbeat, nausea, and headaches!

Well, we can't all produce stunning food with the facility of those chefs on television, but slow cooking can greatly help us to cope with KPA. In my recipes, most of the kitchen work may be accomplished at a leisurely pace in advance, obviating the necessity for stressful, last minute performance while grounding the cook by allowing her to partake in a relaxing, joyful, creative process.

---

thought at first taste. No matter how authentic and promising a dish is, if it doesn't prove to "have legs," I jettison it without regret.

Authenticity is always my guide, but I try not to let it become my straitjacket. In most regional recipes there's plenty of wiggle room. I try to find the best recipe for every dish I offer. Thus many recipes here are my personal adaptations, yet they are always rooted in something real I tasted on my Mediterranean travels.

The famous cookbook author and *New York Times* restaurant critic Craig Claiborne once wrote: "Cooking is at once one of the simplest and most gratifying of the arts, but to cook well one must love and respect food." To me this means buying the best products you can find, and then using them as quickly as possible. You know what savvy real estate agents say about real estate? "Location, location, location!" Similarly, I say about cooking: "Ingredients, ingredients, ingredients!"

The wonderful thing about slow-cooking is that it can bring out the best in your ingredients. Some people fall back on slow-cooking to revitalize or add flavor to foods past their prime. Slow-cooking will usually do this, but I disapprove of this approach. The best slow-cooked dishes (like the best fast-cooked ones) are those that start with the finest ingredients. Please, when following these recipes, try to use only the best.

APPETIZERS

BRUSCHETTAS AND OTHER TOASTS

To my mind, creating stale bread—by leaving it out on the counter to dry so as to acquire texture and absorbency—is the most relaxed form of slow cooking around the Mediterranean. Dry or stale bread is the foundation of numerous gastronomical inspirations. Its very plainness makes it a perfect starting point for culinary creativity, an essential ingredient in appetizers that include *crostini, bruschettas,* and *croutes.* Stale bread with or without crust, slowly grilled, deep fried, or oven baked, served cool, warm, or hot, is the underpinning for a huge assortment of Mediterranean appetizers. A slice of most any kind of dense flavorful bread can become a canvas upon which to paint any number of toppings or dips. Some may be eaten with your hands, while others should be served with a knife and fork.

Appetizers made with stale bread are delicious and easy. All you really need is one excellent topping. The toppings on pages 14 to 24 can be served on stale bread and also as dips if so specified.

The Bread Thick slices of dense day-old bread are great for grilling. Always use a quality bread: some breads made with preservatives will never properly turn stale. And if bread is too stale, it probably won't be useful in toppings or dips.

Grill ¾-inch-thick slices of somewhat stale country bread over coals or on a ridged grill pan. Just rub the warm aromatic slices with garlic, then top with a smear of fresh tomato, tapenade, or ham, and you'll have . . . pure heaven. Grilled bread, still warm, brings out the aroma of garlic and the fruity taste of extra virgin olive oil. The cleverness of such dishes (bruschettas, etc.,) resides in their simplicity.

An alternative to grilling slices of slightly stale bread is to toast them in a 375°F oven until lightly golden, about 12 minutes.

Slice semi-stale baguettes on the diagonal into thin ¼-inch slices for Italian crostini and French croutes.

Dense chewy breads, semolina breads, and brioche are best sliced ¼ inch thick, toasted, then used the same day. Thin Middle Eastern pita bread is cut into triangles, toasted, then used crisp for dipping into mezes or as a base for the Middle Eastern bread salad *fattoush*. Crisp triangles can be stored in an airtight bin for several days.

No stale bread in the house? Place some chunks or slices of good bread in a slow oven until the surface dries out. To enhance with a lightly charred flavor, broil or grill slowly until dry to the touch, but be sure to stop before the slices turn hard.

Finally, try to avoid topping your bread too far in advance lest the bread turn soggy.

YESTERDAY'S BREAD

Mediterranean cooks slip chunks of stale bread into a vegetable casserole, such as the *panade* on page 80, or into a soup such as the Tuscan bread soup on page 82. They cube bread for stuffing or to fry into croutons for salads and soups, and as an enrichment for stews. They grate the crumbs for coatings or thickeners for sauces, or to lighten dumplings and meatballs. Stale bread is used, too, in numerous Mediterranean sweets: French toast, Spanish *torrijas*, Sicilian *budino*, and Turkish cherry bread pudding.

Marinated Summer Tomato Bruschetta

*I*n the summer I like to binge on tomatoes and bread, particularly Catalan *pa y tomate*—a slice of bread grilled on a ridged iron pan, then rubbed hard with half a ripe tomato. The warm bread soaks up the tomato water and liberates its amazing flavor. I sprinkle on some coarse sea salt and a good drizzle of unfiltered fruity extra virgin olive oil. The result is pure heaven!

For an easy summer lunch, I often make this variation: a slice of dense bread is grilled, then topped with chopped tomatoes and left to mellow with seasonings for several hours at room temperature. This simple dish relies on careful dicing, fragrant herbs, fine oil, and the exuding tomato water all working together. Use only the very best summer tomatoes, and be sure to leave long enough (3 to 4 hours) for the combination to marinate and thoroughly blend. Remember: It's this slow melding that really makes the dish.

SERVES 2

½ pound red ripe tomatoes

1 garlic clove, finely chopped

2 pinches of dried Italian oregano
  or marjoram

Pinch of crushed hot red pepper

1 tablespoon extra virgin olive oil

Salt and freshly ground pepper

8 slices of day-old, dense bread or baguette,
  cut ½ inch thick and lightly grilled

1. Peel, seed, and finely dice the tomatoes. Mix with the garlic, oregano, hot pepper, and olive oil. Allow to stand at room temperature for 3 to 4 hours.

2. Just before serving, smear about 2 tablespoons of the tomato mixture on each slice of grilled bread, season with salt and pepper, and dribble with a little olive oil.

Note: When tomatoes are firm but ripe, peel by piercing the core with a long-handled knife, then placing the tomato over a gas flame until the skin blisters on all sides. Then peel, seed, and dice as directed.

Slow-Roasted Mushroom and Garlic Bruschetta

*H*ere's an easy way to prepare large portobello mushrooms. By slow-roasting them whole, you retain their flavor and fine creamy texture. Because they are so spongy, I never marinate them. I simply slice them the minute they come out of the oven, then fan the slices on a slice of garlic-rubbed grilled bread. The mushroom juices seep into the bread, creating a perfect snack.

SERVES 6

3 medium-large portobello mushrooms, stemmed

2 sprigs of rosemary

2 tablespoons extra virgin olive oil

6 slices of stale country-style bread, cut ¾ inch thick

1 garlic clove, halved

Salt and freshly ground pepper

Dash of aged balsamic vinegar

1 tablespoon chopped flat-leaf parsley

1. Preheat the oven to 450°F.

2. Place the portobello mushrooms upside down on a lightly oiled baking sheet and lay the sprigs of rosemary over them. Brush the mushrooms with olive oil and roast for 20 minutes.

3. Meanwhile, grill the bread and rub with garlic.

4. Transfer the mushrooms to a plate and let cool for 5 minutes before slicing. Season the mushrooms with salt and pepper. Scrape any mushroom juices into a bowl and use to moisten the bread. Pile the mushrooms on top of the bread, sprinkle with vinegar and parsley, and serve warm.

Note: Since mushrooms are full of water, roasting them keeps in the moisture. Be careful not to salt until ready to slice and serve.

Crostini with Sardinian Caviar, Tomato, and Celery

*S*ardinian *bottarga,* or mullet roe, should be treated like truffles—you only need a little to make a great dish, but the more the better. The bottarga is marinated in olive oil to soften its texture. For an ultimate food experience, slice bottarga at the last minute over pasta, white beans, risotto, or scrambled eggs. This bottarga recipe was given to me by Luca, the owner of the Duomo Libreria in Iglesias, Sardinia. This is the way his mother prepared crostini with bottarga at home.

SERVES 4

1½ ounces mullet bottarga

Extra virgin olive oil

Half a day-old baguette, cut into 12 slices
    ¼ inch thick

8 cherry tomatoes

2 celery ribs

2 tablespoons chopped flat-leaf parsley

Salt and freshly ground pepper

Juice of ½ lemon

2 tablespoons unsalted butter, softened to
    room temperature

1. Use a swivel-bladed vegetable peeler to cut the mullet bottarga into very thin slices. Soak in olive oil until ready to use.

2. Lightly brush the bread slices with olive oil. Toast on a sheet pan in a 375°F oven, turning once, until golden, about 8 minutes.

3. Just before serving, peel, halve, seed, and dice the tomatoes. String the celery. Using a mandoline, slice the celery into paper-thin strips.

4. In a bowl, combine the bottarga, tomato, celery, and parsley. Add a pinch of salt, a good sprinkling of pepper, and the lemon juice; toss gently. Butter the bread slices, top with the bottarga mixture, and serve.

Note: Please do not substitute grated bottarga in this recipe.

SARDINIAN CAVIAR: BOTTARGA DI MUGGINE

Bottarga di muggine is a form of pressed and dried grey mullet roe produced in Spain, Sardinia, Greece, France, Turkey, and Tunisia and often sold covered with paraffin or some type of shrink wrapping.

While Sicilian bottarga made from tuna roe is salty, sharp, and pungent, good-quality grey mullet bottarga is mellow and almond flavored. It is also usually less salty than tuna bottarga and may require some additional seasoning.

When bottarga di muggine is moist, it is amber in color. It turns dark as it ages or as a result of overchilling. It has a defined shelf life, so be sure to check the date. Once a package is open, keep it well wrapped and use within the week.

You can purchase moist slabs of Sardinian bottarga di muggine from a good Italian market or over the Internet (see Mail Order Sources).

The word *bottarga* comes from an Arabic word *bot/ah/rik*, which means "raw fish eggs." Bottarga in slabs is a wonderful product. In the near future don't be surprised to find not only slabs of Sardinian bottarga, but Spanish *huevo de Mujol*, Greek *avogotarha*, French *poutargue*, Tunisian *botarga*, and Turkish *kaviar* at high-end specialty stores in your area.

Knife-and-Fork Tuscan Kale Bruschetta

*I*n winter, when Tuscan kale (also called Tuscan black kale, lacinata kale, or dinosaur kale) is available, I fry it in olive oil until it wilts, then cook it slowly until tender in a covered pan. The liquid and the greens are then piled on a piece of grilled bread and served hot. You can prepare the greens in advance and reheat them just before serving.

SERVES 4

1 bunch of Tuscan kale (about 8 ounces)

¼ cup extra virgin olive oil

2 garlic cloves

Salt and freshly ground pepper

A few drops of balsamic vinegar or a pinch of crushed hot red pepper

8 slices of day-old, dense country bread, cut ¾ inch thick

¼ cup coarsely shredded pecorino Romano cheese

Extra virgin olive oil, for drizzling, preferably *olio nuovo*

1. Wash the kale and strip the leaves from the stems; cut the leaves crosswise into 1-inch ribbons. Place in a wide saucepan, add 2 tablespoons of the olive oil, half the garlic, and the salt and pepper to taste. Cook gently until the greens are wilted, about 10 minutes.

2. Add 1 cup water, cover partially, and cook until the kale is tender, 20 to 30 minutes. Remove the cover and boil until almost all the liquid is evaporated and the leaves are juicy and glistening. Add vinegar or hot pepper to taste.

3. Lightly grill the bread on a heated grid and rub each piece of bread with the remaining garlic. Place some of the greens on top of each slice. Sprinkle a tablespoon of cheese and a drizzle of additional oil over each. Serve warm.

Avocado-Sardine Toasts

Avocados have been available to cooks in the Mediterranean since the sixteenth century, when Cortès brought them back from the New World. It was in Catalonia where I first tasted this simple dish, a combination of silky, paper-thin slices of ripe avocado and marinated fat strips of salty sardine fillets topped with crisp strings of scallions and chives, which makes for a great textural contrast—easy to duplicate and hard to forget.

The combination is based on a dish from the Canary Islands, but the brilliant execution is the work of the legendary master chef Ferran Adrià, famous for his culinary innovations, which include the use of foams, gelatinized liquid, and savory lollipops.

SERVES 4 TO 6

4 tablespoons extra virgin olive oil

2 tablespoons chopped flat-leaf parsley

1 scant tablespoon sherry wine vinegar

Salt and freshly ground pepper

2 cans (4½ ounces each) Portuguese whole sardines packed in olive oil

1 large firm, ripe Hass avocado

4 to 6 day-old, thin slices of country-style bread

4 scallions (white part only), cut lengthwise into thin strips about 1 inch long

Fresh chives

1. Make a parsley vinaigrette by whisking together the olive oil with the parsley and vinegar in a medium bowl. Season with salt and pepper to taste.

2. Drain the sardines, divide into fillets, and soak in the vinaigrette for at least 1 hour. For easier slicing, chill the avocado in the refrigerator for 1 hour.

3. Using a mandoline or a 1mm slicing blade, carefully slice the avocado paper-thin. Remove the skin and pit as you slice.

4. Grill the bread, turning once on a grill over hot coals or under the broiler until nicely browned on both sides. Drain the sardine fillets and lightly brush the toasts with the vinaigrette.

5. Pile 3 or 4 slices of avocado onto each toast, top with a portion of the sardines, and scatter scallions and a few chives on top. Serve at once.

Spicy Roasted Vegetable and Tuna Canapés

*H*ere, earthy caramelized vegetables, chunks of oil-packed tuna, tiny cubes of Gruyère-type cheese, and pitted chopped olives are mixed and piled on a small baguette slice. It's the treatment of the bread slice that makes this dish so special. First it's dipped on one side only in a spicy liquid; only then is the well-blended topping added.

The best rendition of this Tunisian dish occurs when the cook allows all the roasted chopped vegetables to drain overnight. This slow draining creates intense flavor. The preserved oily vegetable drippings are blended with a dose of fiery hot sauce, to be used as the dipping medium for the bread.

SERVES 8 TO 10; MAKES ABOUT 2 DOZEN CANAPES

1 red bell pepper

2 small Italian frying peppers

2 large, firm red ripe tomatoes

2 large garlic cloves, unpeeled

3½ ounces tuna, packed in oil

1 tablespoon small Spanish salt-cured capers, soaked and drained

½ cup finely diced Gruyère cheese

1 teaspoon pulverized dried mint

1 teaspoon ground caraway seeds

2 pinches of ground coriander

2 tablespoons extra virgin olive oil

½ teaspoon red chile sauce, such as homemade *harissa,* Indonesian *sambal oelek,* or Turkish red pepper sauce (see Mail Order Sources)

1 tablespoon cider or rice vinegar

Salt

2 hard-cooked eggs

18 niçoise-type olives

2 tablespoons chopped cilantro

1 day-old baguette, cut into 24 thin slices

1. Preheat the oven to 400°F. Arrange the bell pepper, frying peppers, tomatoes, and garlic on a baking sheet. Roast until soft and tender, about 30 minutes.

2. Remove the vegetables; peel, seed, core, and dice the tomatoes. Peel, and crush the garlic. Place the vegetables and garlic in a plastic colander set over a bowl. Let drain in a cool place or in the refrigerator overnight. Be sure to reserve the juices that collect underneath.

3. The following day, drain the tuna and crumble into a bowl. Rinse and drain the capers. Add the capers, roasted vegetables, cheese, mint, caraway, and coriander to the tuna.

4. Combine ½ cup of the drained vegetable juices with the olive oil, chile sauce, vinegar, and salt to taste. If necessary add a little more of the juices to thin the dressing.

5. Peel the eggs, halve lengthwise, and thinly slice. Rinse, pit, and slice the olives. Gently toss the eggs and olives with the cilantro, cover with plastic wrap, and set aside, if necessary, for up to 30 minutes.

6. Just before serving, dip the bread slices, on one side only for just a few seconds, into the prepared harissa dressing. Arrange wet side-up on a serving plate. Spoon a small amount of the prepared vegetable-tuna mixture onto each slice. Top with a little of the egg-olive mixture and serve at once.

Variation: Tunisian Bread Salad

Tunisian cooks make a version of the Greek *riganatha* or the Italian *panzanella* with stale bread and the same topping as above. It's called *bahriya,* and it is delicious. Dice the bread, toss with the prepared harissa dressing, place on a serving dish, top with the roasted vegetables, cheese, tuna, and olives and toss again; garnish with eggs and capers and serve.

French Croutes with Onion Jam and Scrambled Eggs

*I*n southwest France, slices of dense baguette, thinly cut on the diagonal, are called *croutes*. Such slices are the perfect size to hold this incredibly savory topping. Needless to say, eating it requires a knife and fork.

This dish is a creation of Lucien Vanel, a former two-star chef from Toulouse, now retired. Typical of his cooking, it reveals his keen talent for contrasting textures and flavors. Here, crumbly bits of cooked black sausage and a dollop of long-simmered onions stud the creamy scrambled eggs.

Vanel taught me to scramble eggs in a small pan set in a larger one filled with simmering water to achieve the appropriate creaminess. (A double boiler gets too hot.) The trick is to undercook the eggs, then allow them to finish cooking off the fire in their receding heat. "If they look done," Vanel told me, "then they're already overcooked."

Combine the topping and the croutes at the last minute.

SERVES 6 TO 8; MAKES 24

2 ounces finely diced meaty salt pork

¾ pound red onions, finely sliced to make about 2 cups

Pinch of sugar

Freshly ground pepper

6 eggs

3 tablespoons butter

¼ cup crème fraîche

Salt

24 thin slices of day-old baguette, thinly sliced on the diagonal

1 small black sausage, sliced and fried until crusty and crumbly (½ cup), optional

1. Cook the salt pork in a small Dutch oven, covered, over low heat until lightly browned, about 10 minutes. Add the red onions and sugar, cover, and cook over low heat, stirring from time to time, for 1 hour, or until the onions are a pale golden reddish-brown and very soft. If necessary, add a few drops of water to produce a spreadable marmalade consistency. Season well with pepper. (*The onion jam can be prepared up to 4 days in advance. Keep covered in the refrigerator.*)

2. Break the eggs into a bowl. Add the crème fraîche and beat until well combined. Place the butter in a small saucepan in a larger pot of simmering water. Add the eggs and cook, stirring, until they are barely cooked and soft and smooth, 5 to 10 minutes. Take the 2 pans off the heat and allow the eggs to finish cooking in the receding heat. Season with salt and pepper.

3. Spoon the eggs onto the bread. Top with a spoonful of onion jam and a good pinch of crumbled black sausage, if you have it. Serve at once.

Dips and Spreads

Slow-Steamed Fava Spread with Cumin and Paprika

*F*ava beans are never out of season, since you can always find them either fresh, dried, frozen, or canned, with recipes available for each type. Early summer farmers' markets will have the best selection of fresh, young favas.

In Turkey, in early spring, when fava beans first come into the market, they are cooked in their skins and pods. Turkish cooks simply cut the stringless immature favas into 1-inch lengths and soak them in acidulated salted water for 10 minutes to soften the exteriors. Then they stew them in olive oil and eat them whole as a cold appetizer.

An Italian-born Sonoma-based vendor of organic vegetables taught me a method of steaming beans in their pods and then peeling off both the pod and the skins at the same time, which has become my favorite way of cooking them. The favas retain their beautiful bright green color, and the flavor is vibrant, intense, and bittersweet, though cooking time is a bit longer.

Many readers are probably familiar with Italian raw favas served with pecorino cheese, or Spanish lightly blanched favas served with ham and mint as a small appetizer. In this Moroccan version, the steaming method yields a succulent yet slightly mealy textured spread of favas, crushed and flavored with garlic, lemon, olive oil, and spices. It's delicious with crackers, toasted pita, or warm semolina bread.

1 pound young fava beans	$^1/_4$ teaspoon ground cumin
1 garlic clove, crushed with a pinch of salt	Pinch of hot paprika
2 tablespoons extra virgin olive oil	Salt
2 teaspoons fresh lemon juice	

1. Steam the favas in their pods until tender, 5 to 8 minutes, depending upon their age. Cool under cold running water. Peel off both the pod and the outer skin of each bean. Drop into a small wide saucepan as you work.

2. Add the garlic, half the olive oil, and $^1/_4$ cup water to the fava beans. Set over low heat and use a potato masher to crush the favas to a chunky puree, about 2 minutes. If necessary, thin with a little more water. Add the remaining oil and season with the cumin, paprika, and salt to taste. Let cool before serving.

Notes: To keep the spread a few days, pack in a small jar, top with olive oil, tightly cover, and keep refrigerated.

If your market only carries fresh favas from time to time, freeze them in their pods until you need them.

If the dip seems too thick when you're ready to serve it, thin with a little water.

"As Good as It Gets" Fava Bean Dip

*H*ere's an earthy fava bean dip called *bissara* from the mountain-residing Berbers of Morocco. It's a dish that's recently become quite fashionable in Marrakech and Rabat. In one luxury establishment, I even saw it served in a silver tureen.

Dried fava beans are one of the oldest food staples in the Mediterranean. When peeled and cooked, they become luscious and smooth, delicate in flavor with a hint of piney resin. Purchase large split fava beans by mail order or at your local Middle Eastern store. I think they have a flavor superior to that of smaller favas. With long, slow cooking and a simple sieving, they attain a smooth, unctuous texture.

This dip can be prepared in advance and reheated. Serve with toasted bread rounds.

SERVES 6; MAKES ABOUT 3 CUPS

10 ounces dried large, split, peeled fava beans	Salt
⅓ cup plus 2 tablespoons extra virgin olive oil	Pinch of ground cumin
5 large garlic cloves	Pinch of cayenne
Juice of 1 lemon	

1. Wash the dried favas and drain. In a large pot, bring 3 quarts water to a rolling boil. Add the favas, ⅓ cup of the olive oil, and the garlic; return to a boil. Reduce the heat to medium, cover, and simmer for 1 hour, or until the favas are soft.

2. Using a slotted spoon, transfer the favas, garlic, and a cupful of the cooking juices to an electric blender or food processor and whirl until smooth. Return to the pot with the remaining juices, add the lemon juice and 1 teaspoon salt, and continue cooking for 1 hour longer, or until the mixture is creamy and reduced to about 3 cups. Correct the salt. Push the favas through a sieve into a bowl for the silkiest texture.

3. Put the bissara in a shallow dish and garnish with a light dusting of cumin and cayenne and a generous swirl of olive oil. Serve warm.

Moroccan Eggplant Jam with Tomatoes and Lemon

Moroccans can turn every vegetable into a rich and thick luscious preserve to be served as an appetizer-salad. This eggplant spread called *zaalouk*, cooked down with tomatoes and seasoned with lemon, paprika, and cumin, in the refrigerator for up to a week.

Serve with pita bread or other flatbread.

SERVES 6 TO 8; MAKES 2 TO 3 CUPS

2 medium eggplants, about 1 pound each

Coarse salt

Olive oil, for frying

1 can (28 ounces) Italian plum tomatoes, drained

Pinch of sugar

3 garlic cloves, crushed with ½ teaspoon salt

1 teaspoon imported sweet paprika

Pinches of ground cumin

Pinches of crushed hot red pepper

3 tablespoons fresh lemon juice

1. At least 1 day in advance, remove the top of each eggplant and discard. Remove 3 vertical strips of skin from each eggplant, leaving it striped; then cut the eggplant crosswise into ¼-inch-thick slices. Soak the eggplant in cold salted water to cover (2 tablespoons salt to 1 quart water) for 30 minutes, or until the eggplant leaches brown juices. Rinse the eggplant slices, drain, and pat dry before frying.

2. Pour ½ inch of olive oil into a large cast-iron skillet. Slowly heat it until hot but not smoking. Fry the slices in batches a few at a time over high heat until golden brown on both sides. Drain on paper towels. When the eggplant is cooked, strain the oil. Return ¼ cup to the skillet and reheat.

3. Add the tomatoes and a pinch of sugar and fry them over medium-low heat for a few minutes, stirring often to avoid burning. Fold in the slices of eggplant with the garlic and mash to a puree. Continue to fry the eggplant and tomatoes in the oil stirring to avoid scorching, until all liquid evaporates and there is only oil and vegetable left.

4. Pour off the oil. Stir in the paprika, cumin, hot pepper, and lemon juice and let cool. Cover tightly and refrigerate. Serve at room temperature.

Herb Jam with Olives and Lemon

In Morocco, this thick puree of greens with herbs and olives is made with a local mallow leaf called *baqqula.* My equivalent is a combination of greens: spinach or chard, celery, cilantro, and parsley, cooked down to a luscious, thick, dark jam perfumed with spices and heady with smoky tones.

In Morocco, our housekeeper, Fatima, prepared this jam in a shallow clay tagine set over charcoal embers. As a result, the greens developed a smoky flavor. I use readily available Spanish *pimentón de la Vera* to infuse a similar smoky quality.

The greens are first steamed over boiling water to preserve flavor and color, then they're slowly fried in a skillet until all the moisture has evaporated.

Greens cooked this way become quite delicious. The addition of some chopped oily black olives improves the texture. The jam will keep for up to 4 days. When you wish to serve it, simply thin to a spreadable consistency with water and olive oil and use as a spread or dip. It goes especially well with an earthy flavored semolina flatbread baked on stone or cast iron (see page 41).

SERVES 6; MAKES ABOUT 1½ CUPS

4 large garlic cloves, halved

1 pound baby spinach leaves

1 large bunch of flat-leaf parsley (about 4 ounces), stems discarded

½ cup celery leaves, coarsely chopped

½ cup cilantro leaves, stemmed

¼ cup extra virgin olive oil

12 oil-cured black olives (about 1 ounce), pitted, rinsed, and coarsely chopped

1¼ teaspoons Spanish sweet smoked paprika (pimentón de la Vera)

Pinch of cayenne

Pinch of ground cumin

1 tablespoon lemon juice, or more to taste

Salt and freshly ground pepper

Crackers or semolina bread (page 41)

1. Put the garlic cloves in a large steamer basket set over a pan of simmering water and top with the spinach, parsley, celery, and cilantro. Cover and steam until the garlic is soft and the greens are very tender, about 15 minutes. Let cool, then squeeze the greens dry, finely chop, and set aside. Using the back of a fork, mash the garlic cloves.

2. In a medium cazuela set over a flame-tamer or in a heavy-bottomed skillet, heat 1 tablespoon of the olive oil until shimmering. Add the mashed garlic, olives, paprika, cayenne, and cumin and stir over moderately high heat for 30 seconds, or until fragrant. Add the greens and cook, mashing and stirring, until soft and dry and somewhat smooth, about 15 minutes.

3. Remove from the heat and let cool to room temperature. Mash in the remaining olive oil. Refrigerate, closely covered, for at least 1 day and up to 4 days.

4. To serve, return to room temperature. Stir in the lemon juice and season with salt and pepper. Pack in a serving dish and serve with crackers or semolina bread.

Sesame-Studded Tomato Jam

*T*o make this marvelous preserve, tomatoes are first scorched in a hot oven to bring out their natural sweetness, then cooked down in a skillet. The jam is delicious with hot Semolina Griddle Bread (page 41) or served in dollops on freshly steamed couscous.

Toasted sesame seeds add an inimitable nutty flavor. For a different taste, substitute a pinch of North African *baharat,* a spice mixture made with equal amounts of dried orange rind and dried ground rosebuds, and pinches of ground ginger and cinnamon to taste. Chef-owner Fatima Hal, of the Restaurant Mansouria in Paris, often adds pinches of powdered dried rose petals and nutmeg to flavor her tomato jam.

This jam can be refrigerated for up to 1 week. Sprinkle with sesame seeds just before serving.

SERVES 6 TO 8; MAKES 3 CUPS

4 pounds red ripe Roma or other tomatoes

2 tablespoons extra virgin olive oil

3 tablespoons honey, preferably wildflower honey

½ teaspoon ground cinnamon

Salt and freshly ground pepper

1½ teaspoons orange flower water

2 to 3 teaspoons sesame seeds

1. Preheat the oven to 450°F. Arrange the tomatoes on a baking sheet and roast turning occasionally, until charred and soft, about 1 hour. Let cool, then peel, core, seed, and coarsely chop to make about 3½ cups. (Do not use a food processor.)

2. Heat the olive oil in a large skillet until shimmering. Add the tomatoes and cook over moderately high heat, stirring frequently, until all the liquid has evaporated and the tomatoes are sizzling and beginning to brown, about 8 minutes.

3. Add the honey, cinnamon, and salt and pepper to taste. Cook for a minute to bring up the flavors. Remove from the heat and let cool. Add the orange flower water and correct the seasoning, adding more cinnamon if desired. Serve in a flat bowl, garnished with a topping of sesame seeds.

Roasted Garlic Puree

Unpeeled garlic, slow-cooked in extra virgin olive oil, duck fat, or pork fat, produces a soft-textured, sweet, and nutty-flavored puree that is excellent when spread on grilled or toasted bread. I serve it as an hors d'oeuvre or as an accompaniment to soups or mixed green salads.

One of the best uses for this "confit" was taught to me by Lazarou Lefteris of Piraeus, the first Greek chef to earn a Michelin star. He gently sautés the puree along with chopped onion as a base for stuffings, stews, and soups.

2 large heads of garlic, about 6 ounces total
1 cup extra virgin olive oil

1. Wash the garlic heads; divide into cloves but do not peel. Drain well, put in a small heavy saucepan, and cover with the oil. Cook over low heat for 1½ hours, or until the garlic is very tender and pale golden. Turn off the heat and allow the garlic to cool in the oil.

2. Drain the cloves, reserving the oil. Peel the garlic and mash to a puree. Pack into a small jar, top with the reserved oil, and cover with a lid. Store in the refrigerator.

Note: Try to avoid tattered, dried garlic, which may be rancid, and, if so, will impart a nasty flavor to anything cooked with it.

Roast Eggplant and Walnut Dip

When it comes to eggplant, size doesn't matter, only age, firmness, and freshness. Some eggplants are as tiny as your thumb, and some are as long as your arm. Just spend some time in the vegetable market in the Turkish town of Izmir and you'll see an assortment of eggplants that will boggle your mind.

To make this delightful dip, I grill eggplants very slowly to achieve a deep, smoky aroma. Depending on the weather, I grill either on a V-shaped roasting rack over a gas burner or slowly over coals outdoors.

While many Turkish cooks blend eggplant with yogurt, the lushest creamiest texture comes by blending in *lor,* a local ricotta. In northern Greece, a similar salad is made by blending the eggplant with feta and mayonnaise.

Just before serving, scatter fresh chopped walnuts on top for a pleasing rush of crunch. Serve with pita crisps.

SERVES 6

2 eggplants, ¾ pound each

1 green bell pepper

2 garlic cloves

1 cup chopped walnuts (3 ounces)

½ teaspoon salt

1 scant cup ricotta cheese

2 tablespoons extra virgin olive oil

1½ tablespoons wine vinegar, or 3 tablespoons verjus (see page 58)

Salt and freshly ground pepper

2 tablespoons chopped flat-leaf parsley

1. Pierce the eggplants with a sharp fork in 2 or 3 places (to keep them from exploding) and straddle them as high as you can on a V-shaped roasting rack. Set over a medium-low gas flame or over hot coals and grill for 15 minutes to a side, or until they are completely soft and the skin is black and blistery. The longer and slower the grilling, the creamier the eggplant will be. When the eggplants collapse, remove from the grill and let cool slightly. Remove the black parched skin, then squeeze gently to remove any juices. Crush the pulp to a puree with a fork.

2. Meanwhile, grill the pepper, turning, until soft and blackened all over. Cover with a sheet of plastic, allow to cool, then core, seed, and slip off the skin. Finely chop the pepper and mix with the eggplant.

3. In a mortar or food processor, mash the garlic to a paste with half the walnuts and the salt. Add the ricotta, olive oil, and vinegar or verjus. Season with salt and pepper and pulse to combine. In a serving bowl, combine the garlic-walnut mixture with the eggplant-pepper pulp and mix well. Correct the seasoning. Mix the parsley with the remaining walnuts and sprinkle over the top.

Note: When large eggplants are roasted whole, you may notice black juices seeping out of the skin. If this happens, immediately slit the eggplant on one side and leave to drain on a slanted board in the sink until all the "bitter" juices are expressed.

With thanks to Dr. Ayşe Baysal for sharing this recipe.

Overnight Gorgonzola with Saba Spread

Since I'm serious about all kinds of slow-cooking, I'm including this recipe for Gorgonzola cheese left to mellow overnight with flavorings as an example of how something magical and transcendent can happen with the delicious condiment *saba*. Serve on toast with an extra dribble of saba on top.

SERVES 4

5 tablespoons unsalted butter, at room temperature

¼ pound Gorgonzola cheese

1 tablespoon heavy cream

1½ teaspoons saba, or more to taste (see page 33 and Mail Order Sources)

In a food processor or blender, combine the butter and Gorgonzola. Add the cream and pulse once. Add the saba and pulse to blend. Store covered in the refrigerator.

AYRAN

This cold Turkish yogurt beverage makes an incredibly refreshing summer drink.

SERVES 5 TO 6

1 quart plain yogurt

1½ cups cold water

Pinches of salt

Place ½ quart yogurt in a food processor or blender. Add ¾ cup water and a pinch of salt and blend until smooth. Pour into a refrigerator jar. Repeat with the remaining yogurt and water. Chill and serve with ice.

NUTS AND CHEESES

As a food journalist I always try to track down stories. Sometimes all I come up with is the equivalent of an urban legend. Here's an example: About a dozen years ago, I met a man in northern Greece who told me that in the 1930s his grandfather created a new way to serve *mezethes,* small plates of nibbles to accompany drinks at his *taverna* in the central Greek town of Volos. Not a huge spread of little plates set on the table at once as is often shown in photos in cookbooks and glossy magazines, but small single plates of tidbits to accompany a glass of ouzo or *tsipouro,* served progressively, each more filling than the one before. The local working men would come to the taverna after work for friendly conversation and a drink. "Grandfather would have been forced out of business if he sent the men home drunk. The wives wouldn't stand for it," my informant told me.

"In summer," he went on, "Grandfather would serve a piece of melon with the first glass. In winter, a few leaves of romaine for dipping in mild vinegar. Following that, he might serve some pickled vegetables, or a piece of dried salty fish called *lakerda,* then some fried potatoes sprinkled with oregano, then a few hard-cooked eggs."

> *A sip leading you to a bite leading you to another sip in one long conversational flow. They do it in the Mediterranean without thinking—even we can do it in the Mediterranean without thinking, when on holidays—but can it survive here without the long hours of sunshine, the droning buzz of bees, and the escapist joy of being abroad?*
>
> — TERRY DURACK
> (A FOOD WRITER BASED IN LONDON),
> THE INDEPENDENT,
> NOVEMBER 18, 2001

Whether true or not (and the claim of having invented *"a new way to serve mezethes"* is quite huge!), I think there is a moral to this story: one should always serve a little something— (not too filling)—to accompany a drink before dinner, slowing down the consumption of both food and drink.

My close friend, Greek food writer Aglaia Kremezi insists that Greek tavernas have always served something with ouzo. "Drinking *kserosfyri* [without eating]," she told me, "has always been considered bad and reproachful behavior." Well, here are an assortment of little nibbles to accompany an aperitif or enjoy on their own. Most are extremely simple and require just a slow touch of toasting, steaming, or marinating.

HAZELNUTS, PINE NUTS, AND WALNUTS

Toasted and Salted Hazelnuts

Hazelnuts, whether from Turkey or Oregon, benefit from a slow toasting in a preheated 275°F oven for about 30 minutes. To remove their skins, fold them in a terrycloth towel, let them rest for a few minutes, then rub them while still wrapped. Salt and serve when cool.

Pine Nuts

Pine nuts benefit from a gentle toasting in a lightly oiled preheated heavy skillet. Shake the pan frequently so the nuts are evenly toasted.

Toasted and Salted Walnuts

Shake walnuts in their shells to find out if they're still fresh. If they rattle in the shells, they are.

In October, when walnuts start appearing in markets, I buy them shelled. I purchase enough for the entire year and freeze them in small quantities in plastic boxes. If I run out, I buy more packed in vacuum-sealed bags.

Whether defrosted or vacuum packed, preserved walnuts usually need a little lift to bring out their full flavor. To do this, soak them in milk for a few hours before use. Because walnuts have such a high oil content, I find slow-toasting them for 5 minutes in a heavy dry skillet enhances flavor better than oven-toasting. Be careful not to let them burn. Season toasted walnuts and serve warm.

Chestnuts Roasted on a Bed of Salt with Fennel

I've always loved the French way of roasting chestnuts on a bed of sea salt, flavored with a few fennel seeds to infuse a faint licorice taste. (Licorice happens to be one of the best flavors to enhance the natural taste of chestnuts.) Traditionally, French cooks bake the chestnuts with salt in an earthenware pot-bellied dish called a *diable,* but you can use a heavy cast-iron pot and still obtain excellent results.

The chestnuts are served warm accompanied by pats of butter.

SERVES 4

¾ pound large, firm chestnuts
    with smooth shells

1½ cups sea salt or coarse salt

½ teaspoon fennel seeds, bruised

1 to 2 tablespoons unsalted butter,
    preferably Echiré, Beurre de Celles, or
    Isigny Ste. Marie, imported from France

1. Soak the chestnuts in cold water for 1 hour to soften the shells. Preheat the oven to 450°F. Drain the chestnuts. Use a small sharp knife, or a chestnut knife if you have one, to slit the rounded side of each chestnut. Line the bottom of a medium cast-iron pot with foil or parchment paper. Spread salt over the foil or paper and arrange the chestnuts, slit side up, on top in layers. Scatter the fennel seeds over the chestnuts. Cover and bake for 35 to 45 minutes.

2. Remove the pot from the oven; keep covered with a thick towel until ready to serve. (This steaming period helps to detach the inner skins.) Guests peel their own chestnuts and add a dab of butter with each bite.

Slow-Roasted Almonds

*H*ere's a great "single ingredient" recipe of incomparable delight—slow-roasted almonds, which develop a deep rich flavor and also produce a wonderful fragrance. Simply seasoned with salt and served warm with a glass of chilled sherry, these almonds are one of the very best *tapas* I know.

Professional bakers often roast almonds in their shells for an hour in a slow oven (250°F) to obtain the most intense flavor. I've found this method extremely difficult to duplicate at home, as it's nearly impossible to judge when the nuts are done. My method, browning shelled and peeled almonds, is much simpler and never fails.

SERVES 4 TO 8

12 ounces almonds, shelled but not skinned

½ teaspoon extra virgin olive oil

Sea salt to taste

Spanish paprika (*pimentón dulce*), optional

1. To peel the almonds, slip them into a pot of water, bring to a boil, drain, rinse under cold water, and, as soon as possible, loosen and slip one by one out of their skins.

2. Preheat the oven to 275°F. Spread out the almonds in a single layer on an oiled jellyroll pan and set in the oven to bake until golden, 30 to 40 minutes. Midway, shake the almonds and check to avoid overbrowning. Remove from the oven.

3. Sprinkle sea salt over the toasted almonds, toss, let cool on paper towels, and, if desired, add a dash of Spanish paprika. If not planning to serve them right away, store cold nuts in a jar or tin with a tight-fitting lid. Keep in a cool, dry place for not more than 2 weeks. Toasted almonds turn rancid very quickly.

Notes: You can make a delicious Moroccan spread *(amlou)* with leftover toasted, salted almonds. To do this, finely crush the toasted almonds in a food processor. Add 2 tablespoons argan oil for every 1/3 cup (about 2 ounces) almonds and blend. Scrape into a small serving bowl and stir in 1 tablespoon warm honey to make about 1/3 cup. Stir until well blended, cover with plastic film, and store at room temperature. Serve on semolina bread (page 41) or dribble it over steamed couscous. Rich, nutty flavored argan oil from the Sousse region of Morocco is used as a finishing touch on tagines, couscous, grilled vegetables, small brown lentils, and salads (see Mail Order Sources).

The so-called queen of almonds is the Spanish marcona, which is best slowly toasted in a skillet with a drop of olive oil until golden, then simply salted. In autumn, you can purchase marcona almonds from The Spanish Table (see Mail Order Sources).

ROSATA, A TUNISIAN APERITIF

Tunisians convert peeled almonds to make an apéritif, a delicious cold milky drink called *rosata.* Tunisian cooks often soak some imperfect and too-dry almonds in hot milk to make their rosata creamier and more delicate. This drink is best made a day in advance.

The French writer Colette had her own peculiar opinion about consuming almond milk. In her novelette *Gigi,* the old aunt cups her hands like conch shells over Gigi's bosom, then makes her promise "not to eat too many almonds, since they add weight to the breast."

SERVES 8

1 1/4 cups ground blanched almonds

1 1/2 cups sugar

1 tablespoon almond extract

1 tablespoon vanilla extract

In a large saucepan, combine the almonds, 2 quarts water, and sugar, and cook until the sugar is dissolved. Strain through a fine mesh sieve, chill overnight, then flavor with the almond extract and vanilla. Serve chilled.

With thanks to Aliza Green for sharing this recipe.

GREEN ALMONDS

In early spring, in sophisticated circles in Istanbul and other eastern Mediterranean cities, one star of the *meze* table is the crisp, fuzzy, bright, green ovoid almond fruit. This fruit has an intense sour taste that reminds me a little of sour green grapes. It is quite delicious when accompanied by a glass of anise-perfumed *raki*.

Istanbulites split the hull in half, discard the membrane and the gelatinous liquid, then use a pair of silver tongs to pick up one of the halves, moisten it with water, dip it into salt, then pop it into their mouths. In other parts of the eastern Mediterranean, the hulls are soaked in salted water overnight to remove some of the sourness.

By midsummer this fruit mutates. The membrane turns into a hard shell, and the fluid inside turns into what we know as the moist, somewhat firm, sweet teardrop-shaped fresh green almond, eaten in salads, or soaked in salted water with a little milk to firm it up so it can be sliced or sautéed.

Gascon-born Laurent Manrique, chef at the San Francisco restaurant Campton Place, celebrates the seasonal arrival of sweet green almonds by devoting an entire meal to them. One of his best green almond dishes consists of gently sautéed fresh young almonds, which he scatters over a brilliant fig marmalade.

In Tunisia, sweet green almonds are scattered over orange and mint salads; Moroccans stew them in a butter-rich *kdra*-style tagine along with chicken.

I remember trying to duplicate the texture of soft, delicately flavored fresh green almonds in my first cookbook, *Couscous and Other Good Food from Morocco*. It took two hours of simmering to transform regular blanched almonds to the proper soft state. Years later I learned that Moroccan cooks often simulate the texture of these sweet almonds by soaking dry almonds overnight in water with a tiny pinch of baking soda. If you try this trick, be sure to thoroughly rinse the almonds to remove the soapy flavor of the soda.

By far the most famous Mediterranean recipe for fresh almonds is the white gazpacho of Andalusia. Spanish cooks often soak dry almonds in cold water overnight to make them creamier before drying and pounding them to a smooth paste to make the unctuous, almond-garlic soup *ajo blanco*.

Steamed Chickpeas

North African Berbers claim they developed the art of culinary steaming, which then spread throughout the Mediterranean world. If true, they made a huge contribution! Steaming has been used to cook innumerable dishes, not only couscous, but also vegetables, fish, lamb, chicken, fava beans, and soaked chickpeas.

Chickpeas steamed over boiling water, then dusted with coarse salt and ground cumin are a revelation. You taste the nuttiness without any toasting. The trick is to start with perfectly swollen chickpeas, requiring a full 12-hour soak. Steaming will then create moist and pure-flavored chickpeas with a fine creamy texture. Steamed chickpeas are best served hot. Cool, they lose all their charm. Eat them as you would nuts, a few at a time.

Though the soaking is long, the steaming is quick. This recipe works best for small amounts.

MAKES ABOUT 1 CUP

⅓ cup dried chickpeas

¾ teaspoon extra virgin olive oil

¼ teaspoon sea salt

⅛ teaspoon ground cumin

1. Soak the chickpeas in a bowl with water to cover by at least 2 inches in the refrigerator for at least 12 hours; drain.

2. Fill the bottom of a couscous cooker or deep pot with water and bring to a boil. Lightly oil the inside of the perforated top or a colander and fasten onto the cooker. Use a strip of cloth as padding to keep steam from escaping between the cooker and the top. Add the drained chickpeas, cover, and steam for 45 minutes. Do not remove the cover during this time.

3. Remove from the heat, toss the chickpeas with the sea salt and cumin, and serve at once while still hot.

Marinated Mushrooms with Saba

*T*his terrific innovative recipe, from San Francisco chef Mark Gordon, employs the delicious saba now readily available at fine food stores to finish off a dish of marinated mushrooms.

What makes saba from Emilia-Romagna the syrup of choice for this recipe is that it's blended with aged balsamic vinegar, then stored in barrels to age.

There are many things you can do with these delicious mushrooms besides serving them with drinks. Sometimes I combine them in a salad with thinly sliced fennel and red onion; toss them with spinach and slivers of Parmigiano-Reggiano; mix them with roasted chestnuts and small tender greens; or serve them over grilled polenta. They must marinate overnight, however—that's the slow part—so do plan accordingly.

SERVES 4 TO 6

¾ cup plus 1½ tablespoons extra virgin olive oil

¾ cup inexpensive mild balsamic vinegar or Greek *glyko* vinegar

2 bay leaves

1 small sprig of rosemary

1 small bunch of thyme sprigs

1½ tablespoons wildflower honey

Salt and freshly ground pepper

1½ pounds small brown (cremini) mushrooms, cleaned and quartered

2 teaspoons saba balsamic (see Mail Order Sources), or more to taste

1. In a large nonreactive saucepan, combine ¾ cup of the olive oil, the vinegar, bay leaves, rosemary, thyme, honey, and salt and pepper to taste. Bring to a boil.

2. Add the mushrooms and return the liquid to a boil. Cover with crumpled parchment paper and lower the heat to a simmer. Cook gently for 5 to 8 minutes, depending on the size of the mushrooms. Remove from the heat and let stand for 1 hour at room temperature. Cover and refrigerate.

3. The following day, drain the mushrooms. Toss them with the saba and the remaining 1½ tablespoons olive oil. Correct the seasoning with salt and pepper. Serve with toothpicks.

Note: The mushrooms will keep for up to 3 days. They are always better the second or third day.

SABA: UNRIPENED GRAPE SYRUP

Saba from Emilia-Romagna, *sapa* from Sardinia, *arrop* from Spain, *pekmez* from Turkey, and *petimezi* from Greece are all Mediterranean syrupy reductions made from grape must. In each case the flavor is pure, clean, and concentrated. Any of these syrups can be thinned and used as a dip for roasted chestnuts, grilled sausages, or boiled carrots. Or they can be dribbled over mild ricotta or sweet Gorgonzola, vanilla ice cream, or even a meat stew.

GREEN WALNUTS

Around the Mediterranean, the walnut season begins in early summer when the walnuts are still sour and green. The French and Italians often use unripe walnuts in their husks to make a liqueur to be served to visitors as a drink of welcome.

When I visited a home in the Turkish town of Samsun on the Black Sea, I was served a Day-Glo red syrupy spoonful of preserved, unripe walnuts as a welcoming sweet. The unripe walnuts had been soaked to remove bitterness, then cooked in rose hip jam until they turned red as ketchup.

Greeks, Armenians, and Georgians also use unripe walnuts to make welcoming preserves by soaking them in many changes of water to remove bitterness, then soaking them in ash and water to keep them firm, finally simmering them in sugar syrup to sweeten. Cooled and bottled, they are served as a crisp, dark, deep-tasting nibble to accompany a cup of sweetened tea. You can buy these prepared walnuts at most Middle Eastern groceries (or see Mail Order Sources). Their blackness is particularly striking when used as a topping over vanilla ice cream.

In late summer, the French make an appetizer called *cerneaux au verjus,* or walnuts with sour grape juice. Ripe but still green walnuts are opened, cleaned, and chopped; seasoned with salt and pepper; soaked in unripe green grape juice; then sprinkled with walnut oil. The resulting mixture is served with cubes of crisp apple and a few crunchy greens as an appetizer.

Spanish Manchego Cheese Marinated with Olives and Herbs

We're used to pairing cheese and wine, but in the same vein, I've found that particular cheeses have an affinity for particular olives. For example, moist slices of fresh mozzarella are delicious served with Italian gaeta olives; Gorgonzola goes well with large, apple-green cerignola olives from Apulia; sheep's milk cheeses, such as *kasseri* or feta, are excellent with cracked green Greek olives, especially if the cheeses are sprinkled with a little crushed oregano.

At the other end of the Mediterranean, Spanish *cabarales* blue cheese is a match for manzanilla olives, while Spanish *manchego* cheese, marinated in olive oil with herbs and seasonings as presented here, goes perfectly with small juicy *arbequina* or *niçoise* olives. I think a dense cheese like manchego is so much better when marinated; it doesn't dry out. Manchego is easily infused by oil and herbs in about a week.

I serve slices of this marinated manchego with toothpicks, but you can also set them on grilled bread alongside an arugula salad, or with grilled mushrooms and a bitter green salad garnished with some toasted walnuts. Any olive oil left over from the marinade is absolutely delicious for dressing salads or stirred into a bean soup just before serving.

SERVES 6

1 pound manchego cheese

5 sprigs of thyme

1 sprig of rosemary

1/8 teaspoon cumin seeds

12 arbequina olives, rinsed and completely dried

Extra virgin olive oil

1. Remove the rind and cut the cheese into 1/4-inch-thick slices. Spread the thyme, rosemary, and cumin seeds over the bottom of a wide-mouth jar. Arrange the cheese slices on top of the aromatics. Put the olives on top of the cheese. Cover with olive oil and seal the lid.

2. Store in a cool place for at least 1 week before serving. Refrigerate after opening. Return to room temperature before removing the slices.

With thanks to Steve Winston of The Spanish Table for sharing this recipe.

STUFFED FLATBREADS

Turkish Flatbread Stuffed with Melted Cheese

I first heard the expression "winged nostrils" from an Italian chef who was showing me how to roast a pigeon. It was his term for a chef's instinctive olfactory understanding of when a particular dish is done.

Recently I heard an almost identical turn of phrase while attending an outdoor cooking demonstration in a small Turkish village not far from Izmir. The cook was showing me how to prepare a local dish called *peynirli bogaca*—a traditional hearth bread made with two unleavened olive-oil bread sheets stuffed with a fast-melting cheese called *kesik* and some chopped parsley. The bread is assembled in an oiled clay dish set over olive-wood embers, covered with a flat iron lid, then topped with more hot embers. It bakes quickly. "Your nose will tell you when it's done," the Turkish cook advised.

There came a certain point during the cooking when, indeed, the aroma changed. One instant I smelled baking bread, the next a finished dish—a wonderful and unusual nutty aromatic blend of sesame and cheese. I nodded at the cook. She smiled and nodded back, then quickly removed the bread from the clay dish.

It was wonderful! The hot, slightly burned, crunchy sandwich had a wafer-thin crisp bottom, a crackly top, and a marvelous luscious, oozing, bubbling cheese filling. At her suggestion I drank a glass of *ayran,* yogurt mixed with cold water, as an accompaniment.

This Turkish flatbread, which is almost identical to a Genoese flatbread called *focaccia col formaggio di Recco,* is just one of many flaky hearth breads found in different guises around the Mediterranean. (Also similar are the French *fouace,* the Bulgarian *pogacha,* and the Algerian *bourak b'l-djbene.*) Please don't confuse this with the much better known, puffy, yeast-based

Italian focaccia, which is served at room temperature. The Genoese focaccia is made without yeast and is always served hot from the hearth.

Another variation, using this same particular pastry and method, is a wonderful *torta* from the Ligurian-Tuscan coast made with greens and squash (see page 40), and on the Black Sea a delicious bread pie filled with buffalo-milk mozzarella and feta served hot.

Long ago all these breads were baked in the fireplace. A clay flat-rimmed pan, called a *cerepene* in Turkey and *testo* in Italy, was thrust into the coals, then more coals were piled on top, imbuing the dough with a smoky flavor.

My versions are easily baked on a pizza pan on a preheated stone in a hot oven. Please be sure *not* to open the oven door while they cook, lest you reduce the intense heat. There is no need to check to see how the breads look; your "winged nostrils" will tell you when they're done.

The quick-to-make dough needs to rest overnight, so plan accordingly.

SERVES 4 TO 6; MAKES ONE 15-, 16-, OR 17-INCH ROUND

1½ cups bread flour

½ teaspoon salt

3 tablespoons extra virgin olive oil, plus more for brushing

2 to 3 teaspoons orange juice, lemon juice, cider vinegar, or white wine

7 ounces runny, soft teleme, crescenza, or mozzarella cheese

Coarse sea salt

1. In a food processor, pulse the flour with the salt. Add the 3 tablespoons olive oil and the orange or lemon juice, cider vinegar or white wine. With the machine on, pour in 5 tablespoons cold water and process until the dough resembles wet sand. Transfer the dough to a lightly floured work surface and knead until smooth. (You might need another 1 tablespoon water.) Divide the dough in half and pat into 2 disks, brush lightly with olive oil, wrap in plastic, and refrigerate overnight. Let the disks of dough return to room temperature before proceeding.

(continued)

2. Set a baking stone on the top rack of the oven and preheat the oven to 550°F. On a lightly floured work surface, roll out each disk of dough to a 10-inch round. Cover with plastic wrap and let rest for 10 minutes.

3. Working with 1 round at a time, stretch the dough: lift and pull from the center out toward the edge, rotating as necessary, until you have pulled the dough to a thin round just large enough to fit into a lightly oiled pizza pan. If the dough is resistant, let it rest a few minutes, then continue to press it out. You may need to do this 2 or 3 times to press it out to the edge without its springing back. Trim off any thick edges. If there are any cracks or tears in the dough, pinch or patch together. Scatter the cheese evenly over the dough in the pan to within 1 inch of the rim. Lightly moisten the rim with water. Repeat with the second round of dough, cover, and press the edges together to seal. Trim the edges if necessary. Brush the top with olive oil and sprinkle with sea salt. Make four or five 1-inch slits in the top near the center.

4. Bake the bread for 7 to 10 minutes, until soft, golden, spotted brown, and bubbling. Slide the bread onto a work surface and cut it into squares or wedges.

Notes: You can keep the dough in the refrigerator for a few days or freeze it for up to 1 month.

If you are new to handling thin sheets of dough, allow the rounds to rest a few minutes between rolling out. This allows the dough to become pliable and thus much easier to stretch. Oiled palms also make handling the dough much easier.

About 2 hours before serving, set the oven rack on the highest rung. Place a baking stone on the rack and turn the oven to 550°F. Bake for 7 minutes. If your oven only reaches 500°F, bake for 10 minutes.

At certain times of the year, teleme is very runny and spoonably creamy, making it difficult to cut. This is also when the cheese is at its most flavorful. I use a melon baller dipped in water to scoop out marble-sized balls of cheese, then place them evenly on the sheet of dough, making for an even sheet when the cheese melts.

For easier cutting of the finished bread, use a rolling pizza blade to carve it into squares or wedges.

To turn this flatbread "Italian," add a drizzle of white truffle oil just before serving. The aroma will send you straight to heaven. In season at the Ligurian restaurant Rose Pistola in the North Beach neighborhood of San Francisco, the chef inserts a few thin slices of fresh fig or some morels between the layers of dough to flavor the cheese. This variation, too, is heavenly!

Izmir-Style Flatbread with Cheese, Parsley, and Sesame Seeds

This is another Turkish version called *Peynirli bogaca*. It's particularly good with a glass of chilled *ayran* (see box on page 15). You may substitute shavings of the Eastern Mediterranean *basturma* for the parsley and omit the sesame seeds. Basturma, the Turkish/Armenian preserved meat, is seasoned with fenugreek, paprika, cumin, and many other spices. You can buy it fat or lean from Middle Eastern grocers. It can be thinly sliced and kept frozen until needed.

SERVES 4 TO 6

1 bunch of flat-leaf parsley

7 ounces fresh cheese, such as queso fresco, or a brined cheese, such as feta

2 tablespoons grated Parmigiano-Reggiano, kasseri, or pecorino cheese

2 teaspoons extra virgin olive oil

2 tablespoons sesame seeds

Coarse sea salt

1. Prepare the flatbread dough through Step 3.

2. Blanch the parsley in boiling water for 10 seconds. Drain, squeeze dry, and finely chop to make ½ cup.

3. Crumble the fresh cheese. Combine the crumbled fresh cheese and grated cheese with the chopped parsley and sprinkle over the dough. Top with the second round of dough. Brush with olive oil and sprinkle with sesame seeds and coarse sea salt before baking.

Flatbread Stuffed with Cheese, Winter Squash, and Wild Greens

*T*his savory stuffed Ligurian flatbread is traditionally made with a wide variety of greens, ranging in flavor from peppery to sweet. I salt the greens, leeks, and grated squash to draw out moisture, concentrate flavor, and reduce volume.

½ pound mixed greens, for braising

Coarse salt

½ cup chopped leek (white part only)

½ cup grated winter squash

1 tablespoon extra virgin olive oil, plus more for brushing

¼ cup freshly grated Parmigiano-Reggiano cheese

¼ cup ricotta cheese

½ cup shredded mozzarella cheese

Freshly grated nutmeg

Freshly ground pepper

1. Prepare the flatbread dough through Step 3.

2. In a large nonreactive colander or bowl, rub the greens with ½ tablespoon coarse salt. Let stand for 1 hour. In another bowl, toss the chopped leek and winter squash with a good pinch of salt and let stand for 1 hour.

3. Rinse the greens and squeeze dry. Shred coarsely. Rinse the leek and squash and squeeze dry.

4. In a large nonstick skillet, heat 1 tablespoon olive oil. Add the leek and winter squash and cook over moderately high heat, stirring, until tender, about 3 minutes. Add the greens and cook, stirring, until wilted, about 3 minutes. Transfer the vegetables to a bowl and let cool. Add the cheeses; season with nutmeg and pepper. Mix well and correct the seasoning with salt, if necessary.

5. Spread the filling over the dough. Cover the filling with the second round of dough. Using a fork, pierce the surface 2 or 3 times to allow steam to escape during the baking. Brush with olive oil and bake as directed for 10 minutes, until browned. Serve hot or warm.

Small Semolina Griddle Breads

*H*ere's a fast bread for slow foods. Small as a pancake, these easy-to-make, grainy-textured griddle breads are similar to those sold on the streets of Casablanca and Tunis. No yeast is required. A combination of coarse semolina and fine pasta flour provides a butter-colored interior and blotchy black exterior.

Serve these breads as a hot hors d'oeuvre with North African herb or tomato jams or for breakfast brushed with butter or argan oil and honey.

MAKES TWELVE 5-INCH ROUNDS

2 scant cups (14 ounces) pasta flour

1 cup (6 ounces) coarse semolina (see Mail Order Sources)

1 stick plus 2 tablespoons (5 ounces) unsalted butter, melted and cooled

4 teaspoons sugar

½ teaspoon salt

1 small onion, halved

1. In a mixing bowl, combine the pasta flour and semolina. Add the stick of melted butter and rub the mixture together with your hands until sandy. Mix in the sugar and salt. Mix ½ cup of warm water into the dough; it should be crumbly. Let stand a few minutes, then gradually add more water until you have a soft dough, about 1 cup in all.

2. Transfer to a food processor and pulse 30 times to blend. The texture should now be very soft and moist. Turn the dough out onto an unfloured work surface. Using lightly buttered hands, knead it until silky, 1 to 2 minutes. Cover the dough loosely and let rest for at least 30 minutes.

3. Preheat a cast-iron grill or a ridged pan over medium heat. Preheat the oven to 250°F. Lightly grease the cut side of the onion with melted butter or oil and quickly rub the heated pan. Cut the dough into 12 equal pieces. On a buttered or oiled baking sheet, press out one portion of dough into a 5-inch round. Cover loosely with plastic and repeat to form the remaining flatbreads. Grill the breads, one at a time, until they are golden and speckled with black spots, turning once; it should take 4 minutes total. Serve the breads hot off the grill, or wrap in foil and keep them warm in the oven for up to 30 minutes.

Mediterranean Salads and Cold Vegetable Dishes

---※---

Many Mediterranean salads are not salads in the sense we think of that word, as mixtures of greens doused with dressings. Rather they are more like southern Italian antipasti—spiced or sweetened dishes of cooked or raw vegetables, bowls of seasoned olives, pureed olive oil–rich legumes, all served at the beginning of a meal to excite the diner's appetite and stimulate the palate.

The North African coast is a rich agricultural region where numerous rich, dense, fruit and vegetable–based salads were developed to preserve the harvest. Here, tomatoes, peppers, eggplants, pumpkins, and edible wild greens are individually reduced to thick aromatic purees, then served cool or at room temperature. Vegetables such as radishes, cucumbers, carrots, and beets are shredded and macerated overnight in fragrant waters. Many of these salads are seasoned with spices to achieve balance, harmonize flavors, and preserve them for up to a week.

A typical North African dinner or lunch might start with the presentation of three salads. A North African diner typically dips a slice of warm fresh bread into one and then nibbles at it, using the bread as a scoop. You can alter this traditional presentation by serving these compoted purees on thin slices of toasted baguette. (See "toppings," pages 14 to 24, for many more North African salad-like purees.)

Artichoke and Orange Compote

This rich Algerian-Jewish combination of artichokes and oranges is one of the most alluring dishes in North African–Jewish cuisine.

SERVES 4 TO 6

1½ lemons

4 large artichokes

2 tablespoons extra virgin olive oil

2 garlic cloves, sliced

⅓ cup fresh orange juice

1 teaspoon salt

½ teaspoon freshly ground pepper

2 thin-skinned oranges, peeled and sectioned

Pinch of ground coriander

1 tablespoon sugar

4 sprigs of mint

1. Place about 4 cups cold water and the juice of ½ lemon in a bowl. Clean the artichokes: Break off the leaves as far as they will snap. Cut off the tips. Quarter the artichokes and remove the hairy chokes. Rub with what's left of the lemon half and drop into the acidulated water.

2. Heat the olive oil in a shallow flameproof earthenware dish or stainless steel saucepan, add the garlic, and sauté gently for 1 minute. Stir in the orange juice, the juice of 1 lemon, and the salt and pepper. Drain the artichokes and add to the pan with ¼ cup water. Cover with crumpled wet parchment paper and a tight-fitting lid and set over the lowest heat to cook for 45 minutes. Remove the artichokes to a side plate. Reserve the cooking juices.

3. In a skillet, combine the orange sections and any collected juices, the ground coriander, and the sugar. Cook over medium-low heat, stirring, until the orange sections are glazed, about 10 minutes.

4. With a slotted spoon, transfer the oranges to a serving dish. Add the artichokes to the skillet and cook, stirring, until glazed all over. Transfer the artichokes to the serving dish. Add the reserved artichoke cooking juices to the skillet; boil quickly until reduced to a few tablespoons, season with salt and pepper to taste, add a few drops of lemon juice and a drizzle of fresh oil, and pour over the artichokes and oranges. Serve cool or chilled, garnish with the mint.

Turkish Chopped Salad

*H*ere's a tart, refreshing, no-oil summer salad with plenty of character. It's soupy on purpose, used for dipping bread.

Try to find thin-skinned sweet peppers at your local summer farmstand. Otherwise you'll need to pare them when raw, a tedious process. Choose fresh firm tomatoes so you can cut them into the smallest of dice. Prepare the vegetables early in the day, mix them well, then salt and leave them to mellow. Avoid using your food processor for this dish, lest you end up with a mushy salad. Serve well chilled.

SERVES 4; MAKES ABOUT 5 CUPS

1 pound firm ripe tomatoes, peeled and diced

1 cup finely diced green bell pepper

¾ cup finely diced red bell pepper

½ cup finely chopped flat-leaf parsley

2 tablespoons shredded fresh mint leaves

½ cup chopped scallion or red onion

½ teaspoon Turkish red pepper flakes (see Mail Order Sources)

1 tablespoon dried mint

2 small garlic cloves crushed with 1½ teaspoons coarse salt

½ to ⅔ cup verjus or sour grape juice

A few drops of lemon juice or pomegranate concentrate, optional

Combine the tomatoes, green and red peppers, parsley, mint, scallion or red onion, red pepper flakes, dried mint, garlic, and verjus in a bowl. Stir well, cover, and chill for a few hours. The salad should be liquidy. Dilute with 1 cup cold water and serve chilled. If not tart enough, add a drop of pomegranate concentrate or lemon juice.

With thanks to Ayfer Unsal for sharing this recipe, called Antep salatasi.

Panade of Leeks and Mixed Greens with Cantal Cheese (page 88)

ABOVE: *Pot-Roasted Pork Loin with Fall Fruits* (page 170)

OPPOSITE: *Spicy Roasted Vegetable and Tuna Canapés* (page 10)

THIS PAGE: *Sesame-Studded Tomato Jam* (page 20)

OPPOSITE: *Herb Jam with Olives and Lemon* (page 18)

ABOVE: *Shrimp with Orange, Shallots, and Grilled Radicchio (page 104)*
OPPOSITE: *Moroccan Spring Couscous with Barley,
Fresh Fava Beans, and Buttermilk (page 270)*

Pot-Roasted Club Steak with Piquillo Peppers (page 190)

Cypriot Fresh Fava Bean and Purslane Salad

This delightful Cypriot salad should be prepared ahead of time and refrigerated, though it tastes best served at room temperature. The combination of balsamic vinegar and wine vinegar best resembles Cypriot vinegar.

SERVES 6

2 pounds fresh fava beans

1 cup small, tender purslane leaves

1 small seedless cucumber, cut in ½-inch dice

1 small green bell pepper, diced

2 scallions, thinly sliced

1 tablespoon balsamic vinegar

2 teaspoons red wine vinegar

¼ cup extra virgin olive oil

Salt and freshly ground pepper

1 large tomato, seeded and cut into ½-inch pieces

Steam the favas in their pods as described on page 15. (Timing depends on the maturity of the beans—5 to 20 minutes.) Cool in cold water, then remove the pods and outer skins. There should be 1½ to 2 cups. Mix with the purslane, cucumber, pepper, and scallions. Dress with vinaigrette (made from combining the vinegars, oil, and salt and pepper to taste). Add the tomato just before serving.

With thanks to Niki Moquist for sharing this recipe.

Tunisian Chickpea Salad

*T*o enhance the flavor of home-cooked chickpeas, marinate them with spices while they are still hot.

SERVES 4

¾ cup dried chickpeas, soaked overnight in water to cover

1 small yellow onion

4 tablespoons extra virgin olive oil

¾ teaspoon ground cumin

1 teaspoon homemade *harissa* (page 309) or Turkish red pepper paste (see Mail Order Sources)

1 teaspoon minced garlic

Salt and freshly ground pepper

½ cup finely chopped red onion

2 tablespoons finely chopped flat-leaf parsley

1 tablespoon lemon juice

About 12 oil-cured black olives, pitted and halved

4 cherry tomatoes, for garnish

1. Drain the chickpeas and place in a saucepan with the whole onion and 2 tablespoons of the olive oil. Add enough water to cover by 1½ inches, cover with a tight lid, and cook over low heat until the chickpeas are tender, 1½ hours or more. Drain, reserving 1 cup of the liquid.

2. While the chickpeas are still warm, transfer them to a bowl; discard the onion. Pour the reserved 1 cup cooking liquid over the chickpeas and gently fold in the cumin, harissa, garlic, and salt and pepper to taste. Let marinate for at least 4 or 5 hours. Drain off the liquid.

3. Toss the chickpeas with the chopped red onion, parsley, lemon juice, and remaining 2 tablespoons olive oil. Garnish with the olives and cherry tomatoes and serve at room temperature.

With thanks to chef Haouari Abderrazak for sharing this recipe.

Sephardic Oven-Roasted Eggs

William Rubel, author of *The Magic of Fire,* told me that he roasts eggs in the oven for several hours, achieving the same delicious results as if he'd roasted them all night buried in hot ash in the fireplace. The egg shells and whites turn golden, while the yolks remain creamy.

"I have been known to use the oven when I need a dozen golden eggs for a party," he told me. "To more closely mimic the uneven but very beautiful colors you get baking eggs in the fireplace, I stagger the oven removal times, which makes a more beautiful presentation than oven-roasted eggs all removed at the same moment. When roasting eggs in the oven, I can generally tell when they begin to turn deeply golden by the tiny drops of blackened albumen on the outside of the shell, but, of course, you can always take an egg out, run it under cold water, and crack it open to see the color for yourself."

Rubel tells me he likes to serve them with a strongly flavored anchovy vinaigrette made with salt-packed anchovies.

SERVES 5 TO 10

10 very fresh AA eggs
Coarse sea salt and freshly ground pepper

Anchovy Vinaigrette (page 50), optional

1. Set the oven rack in the middle. Soak the eggs in warm water while preheating the oven to 225°F. Set the eggs directly on the rack. Bake for 4½ to 5 hours. Stagger the removal as described above if you are going for a multihued effect.

2. Roll the eggs to crackle the shells, then drop them into a bowl of cold water to soak for 5 minutes. Slip off the shells, dry, and place attractively on a colorful dish. Serve at room temperature with salt and pepper or the anchovy vinaigrette.

Variation: Slow-Cooker Oven-Roasted Eggs

Place the dry eggs in an empty earthenware electric slow-cooker. Cover, turn the heat to low, and cook for 5 hours, turning the eggs occasionally. Peel as directed in Step 2 above and serve warm with salt and ground cumin.

Anchovy Vinaigrette

MAKES ABOUT ½ CUP

6 salt-packed anchovies, cleaned and filleted, or 12 oil-packed flat anchovy fillets, drained, soaked in cool milky water, rinsed, and drained dry

1 garlic clove, crushed to a puree

1 tablespoon mild wine vinegar

Freshly ground pepper

7 to 8 tablespoons extra virgin olive oil

In a small saucepan over low heat, crush the anchovy fillets with a wooden spoon or fork until creamy and smooth. Scrape them into a small bowl or blender jar. Add the garlic, vinegar, and pepper. With the machine on, gradually add the olive oil. Let the vinaigrette stand at room temperature for at least 1 hour before serving.

Sephardic Long-Simmered Eggs

Huevos haminados, a Sephardic specialty of the Passover table, is made with eggs long simmered in a low-temperature water bath filled with red onion skins or Turkish coffee grounds for up to twelve hours at 160°F. (Salmonella in eggs are killed at 140°F after one hour.) I do this in a slow-cooker. The eggshells emerge in beautiful maroon to purple hues while the yolks and whites attain a unique flavor.

Serve with salt and ground cumin along with a salad, or with long cooked fava beans.

SERVES 6

6 large very fresh AA eggs

3 handfuls of dried red onion skins

2 tablespoons extra virgin olive oil

Sea salt

Ground cumin

Place the eggs, onion skins, olive oil, and salt and 1 teaspoon ground cumin in an electric slow-cooker. Add water to cover and set on low heat. Monitor the temperature of the water with a thermometer. When it reaches 160°F, remove the cover and continue cooking the eggs for up to 12 hours. (Lengthy cooking changes the color of the whites to beige while the yolks turn firm but creamy.)

Notes: You can refrigerate *huevos haminados* in some of their cooking liquid for up to 1 day. Return to room temperature, peel, and serve halved with a good sprinkling of salt, pepper, and cumin.

To facilitate peeling, remove the eggs after they're cooked, allow to cool, roll to crackle the shells, then return to the cooking liquid for 10 minutes before peeling.

THE ONE-HOUR "THREE-MINUTE" EGG

I was delighted when I heard from French scientist Herve This, Ph.D. in molecular gastronomy, about the late British scientist Nicholas Kurti's breakthrough experiment showing that the best way to cook a three-minute egg is to cook it for one hour at a temperature of 60°C (140°F). "The yolk will remain soft, but the white will firm up," Dr. This told me.

The extremely low temperature used for cooking is not dangerous. According to Professor Kurti, the one-hour cooking killed one million salmonellas that had been introduced on purpose.

Using this method, called Low Temperature Long Time (LTLT), I've poached very fresh AA eggs at a temperature between 145°F and 155°F and produced the most delicious "three-minute" eggs.

LONG AND SHORT COOKED EGGS

And new-laid eggs, which Baucis' busy care
Turn'd by a gentle fire and roasted rare.

—OVID, *METAMORPHOSES*

A truly ancient Mediterranean dish: eggs roasted in the ashes of a dying fire, absorbing an exquisite smoky flavor while attaining a silk-and-satin texture.

La Mazille, one of my favorite cookbook authors, wrote in her 1926 volume on Perigord cookery that there aren't thirty-six ways to soft-boil an egg; there is only one, but the most exquisite way to soft cook an egg is in the embers in about three minutes. "The heat," she wrote, "penetrates through and around the egg, providing an exquisite flavor throughout." Yet La Mazille decided not to provide the recipe, stating that such a method was inconsistent with modern life, and lamenting an epoch where people didn't concern themselves "with such details."

Alas, I wish she had provided more details as my own attempts at this form of egg cookery have been mostly unfortunate. The eggs have burst before the whites had set, or else they became overcooked and tough. I've tried various tricks, including soaking the eggs in water before placing them in the embers, and pricking one of the ends. Sometimes they've come out, other times not. Thus I'm not surprised that this method has almost died out.

Melt-in-Your-Mouth Green Beans with Turkish Pepper

The Greeks have a saying that they use frequently to convey the importance of patience: Slowly, slowly, sour grapes turn to honey.

Since you need patience for this green bean recipe, I advise using an electric slow-cooker. The longer the beans remain in contact with the flavorings and oil, the more deeply they will absorb these flavors and the more delicious they will become. If you like your green beans crunchy, this recipe isn't for you. But if you want to try them the Mediterranean way, not overcooked but luxuriously mellow in texture, you'll be very pleased.

Served at room temperature, these beans will melt in your mouth, yet oddly they aren't particularly soft to the touch. You can proudly call this a "seven-hour green bean dish." And in the words of my old friend Emeril Lagasse, the addition of dried Turkish red peppers to the dish "kicks it up a notch."

SERVES 6

1½ pounds thick green beans, trimmed and cut into 1 inch lengths

1 medium onion, finely chopped

3 garlic cloves, thinly sliced

⅓ cup extra virgin olive oil

½ cup peeled, seeded, and chopped canned tomato or 1 large juicy tomato, halved, seeded, and grated

¼ teaspoon Turkish red pepper flakes (see Mail Order Sources)

1 teaspoon sugar

Salt

Lemon juice

Place everything in the clay insert of an electric slow-cooker. Add 2 tablespoons water, cover with a small round of crumpled parchment, and set on the lid. Cook on low for 5 to 7 hours, or on high for 3½ hours, until the beans are very tender. Taste for salt. Allow to mellow overnight. Serve cool with a few drops of lemon juice to taste.

Leeks Simmered in Olive Oil

"*T*he slower, the better, when you simmer the leeks," my Turkish friend and fellow foodie Engin Akin advises me on the phone from Istanbul. Engin, who hosts a weekly food show on Turkish radio, adds: "It's all about creating silky texture and natural flavors and aromas."

I call this method of slow cooking vegetables, which enhances their flavor by forcing them to reabsorb their own moisture, Mediterranean alchemy. It relies on self-basting, usually in a sturdy pot in which the vegetables are cooked in their own juices. To keep the cooking temperature low and constant and to encourage recycling, the pot must be heavy bottomed and tightly covered.

This method is used all around the Mediterranean to cook winter and spring vegetables such as leeks in this recipe, artichokes, cardoons, celery, celery root, fat green beans, favas, and white turnips. The vegetables turn creamy within while remaining firm enough to hold their shape. The method also sweetens slightly bitter vegetables, such as cardoons, by caramelizing them ever so slightly.

Serve these leeks later in the day, or, even better, the following day.

SERVES 6

2 pounds leeks, roots trimmed, thick outer
    skins removed

⅓ cup chopped onion

¼ cup extra virgin olive oil

2 medium carrots, peeled and sliced

2 teaspoons sugar

1 tablespoon rice, preferably medium-grain

Salt and freshly ground pepper

Juice of ½ lemon, or more to taste

¼ cup chopped flat-leaf parsley

1. Soak the leeks in warm water for 30 minutes. Drain and cut into 2-inch lengths. Thoroughly rinse to remove any sand. Drain well.

2. Combine the onion, olive oil, and carrots in a large, heavy casserole and cook over medium heat, stirring, for 2 to 3 minutes. Stir in the leeks and sugar, cover with a sheet of crumpled parchment paper or foil and a tight-fitting lid, reduce the heat to low, and cook for 20 minutes. (Leeks and carrots should cook in their own moisture. If necessary, add 1 tablespoon water.)

3. Meanwhile, in a small bowl, soak the rice in hot water to cover for 10 minutes; drain.

4. Add the rice to the leeks. Season with salt and pepper, and cook, tightly covered, over low heat for 20 minutes longer.

5. Remove from the heat and add the lemon juice. Leave the pan uncovered to cool before transferring the leeks to a serving dish. Spoon the vegetables and rice over the leeks, garnish with the chopped parsley, and serve at room temperature or chilled.

Melting Sweet Red Peppers with Toasted Pine Nuts and Capers

*H*ere's a simple, straightforward salad of red peppers with a from-the-grill smoky aroma, buttery texture, and sweet flavorful taste. This dish will improve greatly if allowed to mellow a few days in the refrigerator. Let return to room temperature, then serve on hot grilled bread.

SERVES 6

4 medium red bell peppers, preferably organic

3 tablespoons extra virgin olive oil

1 tablespoon pine nuts

1 small garlic clove, sliced

12 salted capers, soaked in water for 10 minutes and drained

1 tablespoon chopped flat-leaf parsley

2 teaspoons good-quality sherry wine vinegar, or more to taste

Salt and freshly ground pepper

1. Char the red bell peppers over a flame or under a broiler as close to the heat as possible, turning frequently, until blackened all over, about 6 minutes. Place in a plastic bag to steam for at least 10 minutes. Massage the peppers (still inside the bag) to remove the skins. When the black parts are rubbed off, remove the peppers and wipe dry. Avoid rinsing under water; it dilutes their flavor. Slit the peppers open and remove the stems, membrane, and seeds. Cut the peppers into thin strips.

2. In a medium skillet, heat half the olive oil over moderately low heat and fry the pine nuts until just golden brown, about 3 minutes. Remove to a side plate.

3. Add the peppers, garlic, drained capers, and ¼ cup water to the skillet, cover, and cook until the peppers are thoroughly cooked, about 3 minutes. Sprinkle with the parsley, vinegar, salt, pepper, and toasted pine nuts and toss. Cover and store in the refrigerator for at least one day before serving on toast.

Lemon Tabouli with Tender Romaine

A few years ago, when I was in southeastern Turkey working on my book *Mediterranean Grains and Greens,* I noticed that the women didn't soak their bulgur in water for some summer preparations. When I asked a Turkish friend about this, she let out a laugh. "In Turkey, no man would marry a woman who just used water! For cold bulgur dishes we always soak in tomato juice, onion juice, or fresh pressed and strained sour grape juice to flavor the bulgur first."

When I told this story to my old friend Anne-Marie Weiss Armush, author of two wonderful books on Middle Eastern food, she told me about her own experiments soaking bulgur for tabouli with lemon juice and her spectacular results. Anne-Marie quickly shakes fine bulgur in a sieve to remove any dust, rinses it clean, then soaks it in lemon juice before mixing in the other ingredients. "Make it in the early afternoon," she advises, "then eat it at night, or if you want to serve it for lunch, make it early in the morning."

SERVES 6; MAKES 4 CUPS

½ cup fine grain #1 bulgur

¼ cup fresh lemon juice

2 cups finely diced tomatoes

½ cup thinly sliced scallions

2 pinches of ground cinnamon

Salt and freshly ground pepper

⅓ cup extra virgin olive oil

2 cups finely chopped flat-leaf parsley

2 tablespoons slivered fresh mint leaves

Tender romaine leaves

1. Place the bulgur in a fine sieve, rinse under cold running water, squeeze dry, and soak in the lemon juice for 45 minutes. Use a fork to fluff the bulgur.

2. In a bowl, combine the tomatoes, scallions, cinnamon, and a few pinches of salt and pepper. Drizzle on the olive oil and toss. Fold in the bulgur, parsley, and mint and mix well. Refrigerate, stirring occasionally.

3. Taste and correct the flavors with lemon juice, salt, and pepper. Serve with crisp inner leaves of romaine lettuce for scooping up the salad.

VERJUS, OR SOUR GRAPE JUICE

Once you've tried food preparation with verjus, or unfermented sour grape juice, you are probably going to want to incorporate it into much of your cooking. For this reason I've included here a few traditional Mediterranean dishes to introduce you to this fabulous product, which is more and more readily available. Because verjus, unlike vinegar, won't ruin your palate for wine, it makes a wonderful alternative to vinegar for use in salads. And because of its gentle, fruity tartness, it's able to coax out flavors from hearty peppers as well as delicate greens.

In summer in the eastern Mediterranean, wherever grapes are grown, unripe and freshly pressed grape juice replaces the winter standby, lemon juice, in salads, summer stews, and soups. In old Italian cookbooks, you'll find mention of a condiment called *agresto,* made of verjus combined with almonds or hazelnuts to create a dip for raw vegetables.

California winemakers are now producing verjus. You can find it sold in bottles or shrink packets at fine grocers. (Make your own as described below or see Mail Order Sources.) I particularly like the Fusion brand produced by winemaker Jim Neal. It's milder than most verjus. And when verjus is reduced, it produces a particularly delicious base for a sauce, a perfect balance of sweet and tart. I've also poached fish in verjus with fine results. French cooks use it to deglaze a skillet after sautéing, and in summer, in grape-growing regions of France, it turns up in tangy fruit compotes.

To make verjus: Use the acidic sourest seedless green grapes you can find, usually available in early summer. Simply crush, strain, let the juice settle, then ladle from the top and strain again. Use at once.

To store: Place the strained juice in a saucepan, add a little water, and bring to a boil. (This kills any yeasts.) Remove from the heat and let cool. Store the juice in a covered jar in the refrigerator for up to a few weeks. Use as needed or freeze.

For a refreshing drink: Dilute ¼ cup verjus with 1 cup sparkling water and some ice cubes. You may also add a scented geranium leaf (if you can find one) as they do in Turkey.

If your grapes are not sufficiently sour, you know what to do with them—simply serve them for dessert.

Baked Eggplant Slices Marinated with Verjus and Fresh Herbs

This method of preparing eggplant slices employs a little-known method of salting: pre-soaking the slices in salted water. This keeps the slices extra moist and creamy while baking in a hot oven until their exteriors are browned.

Though the bright acidic finish you get with verjus is highly desirable, you can substitute diluted pomegranate molasses, lemon juice, or rice vinegar.

SERVES 6

2 elongated eggplants (about 1½ pounds each)

Salt

2 tablespoons extra virgin olive oil

1 tablespoon verjus or rice vinegar

1 garlic clove, minced

1 scallion (white and 2 inches of green), thinly sliced

2 teaspoons chopped fresh cilantro

2 teaspoons shredded fresh mint

1. Cut the eggplant into ½-inch-thick rounds. Soak the slices in cold salted water for 30 minutes, or until the eggplant leaches brown juices.

2. Preheat the oven to 400°F. Lightly brush a baking sheet with some of the oil. Spread the slices on the baking sheet in a single layer. Bake for 20 minutes. Turn each slice and continue baking until lightly browned on the outside and soft and creamy within, about 20 minutes longer. Remove from the oven and let cool.

3. In a small bowl, combine the verjus, garlic, scallion, cilantro, mint, and the remaining oil. Whisk to blend. Arrange the eggplant slices attractively on a serving dish. Spoon the herb mixture over the eggplant. Let stand for at least 3 hours before serving.

Fried Green Tomatoes with Skordalia Sauce

*H*ere's an excellent midsummer dish of sliced green tomatoes dusted with flour, then fried until tender inside and crusty on the outside. The fried tomatoes are served with a dollop of rich, garlicky Greek *skordalia* sauce, with some verjus added for tartness.

This dish comes from the town of Pelion in central Greece. Here the sauce is made in a large mortar—pounded until smooth, yet still light and foamy. Most skordalia sauces are enriched by potatoes, walnut, or almonds; this summer version is much lighter, perfect for fried food. The sauce is easy to make and best left to mellow overnight, so be sure to plan ahead. It will keep a few days in the refrigerator, ripening each day.

SERVES 4 TO 6 AS A SIDE DISH

Skordalia Sauce (recipe follows)

2 pounds hard green tomatoes (about 4 medium)

½ cup whole wheat or graham flour

½ cup all-purpose flour

Salt and freshly ground pepper

Pinch of sugar

1 to 1½ cups vegetable oil, for frying

1. Make the skordalia sauce and refrigerate it overnight.

2. Wash and stem the green tomatoes. Cut into slices ⅜ inch thick. There should be 16 to 18 slices.

3. In a shallow bowl, mix the whole wheat and all-purpose flours with a sprinkling of salt, pepper, and sugar.

4. Heat the oil in a large heavy skillet over medium-high heat. Dredge the tomato slices in the seasoned flour, coating both sides completely and shaking off the excess. Working in batches, fry the tomatoes, turning once, until lightly browned and crispy, about 3 minutes on each side.

5. Remove the tomatoes to a cake rack set over paper towels to drain. Season with salt and pepper. Arrange the skordalia sauce in the center of a large, round, shallow serving dish and overlap the tomato slices upright around the side.

Note: Graham flour is a whole-meal flour that is coarsely milled from soft winter wheat; it contains large bran fragments.

Skordalia Sauce

½ pound day-old bread, crust removed

4 medium garlic cloves

1 teaspoon coarse salt

½ cup extra virgin olive oil

¼ cup verjus (sour grape juice), or 2 table-spoons cider vinegar

Finely ground pepper

1. Tear the bread into small pieces to make about 6 cups. Soak the bread in water long enough for it to become wet all over. Press out the excess water. You should have about 2 cups.

2. In a mortar or on a work surface, crush the garlic with the salt until mashed to a puree.

3. Scrape the garlic puree into a blender or food processor. Add the olive oil and verjus. Blend while counting to ten, then add ⅓ cup warm water and continue blending until smooth. Correct the seasoning with pepper and additional salt if needed. Scrape into a bowl, cover, and refrigerate overnight.

Compote of Red Peppers, Zucchini, and Tomatoes

*T*here are numerous Mediterranean pepper, onion, and tomato medleys. This one, called *marmouma,* of Tunisian-Jewish origin, is often confused with French ratatouille or North African *chachouka.* Actually, chachouka never contains eggplant or zucchini, while ratatouille does.

The slower you cook the vegetables here, the more caramelization will develop on the bottom of the pan. The more often you fold these caramelized bits and pieces back into the vegetables, the more delicious your marmouma will become.

This is a good dish to cook in an electric skillet, where it's easy to control the temperature and from which moisture can steadily evaporate while the vegetables caramelize. If you cook in a large ordinary skillet, be sure to use a heavy one to keep the temperature uniformly low. Be careful, as there is a fine line between caramelizing and burning. Too much browning, and the dish will turn bitter.

Marmouma should be refrigerated at least overnight before serving. It will keep for up to a week in the refrigerator, improving as it mellows. Serve as one of a trio of North African salads, or simply smeared on toasted bread.

SERVES 6 TO 8; MAKES ABOUT 1½ CUPS

1¾ to 2 pounds red ripe tomatoes (about 7)
(see Note)

1 pound green frying peppers

1 small red bell pepper

½ pound zucchini

7 large garlic cloves

½ cup extra virgin olive oil

1 teaspoon sea salt

½ teaspoon sugar

⅛ teaspoon cayenne, or to taste

2 pinches of ground coriander

2 tablespoons capers, drained

1. Halve the tomatoes; gently squeeze out the seeds. Place the tomatoes, cut sides down, on paper towels.

2. Core and seed the peppers and cut them into 1-inch pieces. Quarter the zucchini and cut into thin slices. Peel the garlic but leave whole.

3. Heat the olive oil in a large skillet, and when hot, add the tomatoes, cut sides down. Place the peppers, zucchini, and garlic on top and cook, uncovered, without stirring, for 5 minutes. Add the salt. Cover and cook the vegetables for 15 minutes longer.

4. Carefully pick out the tomato skins and discard them. Continue to cook the mixture until all the moisture has evaporated and it starts to fry in the released oil, about 1 hour. If necessary, use a few drops of water to scrape up any caramelized bits stuck to the bottom of the pan and fold them into the vegetables.

5. Stir in the sugar, cayenne, and coriander and continue to fry, stirring, for 10 minutes. When everything is very thick and has reduced to about 1½ cups, remove from the heat and drain in a colander. (About 2½ tablespoons oil can be recouped from the draining; reserve this oil for cooking or for sprinkling over the marmouma.) Garnish with capers just before serving.

Note: If fresh tomatoes aren't red ripe and flavorful, it is better to use canned organic tomatoes.

HOT AND COLD SOUPS

———— �֍ ————

I like all kinds of soups: thin soups, frugal soups, lavish soups, and rich soups, so long as they're interesting and enjoyable to eat. What I don't like are stodgy, boring soups. Soup recipes can be one of the best culinary prisms through which to view new places and gain a feeling for other people's lives. And since I'm writing here specifically about traditional and modern versions of Mediterranean soups, I'm hopeful these recipes will offer insights into the Mediterranean way of life.

For me, at its best the Mediterranean lifestyle is about authenticity. Yet authenticity is not always to be found on the contemporary Mediterranean table. I've visited home cooks from Migas, Spain, to Kars, Turkey, who only want to reproduce the same gorgeously photographed easy-to-cook food they see in food magazines. And many restaurant chefs from Tangier to Istanbul are only too eager to create new dishes. Yet for all the new food magazine and inventive chef recipes, very few measure up to the traditional dishes. The old simple soups, especially, are rarely equaled—proof, I believe, that as Leonardo da Vinci put it so well, "simplicity is the ultimate sophistication."

SAFE STREET FOOD

Mediterranean street food is generally safe to eat. One is able to watch the food preparation and assure oneself that proper hygiene practices are observed. When I asked my friend Dr. Adam Drewnowski, Director of Health and Nutrition at the University of Washington, about the safety of eating street food like *leblebi* (see page 68), he said: "With a fiery sauce like harissa, you can pretty well count on the concept of 'Darwinian gastronomy' kicking in. [Darwinian gastronomy, developed at Cornell, is a theory that cooking methods and use of certain spices and herbs evolved in response to food-borne illnesses.] The capsaicin in chili peppers is a potent bacteriocidal agent and bug repellent. Natural (hot) spices not only make food good tasting, but helps make it safe."

Poor Man's Bread, Kale, and Black Pepper Soup

*A*t a restaurant in Siena a waiter told me: "In Florence they put bread in their soup and here we put soup on our bread." Thus this wonderful thick soup, which you can prepare in advance, then reheat.

SERVES 3 TO 4

1 pound young tender kale (Tuscan, black, lacinata, or dinosaur)

1¼ ounces pancetta, chilled or frozen

3 tablespoons extra virgin olive oil

1 cup minced onion

2 large garlic cloves, crushed

Salt

6 to 8 thin slices of dense, dry country-style bread, grilled or toasted, and rubbed with plenty of fresh garlic

1 teaspoon freshly ground black pepper

3 ounces grated pecorino cheese (about ½ cup)

1. Stem, wash, and finely shred the kale to make about 5½ cups. Use a large-hole grater to shred the pancetta to make about 3 tablespoons.

2. Heat the olive oil in a wide saucepan over medium heat. Add the pancetta, onion, and garlic and cook until soft and golden, 5 minutes. Add the kale, turning it over to mix well, and cook for another 2 to 3 minutes. Add 5 cups water and bring the mixture to a boil. Reduce the heat and cook slowly for about 20 minutes, or until the kale is very tender. (The recipe can be prepared up to this point 5 hours in advance.)

3. About 20 minutes before serving, slowly reheat the soup to boiling. Season with salt to taste. Let simmer 5 minutes. Divide the grilled bread among 3 or 4 wide soup bowls. Ladle the greens and liquid into each of the bowls. Garnish each serving with a generous drizzle of olive oil, ¼ teaspoon black pepper, and 1 to 2 tablespoons grated cheese. Let settle about 10 minutes. Serve with extra cheese and pepper.

Notes: Tuscan kale is available all year round, but it is best after the first frost.

If you have some Parmigiano-Reggiano rinds in the refrigerator, add one to the pot in Step 2. Remember to remove it, rinse, and save to flavor a tomato sauce or another hardy soup.

Tunisian Chickpea Soup with Eggs, Capers, Olives, and Hot Chile Sauce

In my opinion, the prize for most colorful, balanced, freshest, most delicious, and most exciting of all Mediterranean street foods goes to Tunisian *leblebi*. A souplike meal-in-a-dish, it consists of a large bowl of torn stale bread covered with long-simmered chickpeas, a boiling rich broth made with the trotters or bones of veal, and medium-cooked eggs, with the whites firm and the yolks still runny. It is served under an ample amount of the famous Tunisian hot sauce *harissa*, topped with a pinch of capers, a few juicy olives, and roasted sweet red pepper strips. Finally, it's garnished with ground cumin, a lemon quarter, and, at the last minute, a drizzle of some intensely fruity extra virgin olive oil. The resulting melange, in its colorful abstract beauty, resembles a Joan Mitchell painting.

Leblebi is found in hole-in-the-wall stalls in cities and towns throughout Tunisia. The dish is usually served as a breakfast and is almost always cooked by men for men. I eat it whenever I go to Tunisia, enjoying the atmosphere of male camaraderie, the delicious flavor, the reasonable price, and its aroma so early in the morning.

Happily, leblebi is a dish that travels well. And you can enjoy the leblebi experience at home without veal or lamb trotters or a bunch of Tunisian men smoking as they eat it. Whether I serve it for breakfast, lunch, or dinner, people usually ask for more. In the words of Mae West: "Too much of a good thing can be wonderful."

SERVES 8

½ pound dried chickpeas, soaked overnight in
   water to cover with a pinch of baking soda

2 cups rich veal stock

1 pound veal bones, optional

4 garlic cloves, halved

3 tablespoons extra virgin olive oil

Salt

8 very fresh eggs

3 cups cubed stale peasant-style bread

½ cup *harissa, harous,* or *harissa-harous* sauce,
   thinned to pouring consistency with water
   and olive oil (pages 309 to 310)

Ground cumin

Freshly ground pepper

24 pitted black olives

1 heaping tablespoon small capers, drained

1 roasted red bell pepper, diced

Your best olive oil, for drizzling

8 lemon wedges

1 Preheat the oven to 225°F. Drain the chickpeas and rinse thoroughly; place in a deep heavy
pot. Add the veal stock, bones if you have them, garlic, olive oil, a pinch of salt, and enough water
to cover by 1 inch. Bring to a boil, cover, and transfer to the oven to simmer slowly until tender,
about 3 hours.

2. Remove and discard the bones and garlic. Skim off the fat. Correct the seasoning of the liquid. Keep the chickpeas in the cooking liquid. (Up to this point the chickpeas may be made a day
in advance; cover and refrigerate. Reheat to simmering before continuing.)

3. Prepare medium-cooked eggs: Gently lower the eggs in their shells into a saucepan of lightly
vinegared simmering water; remove from the heat. Cover and let stand for 6 minutes in order to
cook the eggs. Remove the eggs from the water, then transfer to a bowl of ice water to cool
quickly; drain. One by one, gently roll the eggs on a hard surface to crackle the shells. Peel, beginning at the rounder side of each egg, dipping occasionally in cool water to facilitate peeling.

4. Divide the stale bread among 8 deep soup bowls. Top with a ladleful of chickpeas and some of
the cooking liquid. Set an egg on the chickpeas in each bowl, then cut the egg so the yolk runs.
Dribble 1 tablespoon harissa or harissa-harous sauce over each serving, dot with pinches of cumin
and sprinkles of salt and pepper. Divide the olives, capers, and diced red pepper among the
bowls. Add more liquid, if necessary. Dribble on your best olive oil and squeeze a wedge of lemon
on top of each. Serve at once.

Chickpea, Celery, and Porcini Soup with Pecorino Cheese

*T*his fine recipe employs the same cooking method described in the preceding recipe, with the addition of oregano, celery, and porcini, an extra swirl of fresh fruity olive oil, and a few curls of pecorino cheese added just before serving. It was inspired by a soup served at the restaurant Oasis in the mountains of Irpinia in Campania. Members of the Fischetti family, who run the restaurant, are adamant about preserving the old culinary traditions of their region. In fact, the motto of the restaurant is *"sapori antichi"* or "old-fashioned flavors." The whole family chips in. Maria Luisa Fischetti cooks; Mamma Giuseppina makes the pasta; her brothers Puccio and Nicola watch over the dining room; and Papa Generoso gardens and provides fresh vegetables and herbs.

When Maria Luisa and Puccio came to the United States to teach at the Culinary Institute of America in the Napa Valley, I had a chance to work with them, observe their talent and devotion, and, of course, taste their simple yet delicious food: authentic flavorful chewy pastas—and soups punctuated with shots of hot red pepper.

I was especially inspired and charmed by this one, and the white bean soup with escarole on page 76, each proving that long, slow cooking and the use of excellent ingredients can result in food one never tires of eating.

SERVES 6

2 cups dried chickpeas

¼ teaspoon baking soda

Salt

½ ounce dried porcini (about ½ cup)

Pinch of sugar

3 imported bay leaves

½ cup extra virgin olive oil, plus more for the table

1 medium onion, peeled and grated in a food processor

2 garlic cloves

2 cups thinly sliced tender celery ribs

⅛ teaspoon Italian or Greek oregano

Freshly ground pepper

Pinch of hot pepper flakes

1½ cups curls of mild sheep's milk cheese such as Sardinian pecorino, *Cacio di Roma,* or if unavailable, a Spanish manchego

1. Soak the chickpeas in plenty of cold water with the baking soda and a pinch of salt for about 12 hours. Soak the porcini with the sugar in 1 cup warm water; refrigerate overnight.

2. Drain the chickpeas; rinse thoroughly, place in a clay pot, add the bay leaves, 6 tablespoons of the olive oil, a pinch of salt, the onion, and enough water to cover the peas by 1 inch, about 6 cups. Cover tightly and bake as described on page 73.

3. Heat the remaining 2 tablespoons oil in a deep heavy pot over medium heat. Add the garlic and cook, stirring, for a minute. Toss in the celery and oregano and cook, stirring, until glazed, about 2 minutes. Drain the porcini and chop into small pieces. Filter the soaking liquid. Add the porcini, its soaking liquid, the chickpeas, its cooking liquid, and 1 quart water and bring to a boil. Cook, uncovered, over medium heat for 20 minutes. Correct the seasoning with salt and pepper. Serve with extra black pepper, a pinch of hot pepper flakes, and curls of a mild sheep's milk cheese. Pass a cruet of extra virgin olive oil at the table.

Notes: Soaking dried mushrooms with a pinch of sugar in water overnight extracts more flavor than the usual recommended 10- to 20-minute soak.

If desired, you may use an electric slow-cooker to cook the chickpeas as directed in Step 2. Cover tightly and cook on low for 8 hours.

Claypot Chickpea Soup

*T*he splendor of this soup is its straight, intense flavor, achieved by using simple ingredients and traditional methods. Though the soup is rustic, the methods used are very precise.

"For a good Sifniot chickpea soup, you absolutely need a crunchy yellow onion that squirts when you cut it," my Greek-born friend Daphne Zepos counsels, after giving me a whole litany of other do's and don'ts, including the proviso that I use rainwater from a cistern and cook my chickpeas in a clay pot with a small opening at a Greek village communal oven.

Daphne remembers how her mother would write the family name in charcoal on the pot. The village baker would push the pot deep into the cavernous oven so it would heat steadily and maintain its temperature throughout the night. The following day, it would be served for lunch.

Two Greek islands, Sifnos and Paros, vie for fame in producing this splendid soup. The only difference between the recipes is that the Sifniots add oregano. I have given the edge to Paros. The recipe here was given to me by Lefteris Menegos of the Music Dance Group of that island. On Paros a special pot with a very small opening called a *skountavlos* is used. I use a Chinese sand pot, but any good bean pot can be substituted.

The chickpeas must be cooked with just enough water to cover, along with some very finely grated onions, bay leaves, a pinch of salt, and *plenty of olive oil.* The pot is sealed with a ribbon of flour, water, and oil to avoid any evaporation, then placed in a slow oven. The chickpeas cook to a silken tenderness that turns them almost buttery on the tongue. Amazingly, their skins become tender and taut. The liquid will thicken slightly as the starch of the chickpeas is slowly released, creating a soup with an earthy flavor.

Serve with just a squeeze of lemon to bring up the taste. You may also serve a chunk of tangy feta cheese on the side.

3 cups dried chickpeas

1 teaspoon baking soda

Salt

3 imported bay leaves

6 tablespoons extra virgin olive oil

1 medium onion, peeled and grated in a food processor

Flour, water, and oil dough for sealing the pot

Freshly ground pepper

Lemon quarters

1. Soak the chickpeas in plenty of cold water with the baking soda and a pinch of salt for about 12 hours.

2. Drain the chickpeas and rinse thoroughly. Place in a clay or sand pot, add the bay leaves, olive oil, a pinch of salt, the grated onion, and enough water to cover the peas by 1 inch, about 6 cups. Seal with a ribbon of flour, water, and a drop of oil. Put the pot in a cold oven, set the heat to 450°F, and bake for 30 minutes. Reduce the heat to 250°F and continue baking for 3 hours. Discard the bay leaves. (*The soup can be prepared 1 day ahead up to this point. Let it cool, then refrigerate.*)

3. To serve, gently reheat the soup to simmering. Adjust the seasoning with salt and pepper. Serve the soup in individual soup bowls and dribble each with a few teaspoons additional olive oil and a squeeze of lemon.

Notes: To prepare a Chinese sand pot (available in most Asian markets), soak it overnight in cold water before the first use, then repeat yearly. You'll find it cooks beans better than most pots and costs less than five dollars (see Mail Order Sources).

If you're lucky enough to own a HearthKit earthen lining for your oven, you'll be able to simulate the Greek village oven approach: place your bean pot in a cold oven; heat the oven to 450°F; reduce after 30 minutes to 250°F; one hour later, turn off the heat, and simply leave the beans overnight in the oven. You can remove them after 3 hours, but the texture is superb when cooked in a clay pot in a clay oven for a longer period of time.

(*continued*)

It is very difficult to overcook chickpeas. If you think they're too soft, let cool in their cooking liquid, then refrigerate for a few hours before reheating. They will be firmer and just as tasty.

Once cooked, chickpeas can be stored, covered, for several days in the refrigerator.

If your tap water is heavily chlorinated, use bottled or filtered water to cook the chickpeas.

If your water is hard, add a small amount of baking soda to the soaking water to help tenderize the chickpeas. Even though you don't lose nutrients if a small amount is added in the cooking (there being very little vitamin C in chickpeas), I personally don't like the soapy taste which will persist after cooking.

You can cook the chickpeas in a slow-cooker on low for 8 hours.

Freeze any chickpeas you don't serve; they can be added to soups, stews, or couscous. Or you can make a Moroccan version of hummus without the tahini, called *serruda*. To do this, crush the chickpeas with grated onion, cayenne, and cilantro leaves, and thin with olive oil to a soupy consistency. Accent with a little lemon juice and salt to taste. Spread on toasted rounds of bread.

The Music Dance Group of Paros has produced a charming cookbook to subsidize their travels. It includes this recipe. You can order the book by writing to parofolk@mail.otenet.gr.

Mediterranean Marinated Fish Soup

*T*his charming fish soup is super light. It's cooked in two stages: first, slices of fish are marinated (my favorite form of slow-cooking), then the fish slices are finished off by pouring on ladlefuls of boiling light herb broth seasoned with bruised fennel seeds, orange peel, and cayenne.

SERVES 6

¼ cup extra virgin olive oil

½ cup dry white wine

2 teaspoons Pernod

1½ teaspoons chopped fresh thyme, plus 1 whole sprig

4 garlic cloves, 2 minced, 2 halved

2 pounds white-fleshed fish such as snapper, grouper, or bass, heads and bones reserved

4 medium red ripe tomatoes, quartered

1 leek, cut up

½ medium onion, cut up

½ large carrot, cut up

½ cup diced fresh fennel

6 sprigs of flat-leaf parsley

1 teaspoon bruised fennel seeds

1 bay leaf

3 inches dried orange peel

2 teaspoons salt

½ teaspoon dried saffron threads, crumbled

Pinch of cayenne

Zest from 1 orange, blanched

1. In a 3-quart dish, combine the olive oil, wine, Pernod, chopped thyme, and minced garlic. Add the fish fillets, cover, and refrigerate for 1 hour.

2. Meanwhile, put the fish heads and bones in a 5-quart casserole. Add the tomatoes, leek, onion, carrot, fennel, parsley, thyme sprig, fennel seeds, bay leaf, halved garlic cloves, orange peel, and salt. Pour in 3 quarts water and bring to a boil. Lower the heat to a simmer and cook, uncovered, for 30 minutes. Skim off the scum as it rises to the top.

3. Strain the fish stock through a fine mesh sieve. Add the saffron and cayenne and bring to a boil. Simmer for 2 minutes.

4. Meanwhile, slice the fish crosswise on a slight bias into strips about 3 inches long and 1 to 1½ inches wide. Divide pieces of marinated fish among 6 soup plates. Pour the very hot fish soup over the raw fish, just to cover. Let stand 5 minutes. The hot soup will finish cooking the fish. Sprinkle the blanched orange zest over each portion.

White Bean and Escarole Soup

Chef Maria Luisa Fischetti knows the difference between a good grandmotherly bean-and-greens soup and one that's positively noble. Her method (which makes all the difference) is a simple long soaking, then slow cooking of the beans so they will cook evenly, and then, when they're almost finished, crushing and stirring them into a dense cream.

Escarole is added just 10 minutes before serving so that it will retain its vibrant green color. Please don't forget to scatter cheese curls on this fragrant soup at the table, then drizzle a little extra fresh extra virgin olive oil on top.

SERVES 6

1 pound dried white beans, such as Great Northern

3 garlic cloves, smashed

1 bay leaf

1 dried thin red chile pepper, rinsed and broken in half

5 sage leaves

Salt

¼ cup extra virgin olive oil

1 small head of escarole, well washed and drained

½ teaspoon dried Italian oregano

Freshly ground pepper

Crushed hot red pepper flakes

Shavings of mild sheep's milk cheese such as Sardinian pecorino, *Cacio di Roma*, or if unavailable, a Spanish manchego

1. Rinse the dried beans and drain. Put the beans in a deep narrow pot, preferably a bean pot. Add water to cover and leave to soak overnight.

2. The following day, drain and rinse the beans and place in a clay pot or enameled cast-iron casserole. Add the garlic, bay leaf, dried red chile pepper, sage, 1 teaspoon salt, and 3 tablespoons of the olive oil. Cover with enough water to cover everything by 1 inch. Cover with foil and a tight-fitting lid. Place in a cold oven, set the temperature to 450°F, and bake for 30 minutes. Reduce the heat to 225°F and bake for 1½ to 2 hours longer. The cooking time of the beans will vary according to the quality and age. Discard the red chile pepper and bay and sage leaves. Leave the beans in the pot.

3. Shred the escarole. You should have about 1 packed quart. Place the greens in a large wide saucepan with the remaining tablespoon of olive oil, the oregano, and salt and pepper. Cook, stirring, until the greens are soft and glazed, about 5 minutes. Use a slotted spoon to transfer the beans to the saucepan. Use a potato masher to crush the beans to a puree. Dilute with as much of the cooking liquid as needed to make the beans creamy. Simmer over very low heat, stirring, for 10 minutes. Correct the seasoning with salt, pepper, a few pinches of crushed hot red pepper, and a dribble of extra virgin olive oil over the soup. Serve hot with curls of cheese.

Notes: If your tap water is heavily chlorinated, use filtered water to cook the beans. The texture and flavor will be much better.

Though it's true that some varieties of dried beans don't require soaking before cooking, nonetheless I soak white beans overnight for this recipe.

You can soak and cook the beans in the same lightly salted water in an electric slow-cooker set on low for about 7 hours.

If you cook your beans in a clay pot in the HearthKit inset, set the beans in the cold oven, turn on to 450°F and bake for 30 minutes, reduce to 225°F and bake for 1 hour, turn off the heat and leave until ready to continue preparing the soup. Cooking beans in a clay pot on a baking tile or in an insulated earthen or clay oven produces the best creamy texture when the beans are stirred with a wooden pestle to a puree.

COOKING DRIED BEANS

You don't have to cook beans in a large amount of water. In fact, it's actually better if you use less. As Harold McGee writes in his brilliant book *On Food and Cooking, Science and Lore of the Kitchen:*

And it turns out, contrary to what we would expect, that seeds will actually absorb more water in a smaller volume of water: the less cooking water, the fewer carbohydrates are leached out, and the carbohydrates will take up about 10 times their own weight in water. This means, then, that seeds will seem softer in a given time if cooked in a minimal amount of liquid. So give the seeds enough water both to soak up and to cook in (many a pan bottom has been charred because the cook forgot that beans imbibe), but don't drown them.

Turkish Red Lentil Soup with Paprika and Mint Sizzle

Among the well-traveled, well-heeled, fast-moving Istanbul set, Restaurant Develi is known as a "carnivore's mecca" for the incredible quality of its lamb kebabs. The kebabs, made from hand-chopped lamb laced with plenty of sheep's tail fat, taste great and literally melt in your mouth.

Good as the kebabs are, it's the red lentil soup that keeps bringing me back. Creamy as crème fraîche, it seems to coat the tongue with satin. It's sharply seasoned, too, garnished with paprika, a mint-infused olive oil sizzle, and tiny cubes of toasted bread. It is amazing how much a simple scattering of bread cubes can lift a dish.

Owner Arif Develi watches over his restaurant as closely as Venetian Harry Cipriani watches over his. Arif considers himself a culinary guardian. Sounding a little like a California chef, he tells me: "I only use young male lambs from the region of Trakya. I buy my lentils from Gaziantep, my butter from Sanliurfa, my red pepper and rice from Kahramanmaras. You see, I use only the finest ingredients!

"When I was growing up in southeastern Turkey," Arif tells me, "my mother, a widow, had to watch every penny. To stretch this soup, she added cubed and toasted bread. I still keep the tradition!"

SERVES 4

1 cup red lentils

⅓ cup grated onion

½ teaspoon crushed garlic

4 tablespoons unsalted butter

2 tablespoons white rice

½ cup canned tomatoes or 1½ tablespoons tomato paste

Sea salt

2 tablespoons flour

2 cups meat stock

1 teaspoon crushed dried mint, preferably Egyptian spearmint (see Mail Order Sources)

2 teaspoons Turkish or Aleppo red pepper flakes

1 cup cubed bread croutons, fried in butter until golden

1. Rinse the lentils and drain. Place the onion, garlic, and 1 tablespoon of the butter in a deep saucepan and cook over medium heat, stirring gently for 5 minutes. Add the lentils, rice, tomato, and 1½ quarts water. Cover, bring to a boil, and skim carefully. Cook, covered, over medium-low heat for 45 minutes, stirring occasionally. The soup should develop a creamy consistency. If desired, cool slightly, then press through a food mill. Correct the seasoning with salt to taste.

2. Meanwhile, in a small skillet or saucepan, make a roux with the flour and 2 tablespoons of the butter until it reaches the color of hazelnuts and has a delightful aroma. Gradually add the stock, stirring constantly until smooth. Scrape the roux and stock mixture into the soup and cook, whisking, for 5 minutes. Add salt to taste and cook for a few minutes longer.

3. Just before serving, make the paprika and mint sizzle: Press the mint and red pepper flakes through a fine sieve or whirl in a spice grinder to a fine powder. In the same small skillet, melt the remaining 1 tablespoon butter. Add the powdered aromatics and heat until just sizzling. Pour over the soup in swirls. Cover and bring to the table. Fold in the aromatic swirls just before ladling the soup into individual serving bowls. Serve with the croutons.

Chilled Green Pea and Borage Soup

This refreshing, moss-green soup from western Turkey, called *bezelye corbasi,* combines tiny peas with cooling borage leaves and stalks, which taste like cucumber. Its peerless flavor is due to small young peas. Old peas, with too much starch, won't yield as fine a result. In Turkey, the soup is generally served warm, but I prefer it chilled.

Think of this soup as a "basic black dress" you can gussy up with some whipped cream, or garnish by scattering some blue borage flowers on top, or simply enhance with a swirl of olive oil or pistachio oil blended with very young borage leaves.

SERVES 4 TO 6

4 cups whole-milk yogurt

2 tablespoons extra virgin olive oil

¼ cup finely chopped young leek (white part only) or scallion

1½ cups chopped fresh borage stalks and young leaves (see Note)

1 package (10 ounces) first-quality frozen petite peas

Pinches of sugar

Salt and freshly ground pepper

Borage flowers, for garnish

1. Make the soup early in the day or the day before. Drain the yogurt in a paper towel–lined colander set over a bowl for 3 to 4 hours.

2. Meanwhile, heat the olive oil in a deep saucepan. When it's hot, add the leek, cover, reduce the heat to low, and cook gently for 4 to 5 minutes. Add the borage stalks and leaves and cook, stirring, for 2 minutes. Add 2 cups water and bring to a boil. Simmer for 10 minutes.

3. Add the peas and cook for 5 more minutes. Remove from the heat and add the sugar and salt and pepper. Let cool, then whirl in an electric blender or food processor with 1 cup water until smooth. Strain through a sieve into a bowl, cover, and store in the refrigerator.

4. Place 2 cups of the drained yogurt in a wide bowl; gradually whisk in the pea soup. Thin with ice water to the desired consistency. Correct the seasoning. Serve garnished with any remaining yogurt and borage flowers.

Note: If fresh borage is unavailable, you can substitute 1½ cups jarred borage stalks available at The Spanish Table (see Mail Order Sources). Or use 1 cup peeled and seeded diced cucumber.

STALE BREAD FOR SOUP

Around the Mediterranean, stale bread is nearly as important an ingredient as fresh bread. Entire books have been written on what to do with it. Many of the most famous Mediterranean soups are thickened with it: the Spanish summer and winter *gazpacho;* French *panade;* Italian *ribollita;* Middle Eastern *fatta;* Israeli matzo ball soup; and Moroccan Berber *refissa,* consisting of dried bread simmered in an onion broth.

The combination of onion and bread is inevitable. Think of French onion soup gratinée. In Istanbul there are bakeries that sell a special bagel-shaped bread called *simit,* which is soaked in broth, then cooked very slowly, then served with sautéed onions on top. In the Turkish town of Sivas, toasted bread is smothered in a combination of pickled Swiss chard leaves and simmered onions.

Ancient Turks had a word for stale bread dipped in hot gravy—they called it *tirit.* The word actually has two meanings: a meal made with toasted bread soaked in broth or milk, and also an old and weak person.

There is an old Turkish saying: "I dipped my bread in the tirit broth, which I paid for. Don't ever think I got it for free!"

This means that stale bread, though inexpensive, is still something one has to pay for. In other words, stale bread has value.

"In Greece today, wood is expensive, and we need a lot of it to heat the bread ovens," my friend, Greek cookbook author Aglaia Kremezi, tells me. "Often, to save fuel, a home cook will have quite a few loaves of bread baking at the same time. Of course, some of the bread gets stale before it's eaten, so we have a whole category of dishes in which stale bread is soaked in a sauce or broth, then eaten like a pudding or custard."

Four Chilled Gazpachos

*I*n Andalusia, the *canicula,* or dog days of summer, are long and hot, requited by wonderful cold soups called gazpachos. The culinary concept dates back thousands of years: stale bread, pounded with garlic and blended with vinegar and olive oil, then diluted with cold water, is used as a base for soothing, nourishing summer soups.

In Córdoba, a cold gazpacho is not seasonal. Chef José Carrasco Jurado of the restaurant El Churrasco makes pine nut gazpacho in winter, fava bean gazpacho in spring, tomato gazpacho in summer, and almond gazpacho in the fall.

Traditional gazpacho, made by farmhands with hand-grated tomatoes, onions, cucumbers, and peppers ground to a pulp, then salted until they turned soupy, is hardly seen these days. Now, Spanish home cooks whiz combinations of soaked bread, tomatoes, and peppers in their blenders, or in their new (and yet to become popular in America) Thermomixes, making light, airy gazpacho-like foams. Such machines have enabled cooks to create all kinds of new delicious blends. The basic dish is the same, but the technique has evolved. There is little chunkiness in the new gazpachos, except, occasionally, in the garnishes.

The secret of a great gazpacho is a good sherry wine vinegar and a fine fruity extra virgin olive oil. To allow the flavors of the vegetables, vinegar, and olive oil to blend, leave your gazpacho to slowly macerate before serving.

UPSTAIRS DOWNSTAIRS GAZPACHO

My friend the Spanish food expert Clara Maria de Amezua tells me: "Though Andalusian gazpacho is thought of as a country dish, it wasn't always that way. During the nineteenth century it was found on bourgeois and aristocratic tables, for which it was laboriously pressed through sieves. True experts and aficionados insist that gazpacho should be mashed in a wooden bowl or huge mortar, moving the pestle with a particular artistry and savoir-faire.

Fava Bean Gazpacho with Sherry, Raisins, and Green Grapes

*H*ere's a unique, refreshing, velvety green gazpacho, especially popular in early spring when young fava beans appear in the plains around Granada. Since fava beans have an underlying hint of bitterness, raisins soaked in a little sweet sherry are added to balance the flavors. Please make this dish in early spring when local favas are still small and bright green; the very first favas of the season don't need to be peeled. For all other young favas, it is still best to shuck them and peel off their thick skins.

SERVES 2; MAKES 2½ CUPS

1 tablespoon black raisins

1½ tablespoons oloroso sherry

¼ cup soft bread crumbs

1½ teaspoons aged sherry wine vinegar

2½ pounds tender yet crisp fresh fava beans

½ garlic clove

Pinch of coarse salt

Pinch of ground cumin

7 tablespoons sweet or mild extra virgin olive oil

2 cups ice water

1 cup seedless green grapes (peeling is optional)

1. Soak the raisins in ½ tablespoon of the sherry mixed with 2 tablespoons water. Moisten the bread crumbs with 1 teaspoon of the sherry vinegar mixed with 1 tablespoon water.

2. Briefly steam the favas until just wilted, about 5 minutes. Refresh in cold water. Double peel and set aside. The favas should be almost raw.

3. Crush the garlic with the salt. Add the garlic paste to a food processor along with the fava beans, bread paste, cumin, salt to taste, the remaining 1 tablespoon sherry and ½ teaspoon vinegar. Blend well. With the machine on, add the olive oil in a thin stream to create a puree. Gradually work in the ice water. Chill for at least 3 hours. Serve with a garnish of grapes and the drained raisins.

Note: Some people of Mediterranean origin are allergic to raw fava beans. Cooked fava beans are easier to digest.

With thanks to Clara María de Amezua for sharing this recipe.

El Churrasco's White Gazpacho with Pine Nuts and Currants

*T*he gazpacho called *ajo blanco* (which means "white garlic") is usually made with almonds, but at the restaurant El Churrasco in Córdoba they often substitute pine nuts. And because raw egg yolks are used, the soup is made a bit like mayonnaise, producing a truly voluptuous gazpacho with a faintly resinous flavor.

SERVES 6

¼ cup dried currants

2 tablespoons aged sherry wine vinegar

1¾ cups dried crumbled stale bread, crusts removed

1½ cups pine nuts

3 large garlic cloves

1 teaspoon coarse salt

2 large egg yolks, preferably fresh organic or Davidson's pasteurized eggs

1 cup extra virgin olive oil

1. Soak the currants in the sherry vinegar and 2 tablespoons water until soft. Drain, reserving the currants and vinegary water separately.

2. Soak the bread in water until soft, then squeeze dry.

3. Process 1⅓ cups of the pine nuts, the garlic, and the salt in a food processor until a paste forms. Add the egg yolks and the bread and process to combine. With the machine on, slowly add the olive oil, as if making a mayonnaise. Dilute with 1 cup cold water and process for an instant. Press through a sieve into a bowl. Whisk in 4 cups more water, or enough so that the soup is the consistency of heavy cream.

4. Stir in the reserved vinegary water from the currants. Chill for at least half a day.

5. Just before serving, correct the seasoning with salt. Serve the soup garnished with the reserved currants and remaining pine nuts.

Note: For a deeper flavor, slowly toast the pine nuts in a small, dry heavy-bottomed skillet, until fragrant but still pale.

Gazpacho with Melon

*H*ere's a delicious gazpacho inspired by a recipe given to me by Navarre-born, Madrid-based chef Carlos Oyarbide. Carlos serves his version with a green pepper sorbet, tiny shellfish, and a compote of honeyed raisins and vinegar to make his point that he has found his ultimate "inner gazpacho."

In my version, I replace some of the water with melon to endow the soup with a fruity dimension, then I top it off with a slick of green pepper. That's *my* inner gazpacho!

This soup will keep for days in the refrigerator.

SERVES 10 TO 12

8 garlic cloves

Coarse salt

3½ pounds red ripe tomatoes, halved, seeded, and grated (about 1 quart)

1 small green bell pepper, diced

½ red bell pepper, diced

1 medium cucumber, peeled, seeded, and cut into chunks

2 bunches of scallions, trimmed and sliced (about 2 cups)

1 small cantaloupe, halved, seeded, and cut up

⅔ cup extra virgin olive oil

3 cups cubed stale crustless bread

½ teaspoon aged sherry wine vinegar, or more to taste

Pinch of sugar

Fine salt

Green Pepper Oil (recipe follows)

1. Peel the garlic and crush it with 2 teaspoons salt. Place in a large bowl and add the tomatoes, green and red bell peppers, cucumber, scallions, melon, olive oil, and bread. Stir, cover, and allow to macerate in the refrigerator at least 6 hours, overnight if possible.

2. Puree the mixture in batches in a blender or food processor, adding a total of 5 cups cold water. Strain through a fine sieve into a bowl. Stir in the vinegar and sugar. Cover and refrigerate for at least 1 hour, then add salt to taste, if necessary.

3. Ladle the soup into small bowls or cups for sipping. Drizzle the green pepper oil on top.

Green Pepper Oil

Makes about ⅔ cup

1 medium green bell pepper   1 tablespoon extra virgin olive oil

2 tablespoons coarsely chopped flat-leaf parsley

Combine all the ingredients in a blender or food processor and puree until smooth. Strain through a fine sieve.

Salmorejo

In Baena, the summer soup called *salmorejo* is king! It's a smooth, thick, almost foamy cold tomato soup, a variation on gazpacho with a small amount of water and far fewer vegetables, heightened by the taste of a quality extra virgin olive oil and a shock of fine sherry wine vinegar.

Salmorejo has become so popular you now find it served throughout Spain. The following recipe is from the American chef Richard Stephens, chef-owner of the restaurant La Gamella in Madrid. He follows the cardinal rule of the dish: the tomatoes must not only be ripe, they must also be aromatic; and the soup must be left overnight to rest so the flavor will properly develop.

This rich, salmon-pink soup is garnished with ribbons of serrano ham and cubed whites of hard-cooked eggs, creating a stunningly beautiful visual contrast.

2 pounds red ripe, meaty, and juicy tomatoes

3 cups cubed stale crustless bread

1 large garlic clove

Coarse salt

Pinch of sugar

⅓ cup cubed green or red bell pepper

⅓ cup extra virgin olive oil

2 teaspoons aged sherry wine vinegar

Salt and freshly ground pepper

⅓ cup thinly slivered cured ham, preferably Spanish serrano ham

2 hard-cooked egg whites, finely diced

1. One at a time, pierce the stem end of a tomato with a long fork and hold over a high flame to char all over until the skin blisters, or sear in a dry cast-iron skillet. Cool, then peel. Cut a slice off the top of each tomato, scoop out the watery seeds, and strain over a bowl to collect the juices. Discard the seeds. Cut up the tomatoes.

2. In a large bowl, mix the tomatoes with the bread and let stand for at least 20 minutes.

3. Crush the garlic to a paste with 1 teaspoon coarse salt. Add to the tomatoes and bread along with the sugar and bell pepper. Puree the mixture in batches in a blender until smooth. If necessary, add a little water. The soup must be very thick and smooth. With the machine on, add the olive oil in a steady stream to form a very thick soup, the consistency of yogurt. Add the vinegar. Whirl the soup on the highest setting until it becomes foamy, about 2 minutes. Scrape the mixture back into the bowl, cover, and refrigerate for at least 12 hours.

4. To serve, thin with ice-cold water to a thick creamy soup. Correct the seasoning. Ladle into small soup bowls and garnish with the ham and egg whites. Serve cold.

Panade of Leeks and Mixed Greens with Cantal Cheese

*H*ere's a delicious winter soup, French in origin, thick enough to hold a fork straight up. Onions, greens, soaked bread layered with milk, stewed leeks, and cheese are all slowly baked in a wide, glazed earthenware dish until they bind. The mixed leafy greens and cheese give this dish a great look, bubbling and golden brown on top. The choice of bread is crucial here. Pick a good chewy bread with a soft crust. Slow cooking will make it silky and soft. Pass a peppermill.

SERVES 8

3 large leeks (white and light green parts only), chopped

1 red onion, chopped

5 green garlic shoots or 8 to 10 garlic cloves, sliced

¼ cup extra virgin olive oil

Salt

1-pound loaf of stale chewy bread with crust

1½ pounds mixed leafy greens (sorrel, chard, parsley leaves, arugula, spinach, and watercress), deribbed and shredded (about 10 cups)

Juice of ½ lemon

Freshly ground pepper

Grated nutmeg

3 cups whole milk, heated to simmering

½ pound Cantal or Gruyère cheese

1. Measure the leeks, onion, and garlic to be sure you have about 1 quart.

2. In a 7- or 8- quart pot, heat the olive oil over medium heat. Slowly stew the leeks, onion, and garlic for 10 minutes. Add 1 teaspoon salt and cook for 5 more minutes. Meanwhile, preheat the oven to 250°F.

3. Cut the bread into 1-inch cubes. You should have about 2 quarts. Spread the cubes in one layer on an oiled baking sheet and bake for 45 minutes, or until just golden. Let cool and store until ready to use.

4. Add the greens to the pot, cover, and cook over low heat for 45 minutes. Uncover and boil away excess liquid. Allow to cool. Add the lemon juice, pepper, and nutmeg to taste. Correct the salt. (Up to this point the recipe can be prepared 1 day in advance. Cool, cover, and refrigerate. Bring to room temperature before continuing.)

5. About 2½ hours before serving, oil a deep 3-quart casserole, preferably earthenware. Place one-third of the bread cubes in the dish, top with half the greens, and repeat, ending with the bread cubes and patting lightly to make an even topping. Gradually pour the hot milk down the insides and over the top of the panade so everything is moist. If necessary, add ½ cup water. Cover with the grated cheese and a sheet of foil.

6. Bake in a preheated 250°F oven for 1¾ hours. Raise the oven temperature to 400°F, uncover, and bake 20 more minutes. Remove from the oven and allow to relax for about 10 minutes before serving.

RICHARD OLNEY ON BREAD SOUPS

"The mind rarely registers weights and measures in terms of visual bulk. The precision of the measures given here could not be of less importance; the thing to remember is that there should be lots of onion, lots of bread, and lots of cheese in relation to the (undetermined) amount of water."

Easter Lamb Soup with Marjoram and Lemon

The combination of egg and lemon beaten into soups, stews, and vegetable dishes provides extraordinary delicate flavor and visual appeal. Usually this ethereal combination, found most everywhere around the Mediterranean, is added to very simply cooked food, bringing it to new heights.

Some humble products such as lamb breast have fallen out of favor, supplanted by such glamorous ingredients as foie gras and other luxurious meats. In fact, lamb breast, being cheap, juicy, and flavorful, makes a great ingredient for soups. Here the bones, rich in natural gelatin, provide body to this *brodetto Pasquale*. Some cooks serve the meat as a separate course, but since there is so little of it, I just cube it and float it in the soup.

In Rome, the cheese of choice is pecorino (which is Italian for "sheep"), but you might find it too strong and salty for such a subtle soup. I usually substitute another sheep's milk cheese, such as a Spanish manchego or even a dry cow's milk Monterey Jack.

SERVES 6

2 pounds breast of lamb in one piece, rinsed well, excess fat removed

2 quarts hot degreased rich meat stock

6 egg yolks

3 tablespoons fresh lemon juice

3 tablespoons chopped fresh marjoram

Salt and freshly ground pepper

1 cup grated pecorino Romano, Spanish manchego, or dry Monterey Jack cheese

18 slices of narrow Italian bread, toasted

1. Place the lamb in a soup pot, preferably earthenware, set over a heat diffuser. Add the hot stock. Bring to a boil; reduce the heat to low and continue to cook, partially covered, until very tender, about 2 hours. Skim off any scum that rises to the surface.

2. Remove the lamb when well done. Cut the meat into fine dice and discard the bones, gristle, and fat. Keep moist with a few tablespoons stock. Carefully skim the remaining stock to remove as much fat as possible. Keep warm over very low heat while preparing the egg yolks.

3. In a medium bowl, whisk the egg yolks and lemon juice until blended. Very slowly, whisk in 1 cup of the hot stock to raise the temperature of the egg yolks. Whisk in a second cup of stock. Whisk the egg yolk mixture into the remaining stock and cook, whisking constantly, until the soup thickens. Do not let it come to a boil, or it will curdle.

4. Stir in the marjoram, correct the seasoning with salt and pepper, and add the cubes of meat. Ladle into individual bowls and garnish with the toasted cheese and bread slices.

Quince-Flavored Tarhana Soup with Chickpeas and Paprika Sizzle

Tarhana is a rustic cereal with a gentle, sour flavor, which comes from the addition of, among other things, yogurt, soured milk, or yeast. There are many versions of rustic pasta in the eastern Mediterranean with different combinations of grains and flavorings.

Most of the tarhana soups I've tasted—even in Turkey, where they are a winter evening staple—have been filling and nutritious, but also somewhat bland. Not so this version from the Black Sea town of Amasra. It is, in my opinion, absolutely wonderful.

SERVES 4

½ cup quince-flavored tarhana (see page 318)

1 dried New Mexican chile

4 tablespoons butter

4 ounces lamb shoulder meat, trimmed of excess fat and gristle, and cut into ¼-inch dice (½ cup)

1 tablespoon plus 1 teaspoon tomato paste

4 cups meat stock

½ cup cooked chickpeas, drained

Salt

2 teaspoons Turkish red pepper flakes (see Mail Order Sources)

1. Soak the tarhana in 2 cups water for a few hours, or until soft. Drain and gently squeeze out the excess moisture.

2. About 1 hour before serving, soak the chile in warm water until soft, about 30 minutes. Stem and seed the chile; cut it into shreds.

3. Heat 2 tablespoons of the butter in a heavy saucepan. Add the meat and cook over medium heat, turning, until lightly browned on all sides, 5 to 7 minutes.

4. Add 1 tablespoon of the tomato paste and fry for an instant. Stir in the chile pepper, drained tarhana, and meat stock. Reduce the heat to low and simmer, uncovered, for 30 minutes.

5. Add the drained chickpeas and cook 5 more minutes. Thin with water to a nice soupy consistency. Correct the seasoning with salt to taste.

6. Just before serving, in a small pan or skillet, melt the remaining 2 tablespoons butter. Add the red pepper and 1 teaspoon tomato paste; heat until sizzling. Dilute with 1 teaspoon water and pour over the soup in swirls. Cover, wait 5 minutes, and bring to the table. Serve right from the pot.

SEAFOOD

———— ✦ ————

At first blush the concept of slow cooking fish seems counterintuitive, but, in fact, the Mediterranean has a large number of such dishes—slow-fried fish; fish slow-poached in olive oil; fish baked slowly in salt or clay; sun-dried fish; oven-steamed fish; fish marinated and preserved in olive oil; and *en escabeche.*

One slow-frying method I like a lot is the eastern Mediterranean approach to fresh sardines, in which they are fried in lots of olive oil at 300°F. These small fish, which have a high oil content of their own, cook slowly at the bottom of the pan, then rise when done: crisp, golden, and oil free.

Cooking and then preserving tuna in olive oil is an ancient process. Today, chefs in Spain, France, Italy, and the United States are slow-simmering salmon, swordfish, tuna, calamari, and clams in olive oil, duck, or goose fat until the flesh feels firm to the touch, then serving them straightaway with ragouts of vegetables, or as a part of a larger presentation.

PAELLA

On a trip to the rice-growing areas of Calasparra and Valencia in southeastern Spain, I learned just how prickly a subject paella can be. People there debate every facet of Spain's most famous dish: Which is the best rice? Does hard water or soft work better? Can paella legitimately be prepared in a kitchen oven, or on top of the stove, or must it be cooked in the field over an open wood fire? Which ingredients are required in an authentic paella? When is a paella not a paella, but an *arroz*?

Señora A—, a representative of the famous Valencian food market, explained the difference between paellas and the family-style rice dishes called *arroces* in terms of gender. Paellas, she told me, are "virile" dishes because they were originally prepared in wide steel pans in the countryside by men who gathered snails, hunted rabbits, and caught ducks or freshwater eels, then cooked them with rice until the grains were plump with flavor yet still dry and slightly firm. "Womanly" arroces, on the other hand, she told me with a straight face, are *meloso*, or soft and creamy; they're not cooked in shallow steel pans but in deeper earthenware cazuelas or casseroles.

"In Valencia, they are absolute fundamentalists when it comes to paella," said Norberto Jorge, chef and owner of the popular Madrid restaurant, Casa Benigna. "Because Valencia is coastal, its cooks transformed the rudimentary rabbit-and-eel version of the countryside into an apocryphal seafood, chicken, and sausage version, then never strayed from the recipe so that it has become immutable in its residents' minds."

Norberto, a soft-spoken, guitar-playing, singing chef, is famous for his imaginative paellas. He grew up in Alicante, where cooks are not bound by the paella conventions of Valencia to the north. "Where I come from, we don't worry about what's authentic the way they do in Valencia," Norberto said. "We just try and make good food."

Norberto experiments in a freewheeling manner. "Once," he told me, "I angered a group of Valenciennes by preparing a series of dishes I called paellas *monográficas*—single subject paellas." For these dishes he covered the rice with a thin single ingredient topping. One night it was a layer of lightly marinated fillet of salmon, which gave the rice a beautiful pink color. Another night he used sea bass.

(continued)

I asked Norberto how far he went with this.

"Well," he said, "I scandalized the food critics with what I think of as my greatest success, a dessert paella made with black Thai rice, coconut milk, and granulated sugar, a variation on *arroz con leche,* or rice pudding, a specialty of my grandmother Antonia."

Whether you're cooking in a traditional or improvisational style, preparing rice for paella isn't difficult. Norberto told me the rules: (1) Never wash the rice. (2) Bring the broth or water to a simmer before adding it to the rice. (3) Stir the rice for the first few minutes only. (4) After cooking, allow the paella to rest for at least 10 minutes under a towel to absorb excess moisture.

Norberto doesn't fool around with different kinds of rice. He stockpiles burlap sacks of Spain's premier rice, bomba, in his restaurant. This squat rice, with a starchy inner core, can absorb vast amounts of flavorful broth without falling apart, allowing Norberto to perfect the crusty paellas that have made his reputation in Madrid.

In fact, his paellas are so perfect and well caramelized that he can actually hold a paella pan by one handle, then carry it into his restaurant dining room like a suitcase. The secret is twofold: the variety of rice, and the ratio of rice to olive oil. Norberto explained: "Once the rice has absorbed all the broth, it should be allowed to fry in the oil remaining in the pan so that a golden crust, called *socarrat,* forms on the bottom. Thus one delicious grain becomes tied to another, holding the entire dish together."

SHELLFISH

Paella with Shellfish and Artichokes

I created this paella recipe after visiting Alicante in southern Spain. It's not nearly so daring or inventive as some of the "new paellas" being served in Spain today, but it's been much appreciated when I've served it to my guests. I prepare it with fresh tuna, shrimp, mussels, and artichokes simmered in a saffron and paprika–infused broth, using time-honored paella cooking techniques.

SERVES 8

1 red bell pepper

Fine sea salt

1 pound tuna steak, cut into 1½-inch cubes

8 large shrimp

1 large ancho chile

⅓ cup dry white wine

1 pound mussels, scrubbed and debearded

Freshly ground pepper

5 tablespoons extra virgin olive oil

2 tablespoons coarsely chopped garlic

1¼ cups canned diced tomatoes

2 teaspoons Spanish smoked *pimentón* or sweet paprika

2 pinches of saffron threads

6 to 8 cups fish stock, or 2 packages (8 ounces each) frozen fish fumet diluted with 4 cups water (see Note on adding shrimp shells for a more flavorful fumet)

1 package (9 ounces) frozen artichoke hearts, cut into 1-inch pieces

8 scallions, cut into 1½-inch lengths

2 cups short- to medium-grain rice, preferably bomba

2 tablespoons chopped flat-leaf parsley

Lemon wedges, for serving

(continued)

1. Roast the red bell pepper under a preheated broiler, turning, until charred. Transfer the pepper to a small bowl, cover with plastic wrap, and let steam for 5 minutes. Peel the roasted pepper, discarding the core, ribs, and seeds; cut the pepper into 1-inch pieces.

2. Salt the tuna cubes and the shrimp and let stand for 30 minutes; pat dry with paper towels. Meanwhile, in a heatproof bowl, cover the ancho chile with 1 cup boiling water and let stand until softened, about 20 minutes; drain. Discard the stem and seeds and coarsely chop the chile.

3. Bring the wine to a boil in a medium saucepan. Add the mussels, cover, and cook over high heat until they begin to open, about 3 minutes. Using a slotted spoon, transfer the mussels to a bowl. Pull off and discard the empty top shells, leaving the mussels on the half-shell. Season the mussels with pepper and cover with foil; reserve the cooking liquid.

4. Heat 2 tablespoons of the olive oil in a large skillet. Add the chopped ancho chile and the garlic. Cook over moderately high heat until the garlic is golden, about 2 minutes. Add the tomatoes, pimentón, saffron, and 1 teaspoon salt and cook over moderate heat for 5 minutes, stirring. Transfer to a food processor and puree to a coarse paste.

5. In a medium saucepan, bring the fish stock to a boil. Cover, reduce the heat to low, and maintain at a simmer. In an 18-inch paella pan or a very large skillet, heat the remaining 3 tablespoons olive oil. Add the tuna and shrimp and cook over moderately high heat, tossing, until browned, about 3 minutes. Transfer to a plate and cover. Add the artichokes and scallions to the pan and cook over moderately high heat for 1 minute. Add the ancho-tomato paste and cook, stirring, for 1 minute. Add 4 cups of the fish stock, the reserved mussel cooking liquid, and ½ teaspoon salt and bring to a boil.

6. Scatter the rice evenly into the pan and stir. Reduce the heat to moderate and cook for 7 minutes. Reduce the heat to low and continue cooking until the liquid has evaporated, about 10 minutes. Add another 3 to 3½ cups of simmering stock and cook, shaking the pan and rotating it for even cooking, until the liquid has evaporated again, about 10 minutes longer. Just before the rice is done, during the last 10 minutes of cooking, gently press the roasted red pepper, mussels, shrimp, and tuna into the paella with the back of a spoon. Continue cooking, shaking the pan, until the rice is just tender but still a bit moist.

7. Remove the pan from the heat and cover with a kitchen towel or paper towels and a foil tent. Let the paella rest for about 10 minutes. Uncover, sprinkle with the parsley, and serve with lemon wedges.

Notes: Bomba rice (see Mail Order Sources) produces the most delicious paellas because each grain has the ability to cook up plump and creamy after absorbing a maximum amount of flavorful liquid. An excellent paella can also be made with other short- to medium-grain rices from Spain, California, and Italy. But if you decide to go "the full bomba," remember that a cup of dry bomba rice requires 3 cups liquid; a cup of short- to medium-grain rice requires only 2 cups liquid.

I save shrimp peels in the freezer. When I want to make a fish stock, I defrost then bake the shells in a very slow oven (200°F) for about 1½ hours. I crush the shells to a powder and use it to flavor stock for paellas and *arroces.*

I imbue my kitchen-cooked paellas and arroces with an outdoors wood-smoke flavor by adding some *pimentón de la Vera,* paprika from Spain's western region, Extremadura. This smoky, brick-red paprika has a warm, rounded flavor. It is produced by drying and smoking mature red peppers over oak fires, then stone-grinding them to a smooth powder almost like talc.

A good, dry paella is ideally cooked in a proper paella pan—a two-handled, wide, shallow, flat-bottomed pan with sloping sides. This type of pan allows liquid to evaporate quickly while the rice cooks, uncovered, over low heat. As an alternative, you can choose a very wide and shallow skillet. These and other necessities—including, for purists, round iron grates for supporting a paella pan over a wood fire in your fireplace—are available from The Spanish Table (see Mail Order Sources).

Los Remos' Shrimp and Seaweed Fritters

*I*n the streets of Algeciras and Cádiz, in Spain, these sweet and tender, thin and lacy *tortíllitas,* made from a perfectly seasoned batter studded with live, thin-shelled, shrimplike crustaceans called *camarones (Palaemonetes varians),* were once a simple street food. The shrimp were pulled up in nets in neighboring estuaries, dropped into a chickpea flour–based batter, fried in olive oil, and eaten hot. Today they are a popular *tapa* everywhere in Andalucia.

The mecca for this fritter, or *tortíllita,* is no longer found in the streets but at the Los Remos Restaurant in San Roque, a ten-minute taxi ride away from the port of Algeciras. The back story here makes for a wonderful tale of raggedy fish fritters to riches: Alejandro Fernandez Gavilán and his wife, Nati, used to run a beach bar along the river where Alejandro's fisherman father caught and sold his catch of the day. Now, fifteen years later, Alejandro and Nati run their restaurant out of a Victorian villa, proving that their "street dishes," such as this delicious fritter, are worthy of serving on a white tablecloth.

Here's an adaptation of Nati's recipe.

SERVES 4 TO 5; MAKES ABOUT 20 FRITTERS

½ scant teaspoon finely crumbled dried seaweed

2 to 3 ounces fresh camarones or peeled rock shrimp

2 scallions (white and 1 inch of the green), sliced

1 garlic clove

Sea salt

½ cup graham flour, toasted chickpea flour, or coarse semolina

½ cup all-purpose flour

Olive oil, for frying

1. Three to 6 hours before serving, prepare the batter. Soften the seaweed in ¼ cup warm water for 5 minutes. Meanwhile, rinse and drain the shrimp. Put the shrimp in a food processor, add the scallion, garlic, and a pinch of salt, and pulse to a puree. Add the seaweed, soaking liquid, and both flours and just enough cool water to make a thin batter, about 1¼ cups. Process until well combined. Scrape into a measuring bowl. Cover and refrigerate for 3 to 6 hours.

2. Let the batter come to room temperature. To check if the batter is the right consistency, lift a spoonful; it should fall back into the bowl in a steady stream. If it's too thick, thin with water. Heat the oil in a deep-fryer to 385°F. (The temperature will drop to 370°F when the food is added.) Dip a tablespoon in the oil, then into the batter. Drop globs of batter into the hot oil, 4 to 5 at a time. Fry the fritters, flattening each against the side of the pan into a cake about 2 inches round, until golden and crisp, turning once. Drain on paper towels. Serve hot.

Note: One of Nati's secrets is the inclusion of a local sea lettuce *(Ulva latuca),* a rubbery, bright green leaf that is more delicious cooked than raw. Sea lettuce is easily found along the northern California coast and can be purchased in some Asian markets. If you can't find it, substitute any other rehydrated seaweed.

CHICKPEA FLOUR

Around the Mediterranean, especially in city streets, you'll always find some sort of delightfully grainy snack food. Usually these snacks are savory, but sometimes they're sweet and made with chickpea flour, which used to be cheaper than white flour made from wheat. Chickpea flour turns up in numerous fried fritters, such as the *panisse* in Marseille, *panelle* in Palermo, *tortillita* in Cádiz, and falafel in Tel Aviv. It's also used to make thick crepes, such as *farinata* in Genoa and *socca* in Nice; a fenugreek-flavored butter cookie called *ghoriba homs* in Tunis; a cumin-flavored, egg-based pudding called *karantika* in Tangier and Gibraltar; and *hibes* (a chickpea flour version of hummus) in Antalya on the Mediterranean coast of Turkey.

Chickpea flour is sold toasted or raw and can be purchased in Indian or Pakistani markets, or from Kalustyan's (see Mail Order Sources). Store in the freezer; it has a very short shelf life. Toasted chickpea flour is tastier. If not available, place raw chickpea flour in a heavy skillet and cook, stirring, over low heat for about 10 minutes until aromatic but not brown. Remove and let cool.

Shrimp with Orange, Shallots, and Grilled Radicchio

*H*ere's a colorful dish of marinated shrimp served with a luscious fruity orange and shallot sauce, accompanied by a mound of burnished radicchio and a few drops of your best balsamic vinegar.

My recipe is based on a dish served at the restaurant Franco Rossi in Bologna. The chef confided his personal secret: a white paste composed of shallots ground with butter and olive oil to thicken the sauce.

SERVES 4 FOR LUNCH OR A FIRST COURSE

4 tablespoons olive oil

1 teaspoon chopped garlic

⅓ cup orange juice

½ teaspoon grated orange zest

3 teaspoons fresh lemon juice

Salt and freshly ground pepper

2 tablespoons unsalted butter, at room temperature

2 tablespoons finely chopped shallots

1 tablespoon finely chopped flat-leaf parsley

1¼ pounds large shrimp in the shell (about 2 dozen)

1 large radicchio, preferably Treviso, cored and cut into eighths

A few drops of balsamic vinegar

1 cup baby greens, for garnish

1. Early in the day, make the marinade. Gently heat 2 tablespoons olive oil in a skillet and add the chopped garlic, 3 tablespoons of the orange juice, the orange zest, 2 teaspoons of the lemon juice, and salt and pepper. Remove from the heat and let cool completely.

2. Cream the butter with the shallots, remaining 1 teaspoon lemon juice, parsley, and salt and pepper to taste. Set aside.

3. About 1 hour before serving, marinate the shrimp in the orange juice mixture.

4. Heat a ridged iron grill. Brush the chunks of radicchio with the remaining 2 tablespoons olive oil and grill until all the surfaces are browned and the interiors are tender, about 5 minutes. Place the radicchio in a covered dish, sprinkle with salt and pepper, and keep warm.

5. About 5 minutes before serving, in a heated skillet set over medium heat, sauté the shrimp and marinade, turning often, until they're cooked and the marinade is reduced and syrupy, about 2 minutes. Add the shallot butter and cook, stirring, for 1 more minute. Remove the skillet from the heat and hold.

6. Divide the shrimp and radicchio among serving plates. Pour the remaining orange juice, the balsamic vinegar, and 2 tablespoons water into the skillet. Quickly bring to a boil and reduce slightly. Sprinkle each serving with the deglazed juices and top with a few baby greens. Serve at once.

Notes: Make the oily shallot butter and the marinade in advance; the flavors will improve upon resting.

I buy frozen shrimp in the shell in 5-pound bags, ask the fishmonger to quarter the bags, then keep each section well wrapped in the freezer. Each section will serve three to four. Defrost overnight in the refrigerator in a plastic tub of salted water. The following day, drain, peel, devein, pat dry, and marinate 1 hour before cooking. Avoid overmarinating the shrimp lest they become tough.

If I have time, I use the shells to make a shrimp-flavored syrup, which adds another dimension to the dish. To make this syrup, slowly cook the shells in a drop of oil in a skillet or in a 200°F oven until dry; cover with water and simmer until reduced and syrupy. Strain and add enough water to cover, plus a small amount of chopped onion, garlic, and parsley, and cook for 30 minutes; strain and reduce to 2 tablespoons. Use instead of water in Step 6.

Spicy Mussels with Herbs and Feta Cheese

*T*his dish certainly isn't slow in the traditional sense if you prepare it the way they do in Thrace—quickly in a skillet with hot peppers, garlic, and butter. It is this last ingredient that "only a wacky Thracian" would add. And it is possible to take a slow approach with excellent results.

In this adapted recipe, a variation on the famous Macedonian mussels *saganaki,* the mussels are partially prepared in the morning not merely to remove the sand, shells, and beards but also to infuse the mussels with a Thracian herb and spice mixture. When it's time to serve, simply reheat the mussels and mount their juices with butter.

Try to serve with glasses of ouzo and thin slices of toasted baguette sticking out of the broth, useful for soaking up the spicy juices.

SERVES 4 TO 6

3 pounds small mussels

Sea salt

4 tablespoons unsalted butter

1 cinnamon stick, 2 inches long

⅔ cup dry white wine

1 teaspoon freshly ground pepper

Juice of ½ lemon

¼ cup slivered fresh basil

¼ cup chopped flat-leaf parsley

1 long dried red chile pepper, about 3 inches long

2 teaspoons tomato paste

2 teaspoons chopped garlic

3 ounces cow's milk feta

Salt

Garlic toasts

1. Scrub the mussels, pull off the beards, and rinse in several changes of water. Place the mussels in a bowl of lightly salted cool water and let stand for at least 1 hour so they purge themselves of sand. (Farmed mussels do not need soaking; if soaked, they lose all their flavor.) Drain the mussels.

2. Heat a large nonreactive shallow pan until hot, add 1 tablespoon of the butter, and allow to sizzle. Add the cinnamon stick, mussels, and wine all at once, cover, and cook over high heat until the mussels open, about 2 minutes. If the shells are just beginning to open, leave them 1 minute longer, but do not overcook. Transfer the mussels to a bowl in order to catch their juices. Strain the cooking liquid through a fine sieve and reserve. Discard the cinnamon stick. Shell the mussels and season them with the black pepper and the lemon juice.

3. Wipe out the pan, add another tablespoon of the butter, and set over medium heat. Add half the basil, half the parsley, and the chile pepper and cook for 1 minute, stirring. Add the tomato paste, reserved mussel cooking liquid, and garlic; quickly bring to a boil. Cook over medium heat for 2 minutes, or until the liquid has reduced to about 1 cup. Remove from the heat, add the mussels, and set aside to cool. If making in advance, cool, cover, and refrigerate.

4. About 30 minutes before serving, bring the mussels to room temperature if prepared in advance. If the feta is very salty, soak it in cold water to remove excess salt. Drain the feta and cut into small slices. Dice the remaining 2 tablespoons butter. Scatter the feta and butter over the mussels. Slowly cook until almost boiling. Swirl to allow the butter and cheese to thicken the sauce. Correct the seasoning of the sauce with salt, pepper, and lemon. Garnish with the remaining basil and parsley and serve at once with the garlic toasts.

BUTTER IN GREEK COOKING?
ASK A WACKY THRACIAN

If you want to bug a Latin student, assign a passage that includes the word cream. *The Romans had no word for it, so your student will have to improvise some clumsy translation like* spuma lactis *(milk scum).*

The fact is, the Greeks and Romans scarcely ever consumed milk in any form but cheese. Fresh milk spoils quickly unless pasteurized and refrigerated, especially in the warm Mediterranean climate. Even yogurt (oxygala) *didn't keep well enough to be a significant part of their diet.*

The word butter *does come from Greek, where* boutyron *has the odd literal meaning "cow cheese," suggesting that the Greeks, who mostly herded sheep and goats, picked up the idea from some cattle-breeding neighbors of theirs. They certainly found the very idea of cooking with it terribly amusing, something only a wacky Thracian would do. In ancient Greece and Rome, you used olive oil for cooking; butter was for external application only—rubbing on a burn, for instance.*

—CHARLES PERRY, *LOS ANGELES TIMES*

I was reminded of Charles Perry's remarks when I was in the town of Xanthi in Thrace doing research for this book. Over a glass of beer, the owner of a local *taverna* described the *pièce de resistance* of Thracian winter cooking. "It's called *tsoplekis,*" he told me, "and requires a great sense of balance as to fats and flavors if the cook is to get it right. Lamb or veal is cut small, so it will fit into a narrow-topped clay pot. Butter, fresh horseradish, paprika, and mint are added, then the pot is sealed and buried in the embers of the fireplace overnight." He rolled his eyes skyward. "It is a dish for the Olympian Gods!"

No less celestial was this gentlemen's *midia pikantika*, a mussel dish cooked with spices and butter (page 106), accompanied by a glass of ouzo. The mussels were served as a soupy stew, swimming in a luxurious, buttery liquid flavored with black peppercorns, chiles, basil, parsley, peppers, and a scattering of feta. When I returned home and made it for my husband, he commented: "This isn't Greek food, this is Greek *cuisine!*"

SQUID, CUTTLEFISH, AND OCTOPUS

Squid with Fennel, Spinach, and Sorrel

*I*f there's a fish dish that says "Cook me long and slow," this is the one. Gentle, leisurely long cooking allows squid (or the more authentic cuttlefish) to spread its sweet flavor and reduces chewiness. Cuttlefish is the ingredient of choice here. Its sweeter flesh goes particularly well with fennel and sorrel. Imported frozen cuttlefish are very large; one can serve four people. Squid should either be cooked very quickly or very slowly. Long slow cooking will give you an especially delicious result.

While my Cretan friend Mirsini Lampraki picks sorrel in the hills above Heraklion, I pick it from a box on my terrace. If you don't grow your own sorrel, you'll probably find it at your local farmers' market in season.

SERVES 6

2 pounds squid or cuttlefish, cleaned (see page 111)

⅓ cup olive oil

1 cup finely chopped onion

2 to 3 scallions, finely chopped

1 cup diced fennel bulb

1 garlic clove, crushed

¾ cup dry crisp white wine, such as Pinot Grigio, Sauvignon or Pinot Blanc

1 pound spinach leaves, rinsed, stemmed, and coarsely cut up

1 pound sorrel leaves, rinsed, stemmed, and coarsely cut up

¼ cup minced fresh dill

Pinch of fennel seeds, bruised in a mortar

Salt

1 tablespoon all-purpose flour

Juice of 1 large lemon

Freshly ground pepper

(continued)

1. Early in the day, clean the squid or cuttlefish. Rinse and cut into bite-sized pieces. Without drying the pieces, put them in a large saucepan and cook over low heat until the liquid they exude evaporates, about 20 minutes.

2. Add the olive oil, onion, scallions, and fennel and cook until the squid pieces begin to turn golden and aromatic, 10 minutes. Add the garlic, wine, and ¾ cup water and continue to simmer for 10 more minutes.

3. Add the spinach, sorrel, dill, fennel seeds, and salt. Cover and cook for 45 minutes for squid and up to 2 hours for cuttlefish. Up to this point the dish can be prepared many hours in advance.

4. About 20 minutes before serving, reheat the stew to simmering. In a small bowl, mix the flour and lemon juice until smooth. Stir into the pan juices and bring to a boil, stirring. Season with salt and pepper to taste. Allow to rest for 10 minutes before serving.

Pork Stew with
Prunes and Onions (page 175)

ABOVE: *Maghrebi Veal Meatballs with Spinach and Chickpeas* (*page 200*)

OPPOSITE: *Slow-Roasted Rack of Lamb with Simple Mediterranean Flavors* (*page 208*)

OPPOSITE: *Tunisian Chickpea Soup with
Eggs, Capers, Olives, and Hot Chile Sauce* (*page 68*)
ABOVE: *Slow-Cooked Duck with Olives* (*page 148*)

OPPOSITE: *Spicy Mussels with Herbs and Feta Cheese (page 106)*
THIS PAGE: *Moroccan Lamb, Quince, and Baby Okra Tagine (page 224)*

Sardines en Escabeche with Red Onion, Tomato, and White Wine (page 116)

How to Clean Squid

Rinse the squid, then peel off the outer mottled skin. Pull the head and viscera from the body. (If the transparent quill bone comes out easily, that's a sign that your squid is very fresh.) Collect the thin elongated ink sacs, wrap them in cheesecloth, place them in a cup, press down hard with a spatula, then leave to soak in wine or water for at least 1 hour. Discard the empty sacs. (You can freeze the liquid to use in rice dishes or pasta sauces, since ink sacs aren't required in this recipe.)

Remove the tentacles by cutting just below the eyes, then turn the head over and press out the tough round beak. Discard the beak, viscera, and transparent quill bone. Wash the inside of the body carefully to remove the sand. Cut the pouch into bite-sized pieces. Store the pouch and tentacles in a small amount of lightly salted ice-cold water until ready to use.

How to Clean Cuttlefish

An imported frozen cuttlefish is usually very large and needs to thaw for about 24 hours in the refrigerator. Thaw, rinse well, then separate the body from the head by gently pulling them apart. Cuttlefish have large ink sacs, which are often very sandy. Wrap all the ink sacs in cheesecloth, place them in a cup, press down hard with a spatula, then leave to soak in wine or water for at least 1 hour. Discard the emptied sacs. (You can freeze the liquid to use in rice dishes or pasta sauces, since ink sacs aren't required in this recipe.)

Cut the body open on one side of the wide flat bone. Discard the bone and viscera. Rub both sides of the opened pouch with coarse salt, rinse well, then peel off the skin. Cut the cuttlefish into lengthwise strips or bite-sized pieces. Cut away the beak and eyes from the head and discard. Cut the tentacles into bite-sized portions.

Fricassee of Baby Octopus

For this lovely first course or brunch dish called *moscardini alla genovese,* the baby octopus is cooked in advance, then left to cool in the cooking pot, tightly covered, so that all the juices are reabsorbed into the flesh.

For best flavor, baby octopus needs a little "chew," so be careful not to overcook it.

SERVES 6 AS A FIRST COURSE

2 pounds (15 to 24 pieces) cleaned frozen baby octopus, thawed

3 tablespoons extra virgin olive oil

1 cup thinly sliced red onion

4 garlic cloves, thinly sliced

1½ teaspoons chopped fresh rosemary

½ cup finely chopped flat-leaf parsley

2 tablespoons dried porcini mushrooms, crumbled and softened in lightly sugared warm water, drained, and squeezed dry

1 cup dry white or red wine

⅔ cup fresh tomato puree

Freshly ground black pepper

1 tablespoon butter or 4 pureed walnuts

Salt

6 thin slices of Italian-style bread, toasted and rubbed with garlic

1. Rinse and drain the octopus. To clean the baby octopus, pull out the tentacles and reserve. Cut away the eyes, entrails, and hard protruding parts. Rub off the membranes and wash inside the pouches.

2. Set a 10-inch cazuela on a heat diffuser or a heavy-bottomed straight-sided skillet over low heat. Add the olive oil and then the red onion, garlic, rosemary, 3 tablespoons of the parsley, and the mushrooms. Stew until the onion is soft and golden, about 10 minutes.

3. Add the octopus, raise the heat to high, and cook, stirring, until the moisture evaporates. Add the wine, tomato puree, and pepper to taste. Bring to a boil. Lay a sheet of crumpled wet parchment directly over the octopus, cover with a lid, reduce the heat to a simmer, and cook until tender, about 30 minutes. (Larger octopus will take longer to cook; simmer for as long as 1 hour or more.) Turn off the heat and let the dish stand, covered, for l hour. *If you make the dish a day in advance, let cool, then cover and refrigerate. Reheat, partially covered, before proceeding to Step 4.*

4. Add a few tablespoons water to the pan. Reheat gently to boiling. If desired, add the butter or pureed walnuts and swirl to create a creamy sauce. Taste for salt. Sprinkle with the remaining parsley and serve at once over hot garlic toasts.

Note: Around Christmas you'll find frozen baby octopus in ethnic markets. If only baby squid is available, by all means substitute. To prepare baby squid, see "How to Clean Squid" on page 111. After washing the body and tentacles carefully, cut into bite-sized pieces and add to the stewed onions in Step 2.

TENDERIZING OCTOPUS

In New York City two Greek restaurants have come up with a new way of guaranteeing tender octopus. At Avra and Trata, up to six whole octopi are put into a washing machine with red wine vinegar. The machine, which is not hooked up to a water source, is turned on and the octopi are "pounded" into tenderness by the spinning of the washer. "We found it to be the best way," says Stravos Aktipis, an owner of the restaurant. "Otherwise you have to pound the octopus on the rocks like the fishermen do, and we can't do that here."

—FLORENCE FABRICANT IN *NATION'S RESTAURANT NEWS*

Tunisian Grilled Dried Octopus
with Tomatoes and Green Olives

If you've seen octopus drying on clothes lines in Greece, Spain, and Tunisia and wondered what they do with it, here's a recipe for an appetizer from the island of Kerkennah off the coast of Tunisia that uses dried octopus to good effect.

You can buy dried octopus at Asian markets. Be sure to begin soaking it a day in advance. The baking soda not only eliminates the strong odor, it also tenderizes and whitens the flesh.

SERVES 6

1 large dried octopus

Large pinch of baking soda

¼ cup extra virgin olive oil

Pinch of ground cumin

Salt and freshly ground pepper

Juice of 2 lemons

2 tomatoes, thinly sliced

Brine-cured green olives

1. Soak the octopus in plenty of water with the baking soda for 1 hour. Change the water and soak without the baking soda for 24 hours in the refrigerator.

2. Drain the octopus and marinate it in the olive oil seasoned with the cumin and salt and pepper to taste for up to 1 day.

3. Drain and grill slowly for 45 minutes, depending on the thickness of the octopus flesh. Slice sideways and sprinkle with lemon juice. Arrange on a platter and serve with sliced tomatoes and marinated olives.

Note: In southern Tunisia along the coast, cooks cut rehydrated pieces of dried octopus into cubes, then add them to certain soups for a deep strong flavor. They also add them to their rich bean soups along with slivers of lamb confit and dried apricots.

DRIED SMALL FISH AS A FLAVORING FOR TUNISIAN FOOD

In Tunisia, fish consumption is regional. The coastal population consumes a lot of fish, while people in inland areas eat far less. Fresh fish were traditionally expensive even on the coast, so a special method of preservation was developed using solar heat rather than the salting method used in Spain, France, Italy, and Greece.

One type of fish was particularly well suited to sun-drying: a type of anchovy called the *ouzef* (*Engraulis meletta*), fished off the southern coast of Gabès.

Though these anchovies are the smallest fish eaten by Tunisians, they catch them with the same method that they use to catch gigantic tuna. The method is called the *matanza*. Dozens of men manipulate a series of nets, while others drive the fish into them. Old paintings of the tuna matanza show men jumping onto tuna after capture, then plunging harpoons into their flesh.

One-inch anchovies obviously don't require this level of warfare. Two men standing in deep water, holding the edges of stripped palm fronds, guide the anchovies, which swim in schools, toward sacks made of thin cheesecloth-type material. As soon as the anchovies enter these nets, they're closed, scooped up, then emptied onto the beach, where they're left to dry out for a couple of days.

These dried anchovies are used to flavor certain Tunisian dishes both on the coast and also deep inside the country. In fact, trading dried fish for dates between the coastal areas and the oases was part of the traditional Tunisian economy.

FISH

Sardines en Escabeche with Red Onion, Tomato, and White Wine

You'll find pickled fish (sardines, mackerel, tuna, and, in summer, various "blue" fish) all around the Mediterranean. This recipe, pleasantly pungent with some dried hot pepper and white wine vinegar, is based on a *pied-noir* (French Colonial) dish I ate in Oran in the early 1970s, similar to recipes prepared in southern France and Spain. All are based on simmering whole fish in a strong medium, then boning and leaving them to marinate in the same liquid. A lengthy pickling gives best results. Wait at least three days before serving.

SERVES 4

4 large or 8 small super-fresh sardines

¼ cup all-purpose flour

Sea salt and freshly ground pepper

½ cup olive oil

1 small carrot, thinly sliced

1 small red onion, thinly sliced

4 garlic cloves, peeled

1 dried hot red pepper

1 scant teaspoon black peppercorns

2 large bay leaves

1 tablespoon tomato paste

⅔ cup white wine vinegar

¼ cup dry white wine

Chopped flat-leaf parsley

1. Rinse and dry the fish. Season the flour with salt and pepper. Roll the sardines in the seasoned flour and shake off any excess. Fry in hot oil, allowing 2 to 3 minutes per side, until golden. Drain on paper towels, then place in a single layer in a shallow glass or ceramic dish.

2. Reheat the oil in the skillet over medium heat and gently sauté the carrot, red onion, and garlic until soft but not brown. Add the hot pepper, peppercorns, bay leaves, 1 teaspoon salt, the tomato paste, vinegar, and wine. Partially cover and cook, stirring occasionally, for about 10 minutes.

3. Meanwhile, open each sardine along the stomach and bone the fish. (Boning the fish *after* cooking creates much more flavorful results.)

4. Adjust the seasoning of the sauce, adding a few drops of vinegar, if necessary, and pour while still hot over the opened sardines. Allow to cool, cover tightly, then refrigerate at least 2 days before serving. Sprinkle with parsley just before serving.

Fresh Tuna with Green Olives, Capers, Celery, and Mint

A few years ago, on a visit to Sicily, I was invited for dinner at the home of Giuseppe and Julia di'Martino, who moved to the island forty years ago. After we finished a series of pastas, platters of local dishes were brought out, among them the Siracusan specialty, *stimperata,* a beautifully cooked slab of tuna smothered in a sweet-and-sour blend of capers, olives, mint, celery, sugar, and vinegar.

The word *stimperata* derives from the Latin *temperare,* meaning "to mix properly or regulate." It thus reflects that "Greek spirit of temperance" that had originally drawn the di'Martino family to southeastern Sicily.

Their son, Adolfo, now the owner-chef of the Green Gables Inn on the New Jersey shore, told me that all recipes for stimperata are the same "because once a perfect balance is achieved, there's no point in changing it. You must be very accurate about ingredient amounts and sizes so that everything will come out evenly, fully cooked at the same time. Also important is a long mellowing of the ingredients."

Adolfo paused, then he smiled. "But actually there's more to it. There's the tempering." He was referring to the addition of just the right amount of water to dilute the dish judiciously . . . but not too much. "God save us from a too watery stimperata!" he added.

Listening to him, I was reminded of the "Temperance" card in the tarot pack. The traditional image of Temperance is a woman pouring water from one vessel to dilute wine in another.

"Yes, that's it!" Adolfo said. "Add just enough water to temper the dish. Temperance—that's the key to stimperata—and to the Sicilian way of life."

This succulent dish actually cooks fairly quickly, but the secret to its depth of flavor is in letting it stand for several hours, or preferably overnight.

1¼ pounds fresh yellowfin or bluefin tuna
   steak, about 1 inch thick

Coarse salt and freshly ground pepper

Flour, for dusting

3 tablespoons extra virgin olive oil

2 garlic cloves, thinly sliced

½ cup thinly sliced tender celery

18 green Sicilian-style olives, blanched
   1 minute, drained, pitted, and quartered

3 tablespoons salted capers, rinsed and
   drained

3 tablespoons yellow raisins, soaked for
   5 minutes in warm water and drained

3 tablespoons white wine vinegar

2 tablespoons minced fresh mint, for garnish

1. Rinse the tuna and pat dry. Season lightly with salt and pepper and dust with flour. In a medium nonstick skillet, heat the oil over medium-high heat. Add the tuna and quickly sear on both sides, about 1 minute to a side. Transfer the tuna to a plate.

2. Reduce the heat to medium. Add the garlic and celery and cook until the garlic is golden and the celery tender, about 1½ minutes. Add the olives, capers, and raisins and cook, stirring, for another minute, or until lightly glazed but not browned.

3. Return the tuna to the pan; sprinkle with the vinegar, about 2 tablespoons water, and salt and pepper. Baste the tuna with the skillet juices, cover, and cook until almost done to taste, about 1 more minute. Glide the tuna onto a shallow serving dish and pour the pan juices with the olives, capers, and raisins over the fish. Refrigerate for at least 4 hours, and preferably overnight. Garnish with mint leaves and serve at room temperature.

Salmon Fillet Poached in Olive Oil

While visiting the town of Deia on the island of Mallorca, I watched a young chef at the Residence Hotel simmer various pieces of fish and shellfish in quarts of olive oil. I was fascinated by the way he cooked each variety for a different length of time and at a low temperature to achieve a glistening, almost translucent, texture and an incredible succulence. For example, he cooked thick chunks of squid for up to 6 hours at 140°F; shelled thick clams for 4 hours; and freshened slabs of salt cod for 2 hours. In no case did this lengthy, slow simmering produce overcooked fish

As he explained it to me, "So long as the internal temperature and the temperature of the oil remain the same, the fish will not be overcooked. This is a very old way of preparing and preserving all kinds of chewy textured fish in my hometown of Soller," he told me. "Nowadays, we use the same low-temperature method to cook fish fillets, such as turbot and salmon, but we don't cook them as long. What we do now is flavor the oil with browned garlic and let it steep so it will be flavorful for cooking the fish."

This salmon dish is especially successful when served under a bright and acidic salad made of shaved raw rhubarb, slivers of cucumber, leaves of young arugula and fresh mint.

SERVES 4

1 pound thick center-cut, salmon, preferably sushi grade, skinned and pin bones removed

Coarse sea salt

2½ cups olive oil

3 garlic cloves, sliced

1 sprig of thyme

Freshly ground pepper

Raw Rhubarb, Cucumber, and Mint Salad (recipe follows)

1. Lightly salt the salmon and refrigerate it for 1 hour.

2. Meanwhile, in a cazuela or straight-sided skillet just large enough to hold the salmon, heat the olive oil with the garlic and thyme to simmering. When the garlic turns golden brown, remove from the heat and let stand until ready to cook.

3. Discard the garlic and thyme. Heat the oil to 155°F. Rinse the salmon, pat dry, and slip into the oil. Add additional oil, if necessary, to completely cover the salmon. Bring the temperature of the oil to about 145°F and poach the salmon for 12 minutes. Remove the cazuela from the heat. The fish will continue to cook in the receding heat. The salmon is fully cooked when the flesh flakes. Use a spatula to remove the salmon, which will look amazingly rare but will be fully cooked, Drain on paper towels and sprinkle with pepper.

4. Let the salmon rest for 5 minutes, then cut into 4 pieces. Serve warm, with the room-temperature rhubarb salad arranged on top.

Note: The chef told me that because the oil never rises above 155°F it can be reused again and again, including in fish salads or for poaching more fish. The oil will keep for up to 1 week in the refrigerator.

Raw Rhubarb, Cucumber, and Mint Salad

Raw rhubarb! My Turkish friend and food journalist Ayfer Unsal described observing people in eastern Turkey purchasing wild rhubarb stalks from a wagon, stripping back the threads, then munching on the stalks as though they were ribs of celery.

Ayfer watched these raw rhubarb eaters closely to see if their mouths puckered in reaction to the intensely tart rhubarb juice. This didn't happen. Later she learned that the rhubarb stalk seller had sprinkled some salt on the stalks to soften their sour flavor, just the way one tempers radishes or onions. When she ate a stalk herself, she found it was refreshing and intensely pleasurable. Ayfer decreed it a "great Turkish springtime snack."

A year ago I asked an Iranian taxi driver if people ate raw rhubarb in his part of the world. "Yes, indeed they do!" he said. He gave me the following delicious recipe of thin slices of raw rhubarb tossed with arugula and cucumber. I particularly like the last minute addition of fresh mint.

SERVES 4

2 young rhubarb stalks

1 crisp medium cucumber

2 tablespoons coarse salt

2 handfuls of arugula

1 to 1½ tablespoons lemon juice

½ cup shredded mint leaves

1. Using a vegetable slicer such as a mandoline or a thin-bladed knife, cut the rhubarb slightly on the diagonal into very thin slices. Repeat with the peeled cucumber.

2. Toss the rhubarb and cucumber with the coarse salt and let stand for 10 minutes; rinse and drain.

3. In a salad bowl, toss the rhubarb and cucumber with the arugula. Drizzle on the lemon juice, adding enough for a slight mouth-tingling effect. Scatter the mint leaves on top and serve.

Slow Oven-Steamed Salmon

As all good cooks know, the bottom line of fish cookery is *do not overcook.* The problem is that by the time a fish looks cooked, it may already be too late.

Salmon should be allowed to rest after cooking, the same way meat is allowed to stand to allow the juices to seep back in, but, of course, not for too long. If you're not careful, residual heat can give you a mushy side of salmon.

I learned the following salmon recipe from Michelin three-star chef Michel Bras. It's a wonderful, slow, low-temperature method of steam-roasting salmon that always produces an incredibly silky texture. The steam simulates the fantastic Alto Sham ovens that chefs are using these days to cook fish at low temperatures and arrive at superb textures.

From spring to fall is wild salmon season. I think the best choices are the wild king salmon, also called chinook. Its flavor is deep, and its texture firm and moist. I don't suggest using farmed salmon in these recipes. A French food critic wrote of the texture of farmed salmon flesh as "like a coverlet filled with duck's down." He concluded that "salmon are like men: too soft a life is not good for them."

Serve your salmon at room temperature with a tasty piquant green sauce—either Sauce Martiques, made with capers, anchovies, herbs, and olive oil, or Jean-Louis Palladin's Watercress Sauce.

SERVES 8

Jean-Louis Palladin's Watercress Sauce (page 125) or Sauce Martiques (recipe follows)

2½-pound center-cut king salmon fillet, skinned and pin bones removed

Extra virgin olive oil

Salt and freshly ground pepper

Coarse sea salt

2 tablespoons finely chopped fresh chives

(continued)

1. Prepare the watercress sauce or the sauce Martiques as directed below and let stand at room temperature for 2 to 3 hours to allow the flavors to develop.

2. Preheat the oven to 275°F. Position one rack in the lower third of the oven and a second rack in the upper third. Carefully place a skillet of boiling water on the lower oven shelf. Place the salmon on an oiled baking sheet and generously sprinkle with salt and pepper. Bake until the salmon is firm to the touch, about 20 minutes. Let the salmon rest for 5 minutes before slicing. (The color of the salmon will not turn dull; the texture will be very moist and easily flake.)

3. Place a portion of salmon on a plate, and sprinkle with a mixture of coarse sea salt, pepper, and a few fresh chives.

4. To serve, top with a dollop of watercress sauce or thin the sauce Martiques with a few teaspoons of water, if necessary, and drizzle it around the salmon. Serve at once.

With thanks to Russ Parsons for helping me rethink this recipe.

Sauce Martiques

MAKES ABOUT ¾ CUP

2 tablespoons salted capers

4 anchovy fillets, minced

3 scallions, thinly sliced

3 tablespoons chopped flat-leaf parsley

2 tablespoons chopped fresh chives

2 tablespoons chopped fresh tarragon or
    chervil

1 teaspoon grated lemon zest

⅓ cup extra virgin olive oil

1 tablespoon lemon juice

A few drops of red wine vinegar

Salt and freshly ground pepper

1. Rinse the capers and anchovy fillets under cold running water. Drain and coarsely chop.

2. In a small bowl, combine the chopped capers and anchovies with the scallions, parsley, chives, tarragon or chervil, and lemon zest. Stir in the olive oil, lemon juice, and vinegar. Season with salt and pepper to taste and let stand at room temperature.

Jean-Louis Palladin's Watercress Sauce

The late, great Gascogne chef Jean-Louis taught me this simple, intense sauce, which highlights all the flavor of the peppery greens. I have published many of his recipes in my other books. This is one I found in an old notebook, and it is, perhaps, the easiest recipe in his repertoire.

SERVES 8

1½ bunches fresh watercress

¾ cup heavy cream

Salt and freshly ground pepper

About 1 teaspoon lemon juice

3 tablespoons glace de homard or glace de poisson (see Note)

1. Rinse the watercress carefully; pick over and remove all tough stalks. There will be about 2 cups leaves and tender stems. Boil in salted water for 10 minutes. Drain and rinse under cool running water to refresh; drain again. Squeeze the watercress with your hands to remove as much water as possible. Place the watercress in an electric blender, add ½ cup of the heavy cream, and puree until smooth. Season with ½ teaspoon salt, ¼ teaspoon pepper, and ½ teaspoon lemon juice. Blend to combine.

2. In a heavy saucepan, melt the glace de homard over low heat, whisking. Stir in the remaining ¼ cup cream, then the watercress puree. Correct the seasoning, adding lemon juice to taste. Keep hot.

Notes: Glace de homard is a reduced concentrate of lobster, lobster shells, and mixed vegetables. You can substitute *glace de poisson,* available frozen throughout the United States in fine food stores.

Tunisian Poached Fish with Olives, Preserved Lemons, and Capers

*I*n this dish, known as *kababkou* in Tunisia, the chunks of fish slowly cook in receding heat after a light spicy tomato sauce is brought to a boil, then poured over the fish. As the sauce cools to room temperature, the fish is cooked. It can be gently reheated before serving.

This method can be applied to any meaty white-fleshed fish without your having to worry about overcooking. The flesh will be juicy and perfectly cooked. The dish can be served warm, tepid, or cool.

SERVES 4 TO 5

1¾ pounds fresh halibut steak

Salt and freshly ground pepper

1 teaspoon ground cumin

1 small fresh hot pepper

4 to 6 baby onions, preferably red

3 tablespoons extra virgin olive oil

1 medium red onion, grated

2 medium tomatoes, halved, seeded, and grated

1 head of garlic, cloves separated

1 tablespoon tomato paste

1 teaspoon *le tabil* (page 201) or ground coriander seeds

1 cup brine-cured green olives, rinsed and drained

Flour, for dusting

4 cherry tomatoes

¼ cup capers, rinsed and drained

½ preserved lemon peel, rinsed, drained, and cut into thin julienne

1 tablespoon chopped celery leaves

1. Rinse the fish, pat dry with paper towels, and divide into 6 equal pieces. Season each piece with salt, pepper, and ground cumin. Cover and refrigerate for at least 1 hour.

2. Meanwhile, steam the hot pepper and the baby onions until almost tender, about 10 minutes. Stem, seed, and coarsely chop the pepper. Peel the onions.

3. In a deep-sided medium skillet, heat 2 tablespoons of the olive oil. Add the grated red onion and cook over medium heat, stirring, for 3 to 4 minutes, until softened. Add the tomatoes and cook until excess moisture evaporates, about 7 minutes. Add the garlic, tomato paste, tabil or ground coriander, olives, steamed chopped hot pepper, baby onions, and 1 cup water. Cover and cook over medium heat for 10 minutes. The sauce should be thin, light, and very hot.

4. Heat the remaining 1 tablespoon oil in a large nonstick skillet over medium-high heat. Dust the seasoned fish with flour and fry, skin side down, in the hot oil for 2 minutes, or until the skin is crusty. Turn each piece of fish, fry for 1 minute, then pour the hot sauce over the fish. Add the cherry tomatoes, capers, and preserved lemon peel and simmer over low heat for 1 more minute. Remove from the heat, cover, and let stand for 15 minutes before serving. (The fish will finish cooking in the receding heat.) Garnish with chopped celery leaves.

Note: Preserved lemons can be made with either thin- or thick-skinned fruit. Thin-skinned lemons make a good garnish, but when preparing this dish I use lemons with thicker skins, lest they fall apart during cooking. If you only have thin-skinned preserved lemons on hand, add them at the last minute. (To make preserved lemons, see page 303.)

With thanks to chef Haouari Abderrazak for sharing this recipe.

Tagine of Monkfish Fillets with Fig Leaves, Fennel, and Chestnuts

The following recipe is my adaptation of a dish my friend San Francisco–based chef Laurent Manrique created in my kitchen. I made one change in Laurent's recipe in order to make it easier to prepare. In my version given below, I sauté the monkfish on top of the stove, then let it rest while I make a simple, flavorful sauce. Laurent, on the other hand, brought with him a very delicious and complex Bordelaise sauce, made with reduced white wine, port, chopped shallots, thyme, bay leaf, and veal demi-glace, and enriched with beef marrow.

When Laurent prepared this dish in my house, he used one of my earthenware Moroccan tagines for a stunning presentation. About 12 minutes before serving, he reheated the juicy slices of monkfish, glazed roasted chestnuts, and braised slices of fennel on a bed of fig leaves in the tagine. The fish reheated quickly, and the earthenware kept it warm until we were ready to eat.

SERVES 6

2 bulbs of fresh fennel (about 1 pound), trimmed

4 tablespoons unsalted butter

⅛ teaspoon freshly ground pepper

⅛ teaspoon sugar

1 jar (12 ounces) steamed or roasted chestnuts

2½-pound monkfish fillet

Sea salt

2 tablespoons extra virgin olive oil

¾ cup dry vermouth or dry white wine

¼ cup white or tawny port

2 cups well-reduced unsalted chicken stock

1 tablespoon dry fennel seeds

6 to 12 unsprayed fig leaves, stemmed, washed, drained, and patted dry

2 teaspoons fresh minced tarragon or dill

1. Thickly slice the fennel bulbs and place in a large skillet with half the butter and a sprinkling of pepper and sugar. Set over medium heat, partially cover, and cook, turning, until golden brown on both sides, about 10 minutes. Remove to a side dish. Add the chestnuts to the skillet and cook, uncovered, for a few more minutes to glaze. Cover loosely with foil and set aside.

2. About 1 hour before serving, rinse and dry the monkfish fillets. Cut away the gray membrane and divide the fish into 4 even chunks. Season generously with salt and additional pepper. In a medium sauté pan set over moderately high heat, melt the remaining butter in 2 tablespoons olive oil. When hot, add half the monkfish and cook, without turning, until golden brown, about 5 minutes. Turn the fish over, reduce the heat to moderate, and continue frying for 5 more minutes. Transfer the monkfish to a side dish and cover with foil. Repeat with the remaining monkfish. Allow the monkfish to stand for at least 15 minutes to reabsorb the juices expressed during sautéing.

3. Discard the fat in the pan. Pour in the vermouth or wine and the port and bring to a boil, scraping up any brown bits from the bottom of the pan. Boil until thick and syrupy. Add the reduced stock and simmer, uncovered, for 20 minutes. Strain into a bowl. There should be about ¾ cup flavorful sauce. Correct the seasoning with salt and pepper.

4. Transfer the monkfish to a carving board, and cut into ⅜-inch-thick rounds. If the monkfish throws off liquid, add that to the sauce and boil down to reduce.

5. Meanwhile, put the olive oil in a large tagine, cazuela, or other shallow baking dish. Place in a cold oven and turn the oven temperature to 425°F. Heat until the oil is sizzling, about 15 minutes.

6. Carefully remove the heated dish from the oven and sprinkle the fennel seeds over the oil. Spread half the fig leaves on top, arrange the monkfish fillets overlapping on top of the leaves, and dribble about ⅓ cup of the sauce over the fish. Scatter the fennel and chestnuts around the fish and cover with the remaining fig leaves and a lid or a sheet of foil. Return to the hot oven and bake 10 minutes, or until the fish is cooked through when the internal temperature reaches 145°F on an instant-read thermometer. Pull back the fig leaves, scatter the fresh herbs on top, and serve hot, with the remaining sauce on the side.

Notes: The fig leaves are too tough to consume, but they provide an incredible aroma to grilled and baked fish, an almost cinnamon-like perfume. Fig leaves hold up to 2 to 3 weeks when loosely packed in a plastic baggie in the refrigerator. (See Mail Order Sources.)

You can make this dish without the leaves, but it won't be quite as good.

Monkfish and Clams with a Burned Garlic Sauce

*H*ere is a great fish dish from the Catalan repertoire in which garlic is slowly simmered in olive oil in a heavy-bottomed pan until "burned" to a rich brown color. Marvelously succulent, dense, and meaty, monkfish benefits greatly from this garlic-infused sauce bursting with the flavors of toasted almonds, tomatoes, clams, and an exciting floral touch of oloroso sherry.

Chef Josep Lladonosa i Giro, one of the great living experts on Catalan cooking, told me that the finished sauce must be dark and creamy and have the texture of a béchamel. To achieve this, the cook needs to use a mortar and pestle or an electric mixer to make the finishing *picada*.

Steps 1, 2, and 3 can be prepared many hours in advance.

SERVES 4 TO 6

1½ pounds monkfish tails

Sea salt

12 small hard-shell or manila clams, washed in several changes of water, drained, and kept refrigerated

¼ cup extra virgin olive oil

12 blanched almonds

One ¾-inch-thick slice of crustless stale bread

10 to 12 large garlic cloves, thickly sliced

2 teaspoons chopped flat-leaf parsley

Pinch of cayenne

2 tablespoons oloroso (medium-dry) sherry

1 tomato, halved, seeded, and rubbed on the coarsest side of a 4-hole grater

2 cups rich fish or shellfish stock, heated to boiling

2 cups diced Yukon Gold potatoes, about 1¼ pounds

4 to 8 cherry tomatoes, halved

Freshly ground black pepper

1. Wash the monkfish, cut off the gray membrane, and cut the fish into 12 even pieces, each about 1 inch thick. Lightly sprinkle each piece of monkfish with coarse salt, cover, and refrigerate.

2. Rinse the clams in several changes of water, scrubbing the shells, if necessary, to remove any sand. Drain and refrigerate.

3. Make the picada: Heat the olive oil in a 12-inch earthenware cazuela or cast-iron skillet over medium heat. Add the almonds and fry, stirring often, until golden, about 3 minutes. Use a slotted spoon to transfer to a mortar or electric blender. Add the bread to the pan and fry until golden; add to the almonds. Add the garlic slices to the pan, reduce the heat to low, and cook until the slices turn chestnut brown, 10 to 15 minutes. (Be very careful, because the cloves can quickly turn from chestnut brown to burned.) Add the browned garlic to the bread and almonds. Add half of the parsley, the cayenne, sherry, and 3 tablespoons water and grind to a smooth puree. Scrape the picada into a small bowl and set aside.

4. Add the tomatoes to the remaining oil in the pan and cook over medium heat until scorched and thickened to 1 tablespoon, about 15 minutes. Add the boiling stock and bring to a simmer. Remove from the heat and set aside.

5. About 20 minutes before serving, reheat the liquid in the cazuela to boiling. Add the potatoes (see Note) and simmer for 6 to 8 minutes, until almost tender. Stir the almond picada into the liquid and simmer for a few minutes. Rinse the fish, slip it into the liquid in a single layer, and cook over low heat, partially covered, until the fish is half cooked, 5 to 7 minutes. Turn each piece of fish, add the clams and cherry tomatoes, cover, and continue cooking 8 more minutes, or until the clams open and the fish is fully cooked. Correct the seasoning with salt and pepper and another pinch of cayenne, if you like. Garnish with the remaining parsley and serve hot in soup plates.

Note: If you don't have a large enough cazuela or skillet to accommodate the fish and potatoes in a single layer, you can roast the potatoes separately in an oiled baking dish in a 400°F oven for 45 minutes.

Moroccan Tilefish with Sweet Onions

*H*ere raisins and sweet onions are cooked down to a jam, then just enough lemon juice is added to bring the dish into balance. This simple fish recipe is a perfect example of superb Moroccan home cooking.

SERVES 4

4 thick tilefish steaks (about 2 pounds) or other thick white fish, such as monkfish, halibut, rockfish, or cod

Sea salt

2 pounds onions

¼ cup olive oil

1¾ teaspoons ground cinnamon

¼ teaspoon grated nutmeg

Pinch of ground allspice or cloves

Pinch of dried saffron threads

½ teaspoon ground black pepper

⅓ cup yellow or dark raisins

¼ cup sugar

12 sprigs of flat-leaf parsley

2 juicy lemons, cut into wedges

1. Sprinkle the fish on both sides with sea salt. Cover and refrigerate for 1 hour.

2. Halve the onions and thickly slice lengthwise. Heat 3 tablespoons of the olive oil in a heavy saucepan over medium-low heat. Add the onions, 1 cup water, ½ teaspoon salt, the cinnamon, nutmeg, allspice, saffron, and pepper. Cover and cook until golden, about 30 minutes.

3. Meanwhile, soak the raisins in warm water for 10 minutes to plump; drain.

4. Add the sugar and raisins to the soft onions and continue cooking until the onions have a glazed appearance, about 20 minutes. Set the onion jam aside, uncovered.

5. About 45 minutes before serving, preheat the oven to 400°F. Scatter the sprigs of parsley over the bottom of a 9-inch baking dish. Sprinkle with 3 tablespoons water and add the fish. Spread the onion jam over the fish and bake for 10 minutes. Turn off the heat, leave the oven door ajar, and let remain inside for 20 minutes. Serve with lemon wedges.

Chicken, Duck, and Game Birds

———— ✦ ————

A superb chicken or game bird, crisp on the outside and tender and juicy within, can be prepared in either the fast lane or the slow. Since this book is about slow-cooking, the recipes that follow are all cooked by traditional methods employed mainly by Mediterranean women in their role as home cooks.

Around the Mediterranean, chicken, ducks, quail, guinea hens, squab, and quail are similarly treated—flattered, coaxed, and pushed in one way or another by poaching, braising, steaming, or simply marinating with yogurt, steeping in wine or lemon juice, or brushing with mayonnaise; then slowly roasted or grilled.

Often whether I'm poaching, sautéing, grilling, or roasting, I use mild to low heat to coddle my poultry, creating a delicious moist interior with minimal shrinkage. Then I flash grill, fry, or sear the skin to achieve a wonderful crisp exterior.

Just as I adore both my children, I love all my poultry recipes. Still, I must call your attention to several favorites in this chapter: My updated version of a French Catalan dish, Slow-Cooked Duck with Olives, results in lush inner flesh and juicy, deeply caramelized skin. Another French poultry dish, a crispy fried chicken flavored with country ham, is served under a tender, sweet onion cream. And a tagine-simmered "red" chicken in the style of Marrakech, enhanced by an exciting mixture of Moroccan spices, is finished off under the grill for added flavor and texture.

SLOW-ROASTING POULTRY

Thirty years ago, many American cooks, including me, were much taken by Adelle Davis's book *Let's Cook It Right*. We followed her rules for long, slow cooking of poultry and meat in order to retain maximum nutritional value while obtaining maximum juiciness and flavor.

I tried out many of her ideas, including her most eccentric—cooking over just a pilot light. Her theory of slow poultry roasting was to cook a bird at the same temperature that you wanted it to be when it was done, about 165°F. This meant roasting a chicken for an entire day! Her argument was that roasting a chicken at a very low temperature would not only preserve its flavor and tenderness, but would also keep in all the juices. In fact, her method produced a superb degree of moistness.

Back when I did this, I had no idea I was playing Russian roulette with the health of my family. Slow-roasting a chicken can present a whole slew of bacterial problems—an important consideration since many chickens on the market today can be contaminated. To get around this problem, I scrupulously follow USDA guidelines for slow-oven roasting a chicken by passing through the danger zone (40° to 140°F) as quickly as possible, guided by both a digital probe thermometer and a regular oven thermometer.

For me the breakthrough adaptation of Adelle Davis's recipe was made by Christopher Kimball, editor of *Cook's Illustrated*, in its January/February 1996 issue. Mr. Kimball starts by cooking a 3½-pound chicken set on a rack in a 375°F oven for half an hour, which brings the internal temperature to a safe 140°F. Then he reduces the oven temperature to 200°F and slowly roasts the bird for an additional hour. About 30 minutes before serving, he raises the temperature again to 400°F. The chicken is done in about 15 minutes, when the internal temperature of the thigh reaches 170°F. That final blast of high heat browns the skin to a gorgeous golden crust. A final resting period before serving delivers a wonderful chicken, moist and succulent.

Expatriate Roast Chicken with Lemon and Olives

This super-moist Moroccan roast chicken is first stuffed with a lavish amount of preserved lemon and a bit of hot pepper, scented with ginger and black pepper, and flavored with garlic and good extra virgin olive oil. The bird is then roasted over onion and spices. These subtle and elementary flavors remind me of Morocco—in other words, it is an expatriate's delight.

SERVES 4 TO 6

One 4-pound chicken, preferably free-range or kosher

1 preserved lemon (page 303), rinsed and quartered, pulp and skin reserved

1¼ teaspoons ground ginger

Pinch of cayenne

Freshly ground pepper

3 garlic cloves, chopped

3 tablespoons extra virgin olive oil

Salt

Pinch of saffron threads

1 cinnamon stick, 2 inches long

1 small onion, grated

½ teaspoon sugar

1 cup green olives (about 5 ounces), such as picholine, rinsed

2 tablespoons coarsely chopped fresh cilantro

1. Early in the day, rinse the chicken inside and out; thoroughly pat dry. In a bowl, combine the pulp of the preserved lemon with the ginger, cayenne, ¼ teaspoon of the black pepper, the garlic, and 1 tablespoon olive oil. Place this mixture in the cavity of the bird. Tuck the wings under the chicken and tie the legs together. Cover with paper towels and refrigerate until 3 hours before serving. Let the chicken return to room temperature before roasting.

2. About 2 hours before serving, bring 3 cups water to a boil. Rub the chicken with salt and black pepper. Lightly oil a shallow roasting pan, set an oiled V-shaped rack in it, and put the chicken on the rack, breast side up. Set the pan in a cold oven and pour the 3 cups boiling water into the pan under the chicken. Add the saffron, cinnamon stick, onion, and sugar to the hot water. Turn the oven temperature to 550°F and roast until the breast of the chicken is golden brown, about 45 minutes.

3. Reduce the oven temperature to 275°F. Turn the chicken on one of its sides, brush with olive oil, and roast for 20 minutes. Turn the bird onto its other side, baste again with olive oil, and continue to roast for another 20 minutes. Finally, turn the chicken upside down to brown the back; roast for about 10 minutes. Test for doneness: an instant-read thermometer inserted in the thigh should register 160° to 165°F.

4. Leaving the oven on, remove the chicken on its rack to a carving board, cover with foil, and let rest for 20 minutes. (The internal temperature will rise to 170°F.) Meanwhile, skim the fat off the pan juices. Add the olives and half the cilantro; mix and return the pan to the oven to reduce for 20 minutes.

5. Carve the chicken and arrange in a heatproof serving dish. Spoon the olives around the chicken. Season the pan juices with additional salt and pepper and pour over the meat. Arrange the preserved lemon peels on top. Garnish with the remaining chopped cilantro.

Slow-Roasted Chicken with Sausage and Porcini Dressing

Dinner at La Tupina Restaurant in Bordeaux is like eating at a mythical southwest French farmhouse. The first thing you see as you enter is a huge open wood-burning fireplace where everything appears to be spit-roasting, baking, or stewing over live coals. I use the word *mythical,* because few people today still engage in open-hearth cooking on such a scale.

The restaurant, one of my favorites in Bordeaux, specializes in old-fashioned food—the recipes of chef Jean Pierre Xiradakis's French mother and grandmother, who come from the wine region of La Blaye. This food is true "comfort food." People in Bordeaux refer to Xiradakis as the "keeper of the flame."

Chef Xiradakis and I go back twenty-five years. On my last visit to his restaurant in Bordeaux, I eyed a beautiful, golden-brown chicken about to be cut up for a customer, and I decided to share an order with a friend. The chicken came accompanied by a delicious dressing of pork, mushroom, and bread. The bird had been slow-roasted in the oven and basted with the juicy dressing. Then the still-pale skin was lavishly rubbed with duck fat, sprinkled with salt and pepper, and set before the embers in the fireplace. The result was a deeply flavored, beautifully crisped chicken served with the very moist dressng. When my friend and I tasted it, we practically swooned at first bite.

In my recipe, I roast the chicken upside down on a vertical roaster to produce an incredibly succulent chicken. The porcini and sausage dressing below the chicken prevents splattering.

In winter, I like to serve Yukon Gold potatoes, roasted or sautéed in duck fat, and grilled radicchio as a vegetable accompaniment, because it has a strong and pleasantly pungent flavor, which goes well with the chicken. In spring, I offer grilled asparagus.

SERVES 4 TO 6

1 whole organic, free-range chicken (about 4 pounds)

Salt and freshly ground pepper

¾ ounce dried porcini (1 cup)

Pinch of sugar

2½ tablespoons rendered duck fat

1 small leek (white part only), finely chopped

1 small carrot, finely chopped

½ medium onion, finely chopped

4 ounces fresh pork sausage, casing removed, and chopped

¼ cup chopped dry sausage, such as Boar's Head Abruzzi-style pork sausage; or substitute ¼ cup finely chopped prosciutto

9 large garlic cloves—8 chopped, 1 minced

1 cup chicken broth

2 cups diced stale white peasant bread, crust removed

⅓ cup milk

Freshly grated nutmeg

2 tablespoons chopped flat-leaf parsley

1. Rinse the chicken thoroughly inside and out and pat dry. (Remove the neck and giblets and reserve for stock.) Starting at the neck, loosen the skin and with kitchen scissors, cut off about 1½ inches of the backbone. Generously sprinkle the cavity with salt and pepper, cover with paper towels, and refrigerate.

2. Soak the dried porcini with a pinch of sugar in 2 cups warm water to soften, 2 to 3 hours. Drain the mushrooms, straining the liquid through a coffee filter or paper toweling. Rinse the mushrooms briefly and finely chop. Set aside the mushrooms and soaking liquid separately.

3. In a medium skillet, heat 2 teaspoons of the duck fat over medium-low heat. Add the leek, carrot, and onion; cover and cook until softened, about 5 minutes. Add the porcini mushrooms, fresh and dry sausage, and chopped garlic. Raise the heat to medium and cook, stirring, until caramelized here and there, about 5 minutes. Add the reserved mushroom liquid; raise the heat to high and cook, stirring often, until the liquid is syrupy and glazed, about 5 minutes. Add the chicken broth and simmer until it is absorbed, about 5 minutes longer. Remove from the heat and let cool.

4. Toss the bread with the milk and let soften. Combine the bread paste with the mushroom-sausage mixture and blend well. Add nutmeg and salt and pepper to taste. Pack the stuffing into a 10-inch baking dish greased with duck fat. Cover with foil and refrigerate. *(The dressing can be prepared up to 1 day in advance.)*

(continued)

5. About 3 hours before serving, remove the chicken and the dressing from the refrigerator and let stand for 45 minutes. Set an oven rack on the lowest rung and preheat the oven to 375°F.

6. Stir 1 cup water into the dressing. Rub the chicken with duck fat and season generously with salt and pepper. Carefully position the chicken on a vertical roaster with the legs facing up and set in the baking dish above the dressing. Roast in the oven for 30 minutes. Reduce the oven heat to 200°F and roast for about 1 hour longer, until the internal temperature of the chicken reaches 150° to 155°F.

7. Raise the oven temperature to 400°F and continue roasting until the internal temperature of the chicken reaches 160°F, about 15 minutes longer.

8. Remove the chicken and dressing from the oven. Use oven mitts to carefully lift the chicken off the vertical roaster; cover with foil, and let rest for 20 minutes. Press down on the dressing to express excess fat and discard. Spread the dressing onto a heatproof serving dish and cover with foil.

9. Carve the chicken into 6 or 8 serving pieces. Arrange the chicken pieces over the dressing and return to the oven to reheat, uncovered, to finish cooking, crisping, and browning the birds, about 5 minutes. Sprinkle with chopped parsley and the minced garlic and serve at once.

PROBE THERMOMETER

One of the most important pieces of equipment for slow-roasting is a digital probe thermometer, designed to remain inside the poultry or meat while it cooks and alert you when the desired temperature has been reached. You insert the probe into the food, place it in the oven, and close the door directly over the probe cable. Available at all good kitchen equipment stores.

Garlic and Lemon–Marinated Chicken Kebabs

A leisurely wait in a mellowing spiced mayonnaise marinade makes this an easy dish to ready for last minute grilling. This is an excellent summer dish, served with tabouli (page 57) and a sweet pepper and caper salad (page 56). Everything can be prepared in advance, except for the final quick grilling of the chicken.

SERVES 4

1¼ pounds skinless, boneless chicken breasts

4 large garlic cloves

¼ teaspoon coarse salt

2 pinches of Middle Eastern spices (page 312), or substitute a pinch of ground cinnamon and a pinch of ground allspice

¼ teaspoon freshly ground pepper

2 tablespoons mayonnaise

3 tablespoons fresh lemon juice

1 tablespoon extra virgin olive oil

1. Cut the chicken breasts into 1-inch cubes. You should have 3 to 4 dozen pieces.

2. Pound the garlic with the salt until pureed. Add the spices, pepper, mayonnaise, lemon juice, and oil, and whisk until smooth. Roll the chicken in the mayonnaise mixture to coat. Cover, refrigerate, and let marinate for 3 to 4 hours.

3. Preheat the broiler or light a hot fire in a barbecue grill. String the chicken on 4 long metal skewers. Broil or grill, brushing with the marinade, turning and basting, until well browned and cooked, 8 to 10 minutes. For safety, stop basting 3 or 4 minutes before the chicken is finally cooked.

Note: Please follow the timings here as marinated chicken is tricky—marinate too long and the flesh may turn mushy; marinate too briefly, and the flavors won't penetrate.

Double-Cooked Red Chicken Marrakech-Style

*T*he generous use of Moroccan mild paprika, *felfla hloua,* in this classic recipe explains its Moroccan name, *m'hammer,* or "reddish." The double-cooking method increases the complexity and depth of flavor of the dish. Garnish with slices of preserved lemon, if desired.

SERVES 6 TO 8

5 garlic cloves, smashed

1 tablespoon coarsely chopped fresh cilantro

$1/8$ teaspoon saffron threads, crushed

$1\frac{1}{4}$ teaspoons coarse salt

2 tablespoons unsalted butter, melted

2 whole chickens (3 pounds each), backbones removed

$1\frac{1}{2}$ tablespoons sweet paprika, preferably Spanish or *felfla hloua* (see Mail Order Sources)

1 teaspoon ground cumin

$1/4$ teaspoon freshly ground pepper

Pinch of ground ginger

Cayenne

1 small onion, grated

1. In a mortar or mini food processor, mash or pulse the garlic with the cilantro, saffron, and 1 teaspoon of the coarse salt until a coarse paste forms. Transfer the paste to a bowl and stir in the melted butter.

2. Re-form the chickens and tie them up with kitchen string. Rub the garlic paste all over the chickens, cover loosely with plastic wrap, and let stand at room temperature for 1 hour.

3. Put the cut-up chicken backbones in a large enameled cast-iron casserole. Add the chickens, breast-side up. In a bowl, combine 1 tablespoon of the paprika with $1/2$ teaspoon of the cumin, the pepper, ginger, and a pinch of cayenne. Sprinkle the spice mixture over the chickens and cook over moderately low heat until steam begins to rise, about 5 minutes.

4. Mix the onion into 1½ cups water and pour around the chickens. Bring to a boil over high heat. Reduce the heat to low, cover, and simmer until the juices run clear when the thighs are pierced near the bone with a knife, about 1 hour. Transfer the chickens to a cutting board and remove the strings; keep the chickens intact.

5. Discard the backbones. Skim off the fat from the sauce, reserving 3 tablespoons fat. Boil the sauce until it is reduced to 1 cup, about 15 minutes. Transfer to a small saucepan and keep warm.

6. Preheat the broiler. Stir the remaining ½ tablespoon paprika and ½ teaspoon cumin into the reserved 3 tablespoons chicken fat. Add a pinch of cayenne and ¼ teaspoon salt. Put the chickens in a roasting pan, breast side up, and rub with the spiced fat. Broil 8 to 10 inches from the heat for 10 minutes, or until browned. Carve the chicken and pass the warm sauce at the table.

Notes: Ask your butcher to remove the backbones from the chickens. Or use kitchen shears or a large sharp knife to cut along both sides of the backbones to remove them.

Friends often tell me they love the flavor of preserved lemons but complain that they take too long to make, nearly a month to ripen the lemon pith and skin to a soft voluptuous texture. In response, I offer a quick method recipe in the Mediterranean Larder chapter (page 303), which will soften lemons in less than a week. The only problem is that once they are ready, you have to use the lemons within a day or two. But I believe that once you've tasted them, you'll want to use them in lots of dishes, including garnishes for fish, salads, and lamb. See page 303 for the traditional method.

The chickens and sauce can be prepared through Step 4 and refrigerated overnight. Let the chickens return to room temperature before proceeding. Rewarm the sauce in a small saucepan over low heat.

Chicken Smothered in Sweet Onion Cream with Country Ham

*I*n this famous dish from southwest France, chicken is infused with the flavors of meltingly tender onions, Armagnac, and silky-salty Bayonne ham, for which prosciutto makes an admirable substitute.

If you think slicing up two pounds of onions will result in a lot of eye watering, try this method I learned in southwest France: sprinkle the chopping board with a few drops of vinegar. If that doesn't help, sprinkle a few more drops of vinegar directly on the onions as you slice them. When all the onions are sliced, simply rinse them under running water to remove the vinegar. Washing won't spoil their flavor. In fact, the onions should be wet for this dish so they won't burn but will slowly wilt as they cook. The addition of a little water softens them up before the sugars are released. Once soft, they will naturally turn golden.

SERVES 6

3 tablespoons rendered duck fat or extra virgin olive oil

2 pounds sweet onions, such as Vidalia, quartered lengthwise and thinly sliced crosswise

4 ounces dry-cured ham, such as Bayonne or prosciutto, trimmed

2 garlic cloves, thinly sliced

1 bay leaf

3 chicken breast halves on the bone (about ½ pound each), cut crosswise in half

3 whole chicken legs (about ¾ pound each), separated into drumsticks and thighs

Salt and freshly ground pepper

Flour, for dusting

2 tablespoons Armagnac or other brandy

¼ cup dry white wine

⅓ cup finely chopped, drained canned tomatoes

3 tablespoons heavy cream

1 tablespoon chopped flat-leaf parsley

1. Most dry-cured hams need to be soaked in water before cooking. Rinse the ham; soak in several changes of water if very salty for about 10 minutes. If using prosciutto, there is probably no need to soak it. Drain and pat dry. Finely dice to make 1 cup.

2. Heat 1 tablespoon of the duck fat or olive oil in a large enameled cast-iron casserole. Stir in the onions, ham, garlic, and bay leaf. Cover and cook over low heat, stirring occasionally, until cooked down and very wet, about $1\frac{1}{4}$ hours. Uncover and remove from the heat.

3. When the onions have simmered for 1 hour, begin to prepare the chicken. Working in batches, season the chicken pieces with salt and pepper and lightly dust with flour, tapping off any excess. Place a large skillet over medium-high heat, add 1 tablespoon fat or oil and, when almost smoking, add half the chicken, skin side down. Cook over medium-high heat until crusty and a deep golden brown. Turn and brown the other side, about 10 minutes total. Using tongs, arrange the chicken on top of the onions in the casserole. Repeat the seasoning, flouring, frying, and transferring of the remaining chicken.

4. Pour off the fat from the skillet. Add the Armagnac and wine. Using a long kitchen match, carefully ignite the mixture while it is still warm. When the flames subside, add $\frac{1}{2}$ cup water and bring to a boil over moderately high heat, scraping up any browned bits stuck to the skillet. Add the tomatoes and cook down to a juicy caramelized glaze, about 5 minutes. Stir in the cream, season with salt and pepper to taste, and pour over the chicken.

5. Cover the casserole and simmer over moderately low heat until the chicken is cooked through, about 15 minutes for the breasts and 25 to 30 minutes for the thighs and drumsticks; transfer the chicken pieces to a deep platter as they are done. Keep under a foil tent. If necessary, boil the sauce over high heat, stirring, until reduced to 2 cups. Correct the seasoning with salt and plenty of black pepper. Pour the sauce over the chicken and serve, garnished with a sprinkling of parsley.

Notes: The small addition of good white wine strengthens the flavor of this dish and nicely sets off the sauce.

For Bayonne ham, call D'Artagnan at 1-800-327-8246 and ask for the name of their closest supplier.

In southwest France, very sweet pear-shaped onions called *trebons* from the Haute Pyrenees are used. Vidalia onions from Georgia and Walla Walla onions from Washington state possess the same balance of sweet and sharp flavor as trebons. Look for well-cured onions that are shiny and firm.

Inspired by a recipe in Henri Combret's Saveurs et Traditions Gourmandes.

Pan-Grilled Duck Breast with Chanterelles, Dried Apricots, and Almonds

*T*his easy-to-make, slow-cooked duck breast dish pairs beautifully with a garnish of apricot-colored chanterelles and aromatic dried apricots and almonds.

SERVES 2

½ pound fresh small chanterelles

1 boneless duck breast (about 1 pound), Moulard or Muscovy (see Note)

Coarse salt

½ teaspoon freshly ground pepper

2 tablespoons butter

1 cup rich chicken stock

⅓ cup diced dried apricots (about 5)

1 large shallot, chopped

1 tablespoon fresh lemon juice

15 whole blanched almonds

1 tablespoon minced fresh chives

1. Early in the day, clean the chanterelles. (The fresher the chanterelles, the easier they are to clean.) Drop the chanterelles into boiling salted water for 2 to 3 seconds; scoop out and dip into cold water to stop the cooking. Drain in a colander. Use paper towels to remove any dirt. Wrap in paper towels and refrigerate.

2. About 1 hour before serving, remove the duck breast from the refrigerator, rinse, and pat dry with paper towels. Trim the duck breast of excess fat. Wipe the flesh dry and score the skin in a crosshatch pattern without piercing the flesh. Sprinkle the fat side generously with salt and half the pepper. Cover loosely with plastic wrap.

3. Set a large nonstick skillet over medium-high heat, add 1 teaspoon of the butter and the duck breast, flesh side down, and sear well, about 2 minutes. Add 2 tablespoons stock to deglaze the skillet and boil until thick. Turn the duck over; season with salt and pepper. Reduce the heat to medium-low and slowly cook the duck breast, fat side down, *without turning,* for 15 minutes.

4. Meanwhile, in a large straight-sided skillet set over medium-high heat, sear the chanterelles, stirring, until you hear them squeak, about 30 seconds. Add the apricots, shallot, and remaining butter and cook, stirring, for 2 minutes. Add half the stock and simmer until the mushrooms are just tender, about 5 minutes. Remove from the heat.

5. Turn the duck breast over and finish cooking on the flesh side. To test for doneness, use your thumb and middle finger to pinch the flesh. If it springs back quickly, it is rare. Remove to a side dish, cover with foil, and allow to rest for at least 5 minutes while the juices settle.

6. Pour off all the fat from the skillet. Deglaze with the remaining stock. Scrape the mushrooms into the pan and bring to a boil. Heighten the flavor with lemon juice and correct the seasoning. Fold in the almonds and chives.

7. Thinly slice the breast and fan out the slices on a warmed serving platter. Season lightly with salt and pepper. Serve with the mushroom sauce.

Note: Peking duck breasts may be substituted. Use 1 whole breast, divided, and considerably reduce the cooking time by half in Steps 3 and 4.

Inspired by a recipe created by chef Alain Lorca.

Slow-Cooked Duck with Olives

My son, Nick Wolfert, a film industry assistant director, adores duck confit. Though a fine cook in his own right, he never makes confit himself. He prefers to wait until he comes home for the holidays, at which time he expects to find a crock of the stuff waiting to be crisped up by his loving mom.

This year, when I forgot to put up confit, he was so forlorn I offered to enlarge his horizons by teaching him how to slow-cook a duck in the oven that would have the familiar meltingly tender texture of confit, a crisp skin, and also a sauce. Nick was skeptical.

"Confit is like wine and women," he said teasingly. "It gets better with age"

Still, I thought he would like this "quick" slow version nearly as much. The method I use, Spanish in origin, goes against most of the principles of duck oven cookery that appear in cookbooks. I *halve* the duck instead of cooking it whole. I *don't* put it on a rack. I *never* turn it. I *don't* remove the fat during cooking. Rather, I nestle the duck in a bed of chopped vegetables, and these, along with the fat rendered during cooking, keep the flesh succulent and flavorful. I only remove the duck fat at the end while the bird rests, garnering about two cups, perfect for sautéing potatoes, starting a stew, or preparing a small batch of real confit.

I explained to Nick that this dish would fit perfectly with his lifestyle. He could prepare the duck Saturday morning, clean up his kitchen, separate the fat from the pan juices, begin the base for a delicious sauce, and then go about his errands. That night, all he'd have to do is reheat the duck and crisp the skin just before serving.

He could finish his sauce with sautéed onions, caramelized root vegetables, glazed dried fruits, spiced lentils, or herb-flavored olives. The olive sauce, I explained, would provide an extra dimension of flavor, as good in its own way as the slowly developed flavor one gets from a well-preserved confit put up for one to three months. The base for the sauce should be made well in advance; then the sauce is quickly finished while the duck reheats.

"It would be a great dish to serve to a prospective girlfriend," I added.

Steps 1 through 5 can be done early in the day or the day before.

SERVES 4

1 duckling (5 to 6 pounds), fresh or thawed

2 medium onions, coarsely chopped

1 large celery rib, sliced

8 garlic cloves, halved

1½ tablespoons chopped fresh thyme

¼ cup plus 2 teaspoons coarsely chopped
    flat-leaf parsley

2 bay leaves

2 teaspoons sea salt

1 teaspoon freshly ground pepper

1 teaspoon herbes de Provence

Green Olive Sauce (recipe follows)

1. Preheat the oven to 475°F. Halve the duckling, setting aside the back, neck, and wing tips for the sauce. In a 9 by 11-inch roasting pan, make a bed of the onions, celery, garlic, thyme, ¼ cup of the parsley, and the bay leaves. With the tines of a fork, prick the duck skin every ½ inch. Rub the duck with a combination of the salt, pepper, and herbes de Provence and set it on top of the vegetables, skin side up. Roast, uncovered, for 10 minutes.

2. Reduce the oven temperature to 275°F, cover the contents of the pan with foil, and leave the duckling to cook for about 3½ hours, or until it is very tender. Turn off the heat and let the duckling cool in the flavored fat in the oven for 30 minutes.

3. Carefully transfer the duck to a work surface. Remove and discard any loose bones, chopped vegetables, and clumps of fat. Reserve 1 teaspoon of the fat for Step 5. (Reserve the remaining fat for another use.) Quarter the duck; gently squeeze or press each portion to maintain its shape, and wrap individually in foil or plastic wrap to prevent drying out. Set aside in a cool place or in the refrigerator.

4. About 30 minutes before serving, unwrap the duck quarters and generously season the flesh side with salt, pepper, and more herbes de Provence.

5. About 10 minutes before serving, preheat the broiler and set the rack about 10 inches from the heat source. Dab the duck skin with a little duck fat and run under the broiler to reheat the duck and crisp the skin.

6. Pour the sauce with the olives into a shallow, warm serving dish, place the duck on top, sprinkle with the remaining parsley, and serve at once.

Note: Be sure your oven is calibrated. If the duck is baked at a higher temperature it will overcook and will taste reheated.

Green Olive Sauce

MAKES ABOUT 2½ CUPS

Neck, back, and wing tips of the duck

1 medium onion, sliced

1 tablespoon tomato paste

½ cup dry white wine

Pinch of sugar

1 cup poultry stock

Salt and freshly ground pepper

1½ cups (7 to 8 ounces drained weight) green olives, rinsed and pitted

¼ teaspoon herbes de Provence

1. Slowly brown the duck neck, back, and wing tips in their own fat in a covered nonstick skillet. Add the onion and continue cooking until the onions are glazed and browned, about 10 minutes. Pour off any excess fat.

2. Add the tomato paste to the skillet and cook until lightly charred. Quickly deglaze the pan with the white wine. Add the sugar, stock, and 3 cups water. Bring to a boil, reduce the heat, and simmer for 1 hour; then strain, degrease, and boil until reduced to 1 cup. Reserve, covered, in the refrigerator.

3. About 10 minutes before serving, reheat the sauce, add the olives, and simmer for 10 minutes. Correct the seasoning with salt and pepper, and herbes de Provence to taste.

Steamed and Crisped Duck Legs with Umbrian Lentils

*I*n this recipe, I steam the duck legs so that the flesh will melt in your mouth and not in the pot. If you use large foie gras–style legs (legs of a Moulard or Muscovy duck bred to produce foie gras), you'll need to steam them longer.

SERVES 4

4 large duck legs, preferably Moulard or Muscovy

Garlic, celery tops, bay leaves, parsley sprigs, rosemary, and thyme

⅓ cup diced pancetta (2 ounces)

1 tablespoon extra virgin olive oil

⅓ cup chopped celery

⅓ cup chopped onion

⅓ cup chopped carrot

½ pound small brown lentils such as Colfiorito, Casteluccio, or Pardina, rinsed and drained

3 cups light poultry stock

3 tablespoons saba (see page 33)

2 tablespoons red wine

A few drops of balsamic vinegar or lemon juice

2 tablespoons chopped flat-leaf parsley

1. Rinse the duck legs and let drain. Place the legs in a steamer basket or colander over a bed of garlic, celery, bay leaves, parsley, rosemary, and thyme. Set the steamer over a deep pot filled with boiling water, cover, and steam for 1½ to 2 hours. If necessary, add more hot water to the pot.

2. In a 3 quart or medium-size flameproof casserole, heat the pancetta in the oil; add the celery, onion, and carrot and cook until soft. Stir in the lentils and stock, cover, and cook for 45 minutes.

3. When the duck legs are tender, transfer to a work surface to rest for about 30 minutes. Cut out and discard all loose bones and fat. Place the duck on a rack on a baking sheet in a cold oven. Set the oven temperature to 400°F.

4. Mix the saba and red wine and adjust the seasoning with salt, pepper, and balsamic vinegar or lemon juice to taste. When the skin is hot and taut, brush with the prepared saba mixture and roast for 20 to 30 minutes longer, or until the skin is shiny, crisp, and brown. Nestle the legs in the lentils, add any leftover glaze to the lentils, and garnish with the chopped parsley.

Crispy Squabs with Coriander Spiced Salt

*F*or me, this recipe is magical. Squabs, or baby pigeons, poached in a spiced broth, come out velvety in texture, juicy, and flavorful. They are then dried and fried until the skin turns golden and crisp, contrasting with the pink, juicy, interior flesh. Squab flesh should always be served red. If you prefer it medium, simmer a little longer, but please be careful not to overcook.

This dish was inspired by one in Australian chef Greg Malouf's book *Moorish,* and the chef's touch of rubbing a coriander-based salt into the birds just before the last minute of frying is brilliant. In my adaptation, I poach the squab in an aromatic liquid using typical Egyptian seasonings: cinnamon, cardamom, mastic, and saffron.

Prepare Steps 1 through 3 a day in advance. You will need two thermometers—one for the poaching liquid, the other to monitor the cooking of the flesh.

SERVES 2

2 squabs (about 1 pound each)

Coriander Spiced Salt (recipe follows)

5 cardamom pods, bruised

2 pinches of saffron threads

1 cinnamon stick, 2 inches long

½ teaspoon crushed black peppercorns

1 dried hot red chile pepper

¼ teaspoon mastic (see Mail Order Sources)

⅓ cup plus 1 tablespoon extra virgin olive oil

3 garlic cloves, crushed

1 small onion, quartered

Juice of 1 orange

2 tablespoons honey

Dash of fruit or wine vinegar

1. Rinse the squabs; cut off the wing tips, neck bones, and excess fat and reserve for the poaching liquid. Rub the birds dry with paper towels.

2. Place 1 tablespoon of the coriander spiced salt in a large bowl, add the birds, seal, and shake up and down so they are completely coated with the prepared salt. Refrigerate, covered, for 24 hours.

3. Meanwhile, tie the cardamom, saffron, cinnamon, peppercorns, chile pepper, and mastic in a cheesecloth bag. Slowly brown the squab bones and the trimmings in a saucepan in 1 tablespoon of oil over medium heat. Add the garlic and onion and cook, stirring, until golden. Moisten with orange juice. Add the spice packet to the pan along with the honey, vinegar, and 1½ quarts water. Bring to a boil. Skim and simmer for 10 minutes. Remove from the heat and let cool to room temperature. Strain, cover, and refrigerate. Discard the spice packet, wing tips, necks, and aromatics.

4. The following day, bring the squab and liquid to room temperature. Place the birds in a pot, cover with the cold liquid, and slowly heat *almost* to a strong simmer, 15 minutes. Meanwhile, monitor the internal flesh at the thigh, and when it reaches 125°F, remove from the heat. Partially cover and allow the birds to cool in the liquid for 15 minutes. Lift out the birds and leave to drain on a V-shaped rack set over a plate for 10 minutes. Bring the liquid to a boil, simmer for 5 minutes, strain, and set aside to cool. Freeze to use again.

5. Meanwhile, set a wok or wide skillet over medium heat. Add the oil and when hot, dust the birds with 2 teaspoons of the remaining coriander salt and fry, turning them on all sides until beautifully browned all over. Drain on a rack. Serve at once with the remaining salt as a condiment on the side.

Note: Chicken legs and thighs can be substituted for the squab. Cook for 30 minutes.

Strain the poaching liquid, boil for a few minutes, cool, and store in the freezer. You can use it the next time you prepare the dish. The flavor will be more delicious.

Coriander Spiced Salt

MAKES ABOUT 2½ TABLESPOONS

1 tablespoon sea salt

1 tablespoon ground coriander

½ teaspoon ground cumin

¼ teaspoon ground caraway

Grated zest of 1 orange

Mix all the ingredients together. Store in a tightly covered jar.

Tuscan Quail with Red Grape Sauce

*I*n the Capezzana Wine and Culinary Center, located in a magnificent sixteenth-century villa above the Tuscan town of Carmignano west of Florence, I watched as tall lanky chef Patrizio Cirri demonstrated a local dish to a class of American food enthusiasts and cooking professionals. He had just carved a guinea fowl roasted to crisp perfection and was in the process of smothering it with an intensely flavored and deeply colored red wine grape sauce made with sangiovese grapes, for centuries the backbone of distinguished Tuscan red wines.

"This grape is from our own vineyard," he proudly told the class. "It has produced renowned wines since the time of the Medicis." This was not meant as chauvinism but stated simply as a fact, for Patrizio was, I learned during five days of inspiring cooking lessons, a man of very few words.

Still, I knew that if I was to reproduce this simple, magnificent Tuscan specialty at home, I would have to find a red table grape equivalent to the small, tough-skinned, intensely flavored sangiovese. As if reading my mind, Patrizio added: "Tuscany is a state of mind. Learn our cooking, then apply our concepts to what you have at home."

Developing the following adaptation of Tuscan chef Patrizio Cirri's recipe, I tried the sweet, mildly tart red flame and the sweet, earthy red emperor, achieving a Tuscan flavor through a series of reductions of grape pulp and skin. In the process, I learned that grape color is easily lost if the grape skins are removed too soon.

Although guinea fowl make for a glorious feast, I have substituted quail so I can sauté the birds along with the pureed grape pulp and skin, thus further concentrating the flavors. I reduced the pan juices to produce a shiny, smooth, reddish-brown sauce.

When I was satisfied, I e-mailed my recipe to Florence-based American cookbook author Faith Willinger, an expert on Tuscan cuisine and the director of the week-long Capezzana program. "Is the dish still Tuscan?" I asked her. "Even without the correct wine grape and bird?"

"Yes, of course it's Tuscan," Faith e-mailed back, on account of its honesty, straightforwardness, and deliciousness. Remember," she added, "every cook can make her own Tuscany."

Serve with Oven-Baked Polenta (page 177) and a bitter green salad.

SERVES 4

¾ pound red seedless grapes

8 quail (4 to 5 ounces each), rinsed and patted
   dry

¼ cup extra virgin olive oil

1½ ounces pancetta, finely diced

1 small onion, finely chopped

1 small carrot, finely chopped

6 garlic cloves, roughly chopped

2 teaspoons coarsely chopped fresh rosemary

Coarse salt and freshly ground pepper

Several drops of fresh lemon juice

1. Stem the grapes and puree them in a blender or food processor.

2. Using a small, sharp knife, make a ½-inch slash in 1 thigh of each quail and slip the end of the other leg into it to make a tidy package.

3. In a large, deep skillet or flameproof casserole, heat the olive oil until shimmering. Add the pancetta, onion, carrot, garlic, and rosemary and cook over moderate heat, stirring occasionally, until the onion is soft and golden, about 5 minutes. Push the vegetables to one side of the pan.

4. Generously season the quail with salt and pepper and add them to the skillet. Cook over moderately low heat, turning the quail occasionally, until lightly browned, about 20 minutes. Add half the grape puree, cover, and simmer over low heat until the quail are cooked through, about 20 minutes. Increase the heat to high and cook, turning the birds often, until the juices are slightly reduced, 2 to 3 minutes. Remove the skillet from the heat; tilt it and blot away any excess fat from the juices. Transfer the quail to a broiler pan, breast side up.

5. Preheat the broiler. Add the remaining grape puree and 1 cup water to the skillet and boil over high heat, scraping up any brown bits from the bottom of the pan, until the sauce is reduced to 1 cup, about 5 minutes. Strain the sauce, pressing hard on the solids. Season with salt and pepper and, if necessary, a few drops of lemon juice to counter any excessive sweetness, and keep warm.

6. Broil the quail as close to the heat as possible for about 1 minute, turning once, until the skin is lightly browned and crisp; shift the pan for even browning if necessary. Spoon the sauce onto plates or a platter, set the crisp quail on top, and serve.

Grilled Marinated Guinea Hen

*H*ere's a delicious, easy-to-make eastern Mediterranean guinea hen dish. The trick here is to dip the hens very quickly in simmering acidulated water to firm up the skin without hardening the flesh. The slow part comes in letting the skins dry out. This Chinese-inspired method results in a truly crisp, almost crunchy skin. I like to serve the hens with the slightly wet Turkish Purlane Salad that follows and some dense-textured, lightly toasted bread to mop up the juices.

SERVES 6

2 guinea hens (2½ pounds each)

¼ cup mild vinegar, such as cider or rice vinegar

Salt and freshly ground pepper

3 tablespoons honey

¼ cup orange juice

5 tablespoons extra virgin olive oil

3 tablespoons lemon juice

1. Early in the day, prepare the guinea hens. Remove the giblets from the cavities of the hens. Cut off the wings at the second joint. With kitchen shears, remove the backbone from each hen. Rinse and drain the hens. Bring 2 quarts water with the vinegar to a boil. Turn off the heat. Dip one of the hens into the hot water and let stand for 10 seconds. Remove, rinse under cold water, and wipe dry. Repeat with the second hen. Place the birds, uncovered, in the refrigerator and let dry for at least half a day.

2. About 45 minutes before serving, set the oven rack about 9 inches from the heat source. Preheat the broiler. Carefully separate the leg thigh sections from each hen. (Leave the whole breast in one piece.) Season the hen pieces liberally with salt and pepper. Mix the honey, orange juice, ¼ cup of the olive oil, and half the lemon juice in a small bowl. Brush the mixture over the hens. Arrange on a broiling rack, skin side up, and slowly broil, basting often with the marinade, until crackling crisp and deep brown, about 12 minutes.

3. Turn the pieces over and broil the breasts for 10 more minutes, the legs and thighs 17 to 20 minutes. Transfer the breasts to a rack and let them rest, skin side down, while finishing the rest of the birds.

4. Cut each breast into even serving pieces and place in the center of a serving platter. Surround with the prepared salad and drizzle with a combination of verjus or the remaining lemon juice and oil. Remove the legs and thighs from the broiler, add to the platter, and serve.

Turkish Purslane Salad

You can find purslane at farmers' markets. If you don't see it, simply ask; many sellers will be happy to sell it to you for pennies. If you have your own sunny garden, you may discover you've been weeding it out all summer. Purslane is considered so disposable that one farmer offered me "lifetime rights" to as much as I wanted in return for weeding a row a week from his plot.

SERVES 6

2 cups trimmed young purslane tips, ¾ pound uncleaned

½ cup thinly sliced scallions

2 ripe medium tomatoes, peeled, seeded, and cubed (1 cup)

1 medium cucumber, peeled, seeded, and cubed (1 cup)

3 tablespoons fresh lemon juice

2 tablespoons extra virgin olive oil

Pinch of Turkish or Aleppo red pepper flakes

Salt and freshly ground black pepper

Sprigs of fresh mint, for garnish

1. Wash the purslane and pat dry with paper towels or spin dry in a salad spinner.

2. Combine the purslane with the tomatoes, cucumber, lemon juice, olive oil, and red pepper flakes. Season with salt and black pepper to taste, mixing well. Cover and refrigerate for 1 hour.

3. If the vegetables do not express enough moisture, add a few tablespoons cold water to make the salad a little wet. Serve garnished with sprigs of fresh mint.

Catalan-Style Braised Cornish Hens with Stuffed Cabbage Purses

*T*here's an old Mediterranean saying: "For the one who likes working, there's always something to do" . . . which brings me to this wonderful, slow Catalan specialty. I know it's a ridiculously long recipe, but it isn't hard. While it is traditionally made with partridges, I've found it works well with our readily available Cornish game hens.

The hens are marinated, simmered with aromatic vegetables, smothered with leaves of cabbage, then slowly cooked until everything is tender. The cabbage leaves, perfumed with the birds' essence, are then drained, stuffed, rolled in flour and eggs, and fried. Meanwhile, the sauce is enriched with a *picada,* a sauce based on toasted almonds. This dish is a perfect example of the intricacy of Catalan cooking. The delicious result is the payoff.

SERVES 4

4 Cornish game hens

Salt and freshly ground pepper

Pinch of ground cinnamon

Pinch of grated nutmeg

1¼ teaspoons herbes de Provence

3 tablespoons extra virgin olive oil

1 small green cabbage (about 1⅓ pounds)

1½ ounces pancetta, finely chopped

¾ cup chopped onion

⅓ cup chopped carrot

6 tablespoons chopped flat-leaf parsley, plus 2 sprigs

3 tablespoons sherry, preferably oloroso

2 cups chicken stock

2 whole cloves

5 garlic cloves

½ cup fresh bread crumbs

¼ pound ground veal

2 large eggs, beaten

12 lightly toasted blanched almonds

Olive oil, for frying

Flour

1. Wipe the birds with paper towels and season with salt and pepper. Reserve the neck bones, gizzards, and hearts. Mix pinches of cinnamon and nutmeg, ¼ teaspoon of the herbes de Provence, and 2 tablespoons of the olive oil and rub over the skin. Wrap and refrigerate overnight.

2. About 3 hours before serving, remove the birds from the refrigerator. Bring plenty of water to a boil in a large saucepan over high heat. Cut out the core of the cabbage and remove the leaves, discarding the outermost ones. Blanch them in salted water for 10 minutes. Drain and leave them to dry.

3. Heat a large heavy Dutch oven over medium heat. Add the remaining 1 tablespoon of oil and the pancetta and let sizzle. Add the hens and fry on one side until brown; turn and brown the other side. Add ½ cup of the chopped onion, the carrot, and 1 tablespoon of the chopped parsley and cook, stirring, until the onion is soft and golden. Add the neck bones, gizzards, and hearts. Pour in the sherry, stock, the remaining 1 teaspoon of herbes de Provence, the whole cloves, and 4 of the garlic cloves and cook, uncovered, for 15 minutes over medium-low heat. Spread the cabbage leaves over the hens, cover, and cook until they are meltingly tender, 45 minutes to 1 hour.

4. Meanwhile, in a bowl, moisten the bread crumbs with a few teaspoons of the cooking liquid. Mix in the ground veal, remaining ¼ cup chopped onion and 2 tablespoons chopped parsley, ¼ teaspoon salt, and pinches of pepper and grated nutmeg. Work in a few tablespoons of the beaten egg. Set in the refrigerator to chill and develop flavor for at least 30 minutes.

5. Make the picada: In a mortar or small spice mill, pound or grind the almonds, remaining garlic clove, and 3 tablespoons chopped parsley until pasty. (If necessary, add a few teaspoons of water to make it smooth.) Set aside.

6. Use tongs to transfer the cabbage leaves to a colander set in the sink to drain. Place the birds tail side up in a dish to rest; remove as many loose bones as possible. Cover with foil to keep warm. Strain the cooking liquid into another saucepan; discard the bones, and press on the vegetables to extract all their juices. Degrease the liquid and correct the seasoning. As soon as the cabbage is cool enough to handle, divide into 4 piles and fill each leaf with one-quarter of the veal stuffing. Roll up tightly and flatten into 3-inch rounds.

7. About 30 minutes before serving, preheat the oven to 375°F. Brush the hens with a little oil and set in the oven to brown. Gently reheat the sauce, stir in the picada, and simmer for 5 minutes. Correct the seasoning. Heat ¼ inch of olive oil in a wide skillet until very hot but not smoking. First dip the cabbage rolls in flour, then in the beaten egg. Fry the rolls in hot oil until golden crisp on all sides, 15 minutes. Spoon the sauce on a large warm serving platter and place the hens in it in one layer to absorb the juices and remain moist. Surround with the cabbage and garnish with the sprigs of parsley. Serve at once.

MEATS

When I first moved to Morocco, the word *meat* usually meant lamb. In the international city of Tangier, there were a few Spanish butchers who sold pork and some European butchers who offered cuts of imported veal. But for the most part, lamb was king. Amusingly, my Moroccan butcher sold all lamb parts at the same price. His explanation: "Loins, racks, and legs don't feed as many people as shoulder, shanks, and necks."

Though lamb still is the primary meat in most Mediterranean countries, pork, veal, and beef are well represented in France, Spain, Italy, and Greece. Whatever the choice of meat, there are literally thousands of recipes in which low-temperature slow cooking is employed to make the meat tender, juicy, and flavorful. Slow-pot roasting, slow-grilling, slow-baking, slow-simmering, and slow-braising are all time-honored traditional Mediterranean cooking techniques.

In this chapter, you'll find a variety of methods that use an assortment of cuts to produce rich, tender, and succulent meats. Among my favorites are dishes that employ a similar way of cooking: simple slow-braising in a small amount of liquid in a closed pot. Two good examples are Fall-Apart Lamb Shanks with Almond-Chocolate Picada and Seven-Hour Garlic-Crowned Leg of Lamb.

One of my favorite slow-roasted dishes is Night-and-Day Slow-Roasted Pork Shoulder. I also recommend slow-baked lamb and sheep's milk pecorino cheese, teamed up with chunks of potato and fennel, baked with both wet and dry heat in a shallow clay pot—a hearty winter dish. And for summer, meltingly tender chunks of pork shoulder simmered in olive oil for hours, then served over a bed of Tuscan beans topped with a traditional scattering of vinegared onion rings.

I also include some exciting and "edgy" dishes here that employ the science of slow timing and low-temperature cooking. Pot-Roasted Club Steak with Piquillo Peppers and Slow-Roasted Rack of Lamb with Simple Mediterranean Flavors use the most tender and most delicious cuts with the remarkable result that the meat emerges butter-soft yet still rare!

DARIO CECCHINI'S TONNO DEL CHIANTI

In August 2001, I took part in a splendid event on the University of California Berkeley campus—the thirtieth anniversary of Alice Waters's Chez Panisse, the restaurant that has probably had more influence than any other on the way we eat in America today.

Many famous food personalities were present that gorgeous summer afternoon—chefs, food writers, cookbook authors, gastronomes. People had even flown in from Europe for the occasion. Perhaps the most flamboyant guest was a tall, blue-eyed, curly-haired man wearing a dazzling fluorescent lavender suit and matching boots, standing under an umbrella handing out samples of his head cheese (*soprassata*) and a delicious pork concoction he called *tonno del chianti*.

His name was Dario Cecchini. He owns a famous butcher shop in the town of Panzano in the Chianti region midway between Florence and Siena. But Dario is no ordinary butcher. He has been called "the most cultured butcher in the world." My friend the Florence-based food writer Faith Willinger calls him "the Michelangelo of butchers." I've hung out at his shop, tasted his marvelous home-cured sausages, listened to him intone an entire canto from Dante's *Inferno* by heart. Dario is not only a great butcher, he's also a great showman. When the EEC banned the selling of beef on the bone, he organized a "funeral" for the famous Florentine T-bone steak, *bistecca alla fiorentina*.

Dario had come to the Chez Panisse anniversary party out of a long friendship with Alice Waters, and because he practices his profession in the same spirit she runs her restaurant—employing traditional cooking methods, preserving traditional dishes, working closely with local farmers who produce fresh organic products. The dish he was handing out, his tonno del chianti, was, in fact, based on a hundred-year-old recipe he'd uncovered and resurrected.

The name of the dish is, of course, a joke, a metaphor if you will. One of the most famous of Tuscan antipasto is *fagioli con tonno*—canned olive oil–preserved tuna served on white beans. Dario substitutes a combination of olive oil and wine-preserved pork for the tuna. Although in Berkeley he served it on grilled bread (bruschetta), he normally suggests serving it on white beans garnished with thin slices of red onions marinated in wine vinegar.

PORK

Pork Coddled in Olive Oil with Tuscan Beans and Arugula

This dish from Arezzo originated in a time of great poverty and drought, when pigs had to be slaughtered because there was nothing to feed them. The pigs' legs, of course, were preserved in the form of prosciutto. The local farmers devised a method of preserving the rest of the pork similar to the way fresh tuna is preserved in Sicily: they salted it, cooked it very slowly in olive oil along with some seasonings and a little bit of unfiltered *vin brusco,* and then preserved the meat *sott'olio,* literally "under olive oil."

I guarantee you'll enjoy making this dish, as it will fill your kitchen with a wonderful aroma. When served, the meat is broken apart into small chunks, exposing a juicy pink interior. The chunks are presented on a bed of Tuscan white beans tossed with intense pan drippings from the meat. Thinly sliced vinegared red onions are sprinkled on top.

SERVES 8

2¼ pounds lean boneless pork shoulder

1 tablespoon coarse salt

1 tablespoon crushed black peppercorns

2 imported bay leaves, crushed to a powder

½ teaspoon bruised fennel seeds

2 sprigs of thyme

2 cups plus 3 tablespoons extra virgin olive oil

1 small head of garlic, halved

1 small red onion, sliced paper thin

2½ tablespoons red wine vinegar

Tuscan Beans (recipe follows)

2 large bunches of arugula

1. Trim away all fat, sinew, and membrane from the pork. Cut the meat into 2-inch chunks. In a large sealable bag or bowl, toss the meat with a mixture of the salt, peppercorns, bay leaves, fennel, and thyme. Massage the seasonings into the pork, seal or cover tightly, and refrigerate for at least 6 hours or overnight.

2. Without draining the meat, squeeze the pieces into a medium ceramic or enameled cast-iron casserole in a single layer. Pour on 2 cups of the olive oil. Cover with a sheet of crumpled parchment and a lid, set over very low heat, and cook until the oil comes to a boil, 30 to 45 minutes.

3. Preheat the oven to 250°F. Transfer the pan to the oven. Add the halved head of garlic and cook for 2½ hours longer. Check that the oil bubbles only a little; the meat should not brown. To test if the pork is ready, scoop out one piece and tap it lightly; it should break into smaller chunks and be a soft pink color. Remove from the oven and let stand until completely cool. Refrigerate for up to 5 days. (Be sure the pork is completely covered in oil; add additional fresh oil, if necessary.)

4. Reheat the pork slowly. At the same time, soak the red onion in 1 tablespoon of the vinegar for 30 minutes. Drain the pork into a colander set over a bowl; discard the garlic and thyme. Allow all the juices in the bowl to settle, then pour off the oil and reserve it for future use; reserve the meat juices at the bottom of the bowl separately.

5. In a large bowl, whisk together the remaining 3 tablespoons olive oil and 1½ tablespoons vinegar with the reserved meat juices. Add the room temperature beans and toss to mix.

6. To serve, mound the beans on a large platter. Scatter the red onion slices and chunks of warm pork on top. Garnish with the arugula.

With thanks to Chez Panisse Café chef Russell Moore for sharing this recipe.

Tuscan Beans

2 cups dried white beans, such as cannellini or Great Northern

2 garlic cloves, peeled

1 dried hot red pepper

Pinch of salt

2 bay leaves

Freshly ground pepper

1. Soak the beans in cold water to cover by at least 2 inches for at least 12 hours or overnight. Drain the beans.

2. Place the beans in a large pot and cover with 3 quarts of fresh cold water. Slowly bring to a boil, skimming once or twice. Add the garlic, hot pepper, salt, and the bay leaves, and continue to cook over the lowest heat until tender, about 3 hours.

3. Drain the beans; discard the pepper and bay leaves. Let cool to room temperature. Season with salt and pepper to taste. If the beans are made ahead and refrigerated, let return to room temperature before serving.

Night-and-Day Slow-Roasted Pork Shoulder

If you enjoy slow-cooking, you'll love this dish—a pork shoulder with big, bold, crunchy skin and an interior so meltingly tender in texture and so vibrant in taste that eating it will be a revelation. Slow, low-temperature cooking is the key.

I developed this recipe following some of the precepts of the late Adelle Davis, a food authority of the sixties—"setting the oven temperature at the temperature you want the meat when it is done." Though much of her "nutritional" advice has since been discredited, her slow-roasting methods are still sound and worthwhile *provided* you follow some important safety measures: Choose whole pieces of meat. Don't use a skewer or other utensil to pierce the flesh except a clean, dry, digital probe thermometer. Don't stuff the meat. And use high-temperature roasting at the beginning of the cooking to remove any surface bacteria.

After this first high-temperature blast, you can reduce the oven heat and leave the pork to roast leisurely. It won't burn, and you won't have to watch it much. You can even raise or lower the oven temperature to suit your schedule. Use your digital probe thermometer to monitor the internal temperature.

This is a very forgiving recipe. Once the preferred internal temperature is achieved, the meat will stay at that temperature for a while, remaining moist and tender until ready to serve.

For extra moisture, the pork may be soaked in a salt and sugar brine a few days in advance (step 1 in the recipe for Pot-Roasted Pork Loin with Fall Fruits, page 170). Be sure to begin the preparations that follow a day before you plan to serve the pork.

Serve with Glazed Carrots with Green Olives (page 243).

(continued)

SERVES 6 TO 8

One 6- to 7-pound bone-in fresh pork
   picnic shoulder roast or Boston butt,
   with skin on

1 head of garlic

1 tablespoon coarse sea salt

½ teaspoon freshly ground pepper

1½ teaspoons dried oregano or marjoram

1 teaspoon dried thyme

1 large onion, thinly sliced

1 carrot, sliced

½ cup oloroso sherry

4 cups chicken stock

Crushed hot red pepper

1½ teaspoons top-quality sherry vinegar or
   balsamic vinegar

1. Preheat the oven to 450°F. Score the skin of the pork in a crisscross diamond pattern like a ham, making deep cuts about 1 inch apart. Crush the garlic with the salt, pepper, oregano, and thyme. Rub over all the meaty parts of the roast as well as the skin.

2. Set the pork shoulder skin side up on a rack in an oiled shallow roasting pan. Roast for 45 minutes, or until a deep golden brown.

3. Scatter the onion and carrot slices around the pork. Pour half the sherry and half the stock into the pan. Add a good pinch of hot pepper. Reduce the oven temperature to 180°F and continue roasting, basting once or twice, until a probe thermometer inserted in the center of the meat reads 170° to 175°F, about 12 hours. (It will not hurt the meat to keep it in the oven longer, up to a total of 24 hours.) Avoid opening the oven door any more than necessary. (If the meat is cooked before this time, simply reduce the oven temperature to 160°F and continue to roast the pork slowly while preparing the carrots as directed on page 243.)

4. About 30 minutes before serving, remove the meat from the oven and transfer to a carving board. Cover loosely and set aside in a warm place. Pour the remaining sherry and stock into the pan. Bring to a boil, scraping up the browned bits from the bottom of the pan. Boil until the liquid is reduced to about 1 cup. Strain the pan juices into a bowl, pressing on the vegetables. Skim off as much fat as possible. Stir in the vinegar and correct the seasoning.

5. Lift the skin of the pork and cut it into thick strips; place on a serving platter. Slice the meat across the grain and arrange on the platter. Pour the pan juices over the meat.

Notes: If you have a HearthKit inset, follow Steps 1, 2, and 3. Reduce the oven temperature to 250°F and roast for 1½ hours. Turn the oven off and leave the meat in the oven to finish cooking in the receding heat, about 4 hours. Do not open the oven door, or the loss of residual heat will curtail the process.

Please note that most other cuts of pork need less time to cook until tender.

If you're worried about cooking pork at such a low temperature, ask your butcher to get you "certified" pork, which has undergone a special freezing treatment. You can do this yourself by freezing a shoulder of pork for 3 weeks before defrosting and roasting. According to the National Restaurant Association, slow-cooking at low temperatures (below 325°F) is safe for fish and meats that have been seared first to kill surface bacteria, as in this recipe. It is also advisable not to stuff or insert anything in the meat. For more information on safety in low temperature cooking, check with the USDA. Their Meat and Poultry Hotline is 1-800-535-4555.

When choosing pork, ask your butcher to leave the fat on.

With thanks to Suzanne Hamlin for helping me rethink this dish.

SLOW-COOKED MEATS PREFERRED

In experiments where identical roasts were cooked at different oven temperatures to the same degree of doneness, roasts cooked for 20 to 24 hours were preferred in 100 percent of the taste tests to roasts cooked in 3 hours or less. Although the cooking time seems startling at first, the meat is so amazingly delicious, juicy, and tender, slices so beautifully, and shrinks so little that meats cooked at higher temperatures no longer taste good to you.

—ADELLE DAVIS, *LET'S COOK IT RIGHT*, 1947

Pot-Roasted Pork Loin with Fall Fruits

Greek food charms us by its simplicity, but there are exceptions. Here's a rich-tasting yet modern northern Greek pork dish, *hrino langada*, filled with wonderful warm, sweet tones of caramelized yellow raisins, figs, and walnuts, served under a sauce highlighted with a last minute splash of *glyko*, a syrupy sweet vinegar. You can substitute balsamic or sherry vinegar, or any of the new stylish vinegars, such as currant or fig.

Brining a boneless pork loin guarantees a juicy flavorful roast. The meat is browned, oven-roasted at a medium-low temperature, then left to rest before a final glazing in the syrupy sauce. Begin two to three days in advance by brining the pork and making the fruit compote.

SERVES 6 TO 8

¼ cup sea salt or kosher salt dissolved in 1 cup hot water

3 tablespoons sugar

½ teaspoon cracked black peppercorns

2 bay leaves, crumbled

1 teaspoon dried thyme

1 boneless pork loin (4 pounds) with a thin layer of fat left intact, preferably center cut

6 garlic cloves

Salt and freshly ground pepper

1 tablespoon plus ½ teaspoon grated orange zest

2 tablespoons extra virgin olive oil

Flour, for dusting

12 green grapes, preferably muscat

Fall Fruit Compote (recipe follows)

1 tablespoon fruit-flavored vinegar

2 tablespoons chopped flat-leaf parsley

1. In large glass or plastic container, combine the dissolved salt, sugar, peppercorns, bay leaves, thyme, and 3 cups cold water. Add the pork, cover or seal, and let marinate in the brine for up to 2 days in the refrigerator.

2. About 4 hours before serving, drain the pork loin; discard the brine. Wipe the meat to remove excess moisture. Crush the garlic with a pinch each salt and pepper. Mix with 1 tablespoon of the orange zest and 1 teaspoon water to make a paste. Make deep slits all over the pork; press the garlic paste into the slits. Let stand at room temperature for 30 minutes.

3. Preheat the oven to 350°F.

4. Heat the oil in a shallow enameled cast-iron roasting pan or gratin dish over medium-high heat. Dust the pork with flour, shaking off excess. When the oil starts to sizzle lightly, add the pork and cook, turning, until the roast is brown all over, about 5 minutes. Remove to a plate.

5. Add ¼ cup water and scrape up the brown bits from the bottom of the pan. Scatter the green grapes on the bottom. Set the pork, fat side up, on top. Place in the oven to cook for 45 minutes.

6. Turn the pork over and continue to roast, uncovered, until the internal temperature registers 145°F, about 15 minutes. Remove the pork, cover with foil, and let rest at room temperature for up to 2 hours.

7. Skim the fat from the liquid in the pan. Set over medium-high heat, add the juices from the fruit compote, and boil until they start to thicken and shine, about 10 minutes. Add the vinegar and season with additional salt and pepper to taste. Pour all but 2 tablespoons sauce into a bowl. Add the fruits from the compote to the pan and cook over medium-high heat until they lightly caramelize. Return the pork to the pan, turn to coat with the syrupy juices, and cook over medium-low heat until completely reheated, about 15 minutes. The internal temperature should be 150° to 155°F.

8. Lift the pork out of the pan, allowing excess sauce to drip back into the pan. Thinly slice and arrange the pork over the fruits. Dribble the sauce over the pork and scatter the remaining ½ teaspoon orange zest and the parsley on top. Serve at once.

Fall Fruit Compote

MAKES ABOUT 3 CUPS

2 cups mixed dried fruits (yellow raisins, figs, apricots, and prunes)

1 cup shelled walnuts

1 teaspoon grated orange zest

1 star anise

1 cinnamon stick

¼ teaspoon bruised peppercorns

1 cup sweet white wine, such as orange muscat or sauternes

Juice of ½ lemon

1. In a small bowl, mix the dried fruits, walnuts, orange zest, star anise, cinnamon stick, and peppercorns. Add the wine and lemon juice, cover, and let soak for up to 2 days in a cool place or in the refrigerator.

2. Transfer the fruits in the soaking liquid to a nonreactive saucepan set over low heat and cook for 20 minutes. Remove from the heat and drain the fruits, reserving the liquid for use in Step 6 above. Discard the whole spices. Cut the fruits into ½-inch dice.

With thanks to Sotiris Kitrilakis for inspiring this recipe.

Corsican Brined Pork Chops

*T*he French island of Corsica is famous for its strongly flavored herbs, products of a hot sun, dry earth, and fresh sea air. Herbs play a major role in this Corsican-inspired dish of deeply caramelized pork chops. The recipe is based on my vivid memory of a sauté of pork that had been rubbed with herbs, smothered in a rich tomato sauce, and dotted with green olives, served as a "special" at a tiny Corsican restaurant in Paris, a few doors down from the Bohemian hotel where I stayed in my youth. The restaurant, Aux Deux Marches, on Rue Gît-le-Coeur, was part eatery, part grocery store, and, in true Corsican style, filled with pictures and busts of Napoleon Bonaparte. Dolores, the waitress, remarking on the dried shrubby Corsican herbs that gave the pork its delicious flavor, told me: "These herbs penetrate one's very being! I didn't say that—Napoleon did."

In my recipes, I employ thyme, bay leaf, and sage in a novel way, adding them to a salty brine so their flavors infuse the dense lean meat prior to cooking. Brining is a great way to ensure that your pork chops stay moist and succulent.

SERVES 4

¼ cup sea salt

3 tablespoons sugar

1 teaspoon dried thyme

1 teaspoon crushed juniper berries

½ teaspoon cracked coriander seeds

½ teaspoon cracked peppercorns

¼ teaspoon dried sage

2 bay leaves, crumbled

4 center cut pork rib chops, cut 1¼ inches thick

1½ tablespoons extra virgin olive oil

Freshly ground pepper

1 cup chicken stock

2 tablespoons dry white wine

1 cup tomato sauce

¼ cup orange juice

1 garlic clove, smashed

8 cracked green olives, pitted, rinsed, and coarsely chopped

2 teaspoons finely slivered fresh basil

2 teaspoons finely slivered fresh mint

2 teaspoons finely chopped flat-leaf parsley

(continued)

1. In a large stainless steel bowl or plastic container, combine the salt with the sugar and 1 cup hot water; stir until dissolved. Add 3 cups cold water, the thyme, juniper berries, coriander seeds, peppercorns, sage, and bay leaves. Put the chops in the brine, cover, and refrigerate for 24 to 48 hours, turning them occasionally.

2. Drain the pork chops. Pick any whole spices off the meat and discard. Pat the chops dry with paper towels.

3. Heat the olive oil in a large, deep nonstick or black cast-iron skillet until it shimmers. Add the pork chops and cook over high heat, turning once, until browned, about 6 minutes. Transfer the chops to a plate and season with salt and pepper.

4. Pour off the fat from the skillet. Add the chicken stock and wine and bring to a boil, scraping up any brown bits from the bottom of the pan. Boil until the liquid is reduced by half, about 3 minutes. Add the tomato sauce, orange juice, and garlic and simmer for 5 minutes.

5. Return the pork chops to the skillet, turn to coat with the sauce, and bring to a boil. Cover tightly, reduce the heat to low, and simmer until the pork is tender and fully cooked through, about 10 minutes. Transfer the chops to a platter, cover, and keep warm.

6. Add the olives to the sauce and boil over high heat until the liquid is reduced to about 1 cup. Stir in the basil, mint, and parsley and pour the sauce over the chops.

Salmon Fillet Poached in Olive Oil (page 120) with Raw Rhubarb, Cucumber, and Mint Salad (page 122)

OPPOSITE: *Avocado-Sardine Toasts (page 9)*

ABOVE: *Tuscan Quail with Red Grape Sauce (page 154)*

OPPOSITE: *Paella with Shellfish and Artichokes (page 99)*
THIS PAGE: *Monkfish and Clams with a Burned Garlic Sauce (page 130)*

ABOVE: *Pan-Grilled Asparagus and Oyster Mushrooms
with Pancetta and Garlic Puree (page 235)*

OPPOSITE: *Pan-Grilled Duck Breast with
Chanterelles, Dried Apricots, and Almonds (page 146)*

Artichoke and
Orange Compote (page 45)

Pork Stew with Prunes and Onions

This winter dish from southwest France has a lot going for it: well-caramelized cubes of pork; a deglazing that provides deep flavor; an embellishment of lush, sweet dried plums joined with glazed sweet-and-sour onions. The result is a rich flavorful stew that isn't the least bit cloying and that reheats beautifully.

I suggest you serve this dish over Oven-Baked Polenta, which follows.

SERVES 4

1½ pounds pork shoulder or butt, trimmed of excess fat

2 tablespoons extra virgin olive oil mixed with a pinch each of ground cinnamon, black pepper, crumbled rosemary, and thyme

1 cup finely chopped onion

1 tablespoon red wine vinegar

1 tablespoon Dijon mustard

1½ cups dry white wine

3 garlic cloves

2 medium carrots, halved crosswise

1 bay leaf

Salt

1¾ cups unsalted chicken stock

12 small white onions

1½ tablespoons unsalted butter

1 teaspoon sugar

8 dried large pitted prunes (dried plums), soaked in hot water to soften

Chopped flat-leaf parsley

1. Cut the pork into ¾-inch cubes. Toss the pieces with the spiced oil and leave in a cool place for at least 3 to 4 hours.

2. In a large, heavy flameproof casserole, cook the pork, covered, without the addition of any fat, over medium-high heat for 5 minutes. Uncover and sauté, stirring frequently, until the moisture has evaporated and the pork is thoroughly browned, about 10 minutes.

(continued)

3. Remove the pork to a side dish, reduce the heat to medium, and add the onion. Cook until soft and beginning to brown. Remove the onion with a slotted spoon and add to the pork.

4. Add the vinegar, mustard, and ½ cup of the white wine to the casserole. Heat to boiling, scraping up any brown bits that cling to the bottom of the pan. Boil until reduced to a glaze. Add another ½ cup wine and reduce again. Repeat until all the wine has been reduced to a glaze. Add the garlic, carrots, and bay leaf and let them sizzle for a minute; return the pork and onions and any accumulated juices to the pan. Pour in the stock and season with salt to taste. Bring to a boil, cover, and cook very slowly for about 45 minutes.

5. Cut an X in the root end of each small onion. Blanch in a large saucepan of boiling salted water for 2 minutes. Drain and cool under cold running water. Peel the onions. Combine the onions with ¼ cup water, the butter, and the sugar in a medium skillet. Simmer, covered, until the water evaporates, about 5 minutes. Cook, uncovered, over low heat until tender and well browned, about 8 minutes. Set aside.

6. When the meat has cooked a total of 45 minutes, add the prunes and browned onions. Cover the casserole and continue cooking until the pork is soft, about 15 minutes. From time to time, swirl the casserole to keep the meat, onions, and prunes from sticking. Remove the casserole from the heat, discard the bay leaf, and correct the seasoning. Garnish with chopped parsley.

Oven-Baked Polenta

This is hands-down the best polenta recipe I know, especially since it doesn't require stirring. I first presented this recipe in my *Mediterranean Grains & Greens;* I repeat it here for new readers.

This no-stir method—combining cornmeal, water, and a little salt in an oiled casserole and roasting it in the oven, as opposed to frequent stirring in a pot on the stove—produces wondrous, creamy, and seductive polenta. Cooking it this way takes longer than on top of the stove, but it will leave you free to take care of whatever else you'll be serving.

Varying the proportion of water to cornmeal enables you to adjust the consistency of the polenta from runny to firm, and enables the polenta to take on many guises from a simple steaming bowl of cornmeal mush served with a little grated cheese to a delicious bed for stews and ragouts.

FOR SOFT POLENTA 5 parts liquid to 1 part cornmeal

FOR MEDIUM POLENTA 4 parts liquid to 1 part cornmeal

SERVES 6

2 cups medium-coarse or coarse-grind cornmeal, preferably organic stone-ground cornmeal

8 to 10 cups cool water (see proportions above)

2 tablespoons butter or extra virgin olive oil

2 teaspoons salt

1. Preheat the oven to 350°F. Grease a 12-inch cazuela or ovenproof casserole. Add the cornmeal, water, butter or oil, and salt and stir with a fork until blended. (It will separate, but don't worry—it won't come together for more than half the cooking time.) Bake uncovered for 1 hour and 20 minutes.

2. Stir the polenta with a long-pronged fork, season with additional salt to taste, and bake for 10 minutes more. Remove from the oven and let it rest for 5 minutes before pouring onto a wooden pizza shovel or into a buttered bowl.

Pork and Orange-Flavored Beans

The extent of regional Greek cooking was unknown to American readers in the 1980s. Now it is better known and being well studied. Last year my friend the Greek food writer Aglaia Kremezi and I traveled together to one of her favorite islands, Chios, in the northern Aegean, famous for its mastic gum, ouzo, olives, and delicious citrus-based spoon sweets.

Aglaia wanted me to taste some of the dishes that would appear in her book *The Foods of the Greek Islands.* Once again we fell into our old habit of sharing. While there, she introduced me to chef Stefanos Kovas, at whose ouzo bar we tasted this scrumptious pork-flavored orange-fragrant bean dish.

On Chios I learned how fortunate northern Greeks are to have one of the most delicious beans to work with—the huge, nutty-tasting, white *gigante,* which, when baked slowly, produces a soft, unbroken skin over a meaty, firm, and delicately flavored heart. In northern Greece, gigante beans star prominently in soups, casseroles, and other family dishes.

Serious pork and bean eaters will love this recipe from Chios . . . and I thank Aglaia Kremezi for sharing it.

SERVES 4 TO 6 AS A MAIN COURSE OR 12 AS A MEZE

2 cups dried Greek giant beans, or substitute white kidney or cannellini beans

2 bay leaves

¾ pound boned pork shoulder, in 1 or 2 chunks

Zest from 1 medium orange

Salt and freshly ground pepper

½ cup extra virgin olive oil

2 cups coarsely chopped onion

1 teaspoon Aleppo pepper, Turkish red pepper flakes, or hot red pepper, or to taste

1 teaspoon dry mustard

1 cup sweet red wine (Greek Mavrodaphne, Madeira, or Marsala)

⅔ cup fresh orange juice

⅔ cup grated fresh tomato or chopped good-quality canned tomatoes

1 small celery rib with leaves

Sprigs of parsley, for garnish

1. Pick over the beans and soak them in water to cover by at least 2 inches overnight.

2. The following day, drain the beans and put them in a deep pot, preferably a bean pot. Cover with 6 cups fresh water and slowly bring to a boil, skimming. Add 1 of the bay leaves. Reduce the heat, cover, and simmer for 45 to 60 minutes, until the beans are tender but not mushy. Drain and reserve 1 cup of the liquid. Discard the bay leaf.

3. Meanwhile, place the meat in a separate pot, cover with cold water, add the remaining bay leaf, and bring to a boil. Skim, reduce the heat to medium, and cook for 30 minutes.

4. In another saucepan, blanch the orange zest 3 times. Let the zest dry on parchment paper, then cut into fine strips.

5. Drain the meat; cut it into ½-inch cubes and season with salt and pepper. Strain the cooking liquid through a sieve and measure it. If it is more than ½ cup, boil over high heat to reduce to ½ cup.

6. In a large straight-sided skillet, heat the olive oil. Add the onion and sauté for 5 minutes. Add the pork and sauté for 3 more minutes. Add the beans and cook, stirring, for 1 more minute. Stir in the red pepper, mustard, wine, orange juice, meat broth, 1 teaspoon salt, the tomato, celery, and orange zest. Bring to a boil, reduce the heat, and simmer, covered, for 30 minutes. If more liquid is needed, add some of the reserved bean broth.

7. Preheat the oven to 400°F. Taste the beans and adjust the seasoning, adding pepper to taste. (Do not worry about the decidedly orange flavor; it will mellow.) Transfer to a 2½-quart baking dish and bake until the beans are very tender and most of the liquid has evaporated, 30 to 40 minutes. Serve warm, garnished with some sprigs of parsley.

Note: This pork dish is even better reheated in a hot oven until crusty around the edges.

Baked Rice with Black Sausage and Valencian Meatballs

*F*or this prize-winning recipe—a stunning winter rice dish of meatballs, pork ribs, black sausage, potatoes, and chickpeas—I must thank Bertha Gilberta Ivañez, the cook at the Hosteria del Montsant in Jativa near Valencia.

"On Sundays, when I was growing up," Bertha told me, "we would take this rice dish to the baker's oven before attending mass. You don't need to serve anything else, just a salad. And it's even better the next day, served at room temperature or reheated over boiling water."

Award-winning recipes always have their nuances and special touches. Here are some of Bertha's, which, you'll note, are nearly the same as Norberto Jorge's paella on page 97: the rice of choice is a Spanish medium-grain rice that has what Bertha called "a satisfying chew"; don't ever wash the rice; be sure the liquid is boiling before adding it to the rice; stir the rice only once; let the rice rest for at least ten minutes before serving, allowing it to continue to absorb flavor.

As the meatballs must stand overnight, plan accordingly.

SERVES 8

Valencian Meatballs with Pine Nuts and Golden Raisins (recipe follows)

½ pound morcilla or black sausage (see Mail Order Sources), preferably made with onions, sliced on the diagonal

3 tablespoons extra virgin olive oil

1 medium Yukon Gold potato, peeled and diced

4 small ripe tomatoes, halved and gently squeezed to remove the seeds

1 pound country-style pork ribs, bone in and cracked in half

1 small onion, chopped

1 whole head of garlic, scrubbed

1 cup cooked chickpeas

2 cups (1 pound) Spanish rice, preferably bomba from Valencia (see Mail Order Sources)

½ teaspoon sweet Spanish paprika

¼ teaspoon saffron threads

Salt and freshly ground pepper

Pinches of grated nutmeg

1. Make the meatballs as described in the recipe that follows.

2. In a large flameproof casserole or wide saucepan over medium heat, slowly brown the sausage slices in 1 tablespoon of the olive oil until crisp on both sides, 2 to 3 minutes. Remove to an oiled 12-inch cazuela and set in a cool place.

3. In the same casserole, slowly brown the diced potato until golden but not tender. Transfer to the cazuela. Heat another tablespoon olive oil in the casserole and quickly fry the tomato halves, cut side down; remove them to a side dish.

4. Add the pork ribs to the casserole and sauté over high heat, turning, until browned. Add the chopped onion and fry for an instant. Add the whole garlic head, drained chickpeas, and 10 cups water. Cover and bring to a boil, skimming; reduce the heat, cover, and simmer for 1 hour.

5. Remove the garlic head, rub off one layer of the paper, clip off the top to expose the beehive pattern, and set aside. Drop the small meatballs one by one into the boiling liquid. Cover and poach for 30 minutes. Remove the meatballs and set aside. Remove the pork ribs; discard the bones and cut the meat into bite-sized pieces.

6. Preheat the oven to 425°F. With a slotted spoon, transfer the chickpeas to the cazuela. Add the pieces of pork. Set the cazuela over a heat diffuser and heat until hot and sizzling. Add the rice and stir with the sausage slices until coated with oily juices.

7. Measure the broth, add the paprika and saffron, and boil quickly to reduce to 4 cups. Correct the seasoning with salt, pepper, and nutmeg. Pour the boiling broth over the rice. Cook for a few minutes, then spread the meatballs and tomato halves, cut side up, on top of the rice. Place the garlic head in the center. Sprinkle with the remaining 1 tablespoon olive oil. Bake for 10 minutes.

8. Reduce the oven temperature to 325°F and bake for 30 more minutes, until the rice is almost cooked. Remove from the oven, cover loosely with foil, and let finish cooking in the receding heat, about 15 minutes longer. Serve as is, or reheat under the broiler or over steaming water. Do not reheat in the microwave.

Valencian Meatballs with Pine Nuts and Golden Raisins

MAKES 16 SMALL BALLS

½ pound ground pork

½ cup fresh bread crumbs

⅛ teaspoon ground cinnamon

⅛ teaspoon grated nutmeg

¼ teaspoon salt

¼ teaspoon freshly ground pepper

2 tablespoons chopped toasted pine nuts

2 tablespoons golden raisins, soaked and
    drained

¾ teaspoon crushed garlic

1 large egg, lightly beaten

1. In a medium bowl, combine all the ingredients and blend until evenly mixed. Cover tightly and refrigerate overnight.

2. Divide the meat mixture into 16 equal parts. Roll into small balls. Cook as directed in the preceding recipe.

Cassoulet

Any good cassoulet recipe is long and complicated, but please don't be intimidated: many of the steps are executed in advance, some as far ahead as a week. This will not only make the final preparation easier; it will actually improve the dish, since the flavors will grow stronger and deeper on account of mellowing.

Serve the cassoulet with a bitter-greens salad dressed with walnut oil and sherry vinegar.

SERVES 12

2 pounds dried white beans, preferably imported French lingots (see Mail Order Sources) or Great Northern

½ pound pork rind with ¼-inch layer of hard fat attached

½ pound lean salt pork

1 ham hock

½ cup rendered duck fat from confit (see page 314)

2 pounds meaty spareribs, trimmed of excess fat and cut into 1-inch chunks

1 medium carrot, sliced

1 medium onion, diced

1 whole large head of garlic plus 1½ teaspoons chopped garlic

½ cup crushed, seeded tomatoes

⅓ pound Bayonne ham or prosciutto, in 1 piece

Bouquet garni (4 sprigs of parsley, 2 sprigs of thyme, 1 celery rib with leaves, and 1 bay leaf, tied together)

Zest of ½ orange

1 tablespoon black peppercorns

1 small onion, stuck with 1 clove

2 quarts unsalted chicken or duck stock

1 pound fresh garlic-flavored pork sausages, preferably mildly spiced

Quick Duck and Pork Confit (see recipe, page 314)

Freshly ground pepper and salt

1 teaspoon chopped fresh thyme

1 tablespoon chopped flat-leaf parsley

½ cup soft white bread crumbs

(continued)

1. Two days before serving, prepare Steps 1 through 4. Rinse and pick over the beans. Soak in cool water for a minimum of 5 hours.

2. In a deep saucepan, place the pork rind, salt pork, and ham hock. Cover with cold water. Slowly bring to a boil, reduce the heat, and simmer for 5 minutes, skimming once. Drain, rinse under cool running water, and drain again. Pat the meat dry with paper towels. If the pork rind is still brittle, repeat, simmering for 10 to 12 minutes, or until it is supple. Roll up the pork rind like a rug and tie it with string. Cut the rind off the lean salt pork and reserve the rind. Cut the salt pork into 4 even pieces.

3. Make the pork ragout: Heat ¼ cup of the duck fat in a very large flameproof casserole, preferably 9 quarts. Add the ribs and brown lightly on all sides, about 5 minutes. Add the carrot and onion and sauté over moderately high heat, stirring, until the onion is soft and golden, about 5 minutes. Add the ham hock and salt pork and let brown a little around the edges, about 5 minutes. Add the rolled pork rind, salt-pork rind, head of garlic, crushed tomatoes, ham slice, herbs, orange zest, peppercorns, and the onion stuck with 1 clove. Pour in the chicken or duck stock, bring to a boil, skim carefully, reduce the heat, cover, and simmer for 1 hour, or until the meat is almost tender.

4. Drain the beans. Add them to the pork ragout. Simmer, covered, over low heat for 1 hour. Add ½ teaspoon salt and cook 15 to 30 minutes longer, or until the beans are tender but not mushy. Remove the casserole from the heat and cool. Discard the whole onion, the herb bouquet, the fatty part of the salt pork, and any loose bones from the ham hock and spareribs. Separate the rinds, meats, and beans. Remove all the gristle and fatty parts from the assorted meats. Strain the cooking liquid. Separately cool, cover, and refrigerate the cooking liquid, meats, rinds, and beans.

5. A day before serving, prepare the cassoulet through Step 8. Skim the congealed fat from the top of the cooking liquid. Pour the cooking liquid into a large saucepan. Add the reserved ham hock skin and pork rinds and simmer for 1 hour, or longer if they are not fork-tender. Strain, reserving the liquid and meat separately. Measure the liquid and add enough water to make 7 cups.

6. Scrape all the fat from the assorted pork rinds and discard it. Cut the rinds and ham hock skin into ½-inch squares, so they will easily disintegrate in the final cooking. Cut the ham hock meat into slivers. Finely dice the ham slice and the lean part of the salt pork, then mix all together with the meat from the ribs.

7. Prick the sausages and cook them in 1 teaspoon of the duck fat in a nonstick skillet. Drain on paper towels; cut them into 1-inch pieces. Pour off the fat. In the same skillet, heat 2 tablespoons of the duck fat. Sear the pork confit all over to brown lightly. Cut into bite-sized pieces. Set the skillet aside for later. Add the sausages and pork confit to the other meats. Season generously with pepper and taste for salt. Cool, cover, and refrigerate.

8. Carefully remove the duck skin from the confit in large pieces. Add 2 tablespoons duck fat to the reserved skillet and heat until it ripples. Slowly crisp the duck skin on both sides. Drain on paper towels. Carefully remove the bones from the duck confit and discard. Divide the duck meat into 12 even portions. Generously season with freshly ground pepper and gently squeeze each portion into a ball. Cover with a piece of crisp skin. Arrange the portions on a plate, cover with plastic wrap to prevent drying out, and refrigerate.

9. About 3 hours before serving, assemble the cassoulet. Spread the pork-rind squares all over the bottom of a 6- or 7-quart, wide, ovenproof serving dish—a large ovenproof pasta bowl is ideal. Cover with a layer of beans, then a layer of the pork and ham. Combine the chopped garlic, thyme, parsley, and ½ teaspoon pepper, and sprinkle half of the mixture over the beans. Repeat with the meats, herbs, and garlic, ending with a layer of beans. Reheat the cooking liquid and pour just enough over the beans to cover them. Be sure there is 1 inch of "growing space" between the beans and the rim of the dish. Reserve the remaining liquid to baste the beans during the final cooking.

10. Place in the oven and turn the heat to 450°F. Sprinkle half the bread crumbs over the top of the casserole. Dot them with 2 tablespoons duck fat. Bake for 30 minutes, or until a golden skin forms on top of the beans.

11. Reduce the oven temperature to 350°F. Gently stir in the skin that has formed and baste the beans with a few spoonfuls of the reserved cooking liquid. Taste the beans and liquid for salt and correct. Continue to bake until another golden layer appears on the beans, about 20 minutes. Repeat 2 more times, stirring, basting, and baking the dish until a skin appears on the surface. Baste once or twice, using up as much reserved liquid as necessary to keep the beans from drying out.

(continued)

12. When the dish has baked a total of 1½ hours, break up the skin and press the reserved pieces of duck confit, skin side up, into the top layer of beans. The crisped duck skin should be just even with the beans' surface. Sprinkle the beans and duck skin with the remaining bread crumbs and the remaining 2 tablespoons duck fat. Bake until a well-browned glaze forms on top and the cassoulet is bubbling hot, about 20 minutes. Remove and let rest 10 minutes before serving.

BEEF

Stop-and-Go Braised Oxtails with Oyster Mushrooms

*T*his French Catalan–inspired stew is a perfect example of how fatty meat, cooked on the bone, will produce a memorable succulent dish. Prepare it a day in advance so you can remove all the fat and allow the full flavor to develop.

On the first day, I rub the oxtails with herbs and spices and then brown them under the broiler, which imbues the meat with a faint scent of smoldering aromatics, thus launching the first layer of richness. The following day, I finish the dish with multiple reductions, deglazing repeatedly to develop complexity and a syrupy sauce, produced from nothing more than a little vinegar and dried porcini soaking water.

Serve this unctuous stew with Golden Potato Gratin (page 265).

SERVES 5 TO 6

5 pounds meaty oxtails, cut 1½ inches thick, fat trimmed

1 tablespoon coarsely ground pepper

1 teaspoon crumbled dried oregano

1½ tablespoons fresh thyme leaves or 1½ teaspoons dried

1 teaspoon bruised fennel seeds

¼ cup extra virgin olive oil

½ cup dried porcini mushrooms

Pinch of sugar

2 medium onions, coarsely chopped

2 large carrots, coarsely chopped

1 celery rib, coarsely chopped

2 cups dry white wine

Bouquet garni (celery leaves from 1 small rib, 1 sprig of parsley, 1 sprig of thyme, and 1 bay leaf, tied together)

4 garlic cloves, minced

Salt and freshly ground pepper

2 tablespoons Banyuls or aged sherry vinegar

1 tablespoon bitter orange marmalade

1 tablespoon butter

1½ pounds oyster mushrooms, thickly sliced

2 tablespoons chopped flat-leaf parsley

(continued)

1. One day before serving, place the oxtails in a large bowl with the ground pepper, thyme, oregano, fennel seeds, and 2 tablespoons of the olive oil; turn to coat all over. Let stand at room temperature for 1 hour.

2. Soak soak the dried porcini in 2½ cups warm water with the sugar until softened, about 1 hour. Lift the mushrooms from the water, rinse them briefly, and coarsely chop. Strain the soaking water through a coffee filter or doubled paper towel and reserve.

3. Set the oven rack about 7 inches from the heat and preheat the broiler. Arrange the oxtails in a single layer in a broiling pan without the rack. Broil the oxtails, turning often, for about 20 minutes, until they are nicely browned.

4. Heat the remaining 2 tablespoons olive oil in a large skillet. Add the onions, carrots, and celery and sauté over moderately high heat until well browned and lightly caramelized, 10 to 15 minutes.

5. In a deep roomy pot (enameled cast-iron or ceramic set over a heat diffuser), heat the wine to boiling. Slightly tilting the pot and averting your face, ignite the wine with a long match. When the flames subside, add the oxtails, browned vegetables, chopped porcini, bouquet garni, half the garlic, and salt and pepper. Slowly bring to a boil.

6. Pour the vinegar and 1 cup of the reserved mushroom water into the broiling pan and bring to a boil, scraping up browned bits from the pan; add to the pot. Repeat deglazing the skillet with the remaining mushroom water. Cover the oxtails with a sheet of crumpled wet parchment and a lid, set over very low heat, and cook without uncovering for 2 hours.

7. Transfer the oxtails to a side dish and season with salt and pepper. Strain the cooking liquid, pressing down on the vegetables to extract all their juices. Skim off as much fat as possible. Pour back into the pot and stir in the orange marmalade. Return the oxtails to the pot. Cover and cook over the lowest heat for 1 hour, or until the meat is very tender. Let cool, then cover and refrigerate overnight.

8. The following day, scrape off any solidified fat. About 1 hour before serving, arrange the oxtails and sauce in a shallow ovenproof baking serving dish (I use a cazuela). Cover loosely with foil and set in the oven. Set the oven temperature to 350°F.

9. Heat the butter in a large skillet. Add the oyster mushrooms and sauté over medium-high heat until shiny and light brown, about 8 minutes. Mix in the remaining garlic, half the parsley, and a pinch of salt. I like to splash them with an additional dash of vinegar.

10. Remove the meat from the oven, spoon the mushrooms around the meat, loosely cover with foil, and return to the oven to bake for about 45 minutes, or until the meat is slightly crusty and dark brown and the sauce is reduced to a thick syrup. Serve with the remaining parsley scattered on top.

Note: Store in the refrigerator, then bring to room temperature and reheat slowly.

Pot-Roasted Club Steak with Piquillo Peppers

*H*ere's a dish that's truly prepared in slow motion. A thick, lean cut of beef is lightly salted, slicked with olive oil, and left to marinate overnight. The meat is seared in a deep heavy pot until crusty on the outside. Finally the pot is covered, and the meat is finished over low heat. No liquid is added, but because of its thickness, the meat steams and browns at the same time.

The beef comes out perfectly cooked, rare and juicy. With it, I serve a cazuela filled with small, lush piquillo peppers. These marvelous peppers, purchased in jars or cans, are heated slowly until they release their juices, making an unctuous and colorful garnish.

SERVES 4 TO 6

2 to 2¼ pounds boneless club steak, cut 2¾ to 3 inches thick, well trimmed

½ teaspoon coarse sea salt

3 tablespoons plus 1 teaspoon extra virgin olive oil

8 garlic cloves, peeled but left whole

1 jar (10 ounces) piquillo peppers, preferably from Lodosa

Salt and freshly ground pepper

Several drops of very fine sherry wine vinegar

1. As soon as you bring the meat home, lightly salt it on both sides, set on a flat oiled plate, and dribble 1 teaspoon olive oil over the exposed side. Cover loosely with plastic wrap and refrigerate overnight.

2. The next day, about 2 hours before you plan to serve the meat, place 1½ tablespoons of the olive oil in a deep 2- or 3-quart enameled cast-iron casserole, iron pot, or Dutch oven. (The pot should be just large enough to hold the meat.) Add half the garlic cloves and slowly cook until they turn golden and the oil smells aromatic. Remove and discard the garlic, add the meat to the pot, raise the heat to medium-high, and sear on all sides, about 15 minutes in all.

3. Cover the pot and reduce the heat to medium-low. Cook for 1 more minute. Remove the covered pot from the heat. Allow the meat to rest for exactly 40 minutes without opening the pot.

4. Meanwhile, after the meat has rested for 20 minutes, begin to prepare the piquillo peppers. Place the remaining garlic cloves and oil in a large nonstick skillet or earthenware cooking dish set over a heat diffuser and set over medium-low heat. When the garlic begins to turn golden, add the peppers and all the juices in the can or jar and cook for 10 minutes. During this time, shake the dish often so that juices exuded from the peppers mix with the oil. Do not turn the peppers over, but do move them around a bit so that they do not stick to the bottom of the pan From time to time, tilt the pan and spoon the boiling juices over the top parts of the peppers. Set half off the heat, partially cover, and keep hot. Season with salt and pepper, and, if desired, a drop or two of very fine sherry wine vinegar.

5. After 40 minutes of resting, the meat should be perfectly cooked. Slice the steak and arrange, overlapping, on a large serving plate. Skim the pan juices and dribble them over the meat. Surround with the peppers.

Beef Short Ribs Simmered in Red Wine with Fennel, Black Olives, and Anchovies in the Style of the Camargue

*P*opular Mediterranean licorice-tasting spirits, such as Pernod, raki, or ouzo, are often served accompanied by a small plate of oily black olives or salty fish. In this wonderful beef stew, a single teaspoon of one of these spirits creates great depth of flavor. This stew is best if started a day in advance so that all the fat can be removed and all the flavors are allowed to develop fully.

Serve with saffron-flavored rice and a fresh fennel salad.

SERVES 4

2 tablespoons extra virgin olive oil

2½ to 3 pounds bone-in beef short ribs (8 to 12 pieces)

Salt and freshly ground pepper

¼ teaspoon bruised fennel seeds

3½ tablespoons flour

1 tablespoon red wine vinegar

3 ounces pancetta, diced

1 medium onion, minced

1 small carrot, sliced

1 small leek, sliced

2 cups hearty red wine

5 garlic cloves

½ cup tomato sauce

1½ cups meat stock or water

Bouquet garni (celery leaf sprigs, 1 sprig of thyme, 2 sprigs of parsley, 1 bay leaf, and strip of orange zest, tied together)

24 oil-cured black olives

3 anchovy fillets

2 tablespoons butter

1 teaspoon Pernod, ouzo, or raki

1. Preheat the oven to 300°F. Heat the oil in a large skillet over high heat. Season the short ribs with salt, pepper, and a pinch of bruised fennel seeds. Dust lightly with 2 tablespoons of the flour, shake off the excess, and place in the hot oil to brown on all sides, about 10 minutes. Transfer the meat to a 5- or 6-quart earthen or enameled cast-iron casserole. Pour off all the fat from the skillet, return it to medium heat, and deglaze the skillet with the wine vinegar and 3 tablespoons water. Pour over the meat.

2. Add the pancetta and onion to the skillet and sauté over medium heat until just beginning to brown, about 5 minutes. Add the carrot and leek and fry until they begin to turn golden brown, about 5 minutes. Add the remaining 1½ tablespoons flour and cook until everything turns a deep brown. (Be sure to adjust the heat as necessary to keep the flour from burning.) Pour in the wine and boil until reduced by half. Add the garlic, tomato sauce, and stock or water and bring to a boil. Tuck in the herb bouquet. Wet a sheet of crumpled parchment and place directly over the contents of the casserole, cover with the lid, and set in the oven to bake until the meat is very tender,
3 to 3½ hours, turning the ribs once midway.

3. Transfer the short ribs to a work surface. Pour the vegetables and liquid through a fine strainer into a large bowl; discard all solids. Skim off as much fat as possible from the liquid and return to a clean casserole. Bring the liquid to a boil over high heat and reduce to about 2½ cups. Remove from the heat and set aside.

4. When the meat is cool enough to handle, remove and discard all bones, gristle, and hard pieces of fat. Place the meat in a tall container, pour the reduced liquid on top, cool, cover, and refrigerate.

5. The following day, about 2 hours before serving, lift off the congealed fat; discard. Let the meat come to room temperature.

6. Pit the black olives and soak in water for 15 minutes. Rinse and drain the anchovies. Cream the butter with the anchovies and Pernod.

7. About 30 minutes before serving, place the meat in an ovenproof serving dish with 1 cup of the cooking juices. Set in a cold oven and turn the oven temperature to 325°F. The short ribs will take about 30 minutes to reheat.

8. Shortly before serving, heat the remaining liquid in a saucepan to simmering. Stir in the olives and anchovy butter and cook over low heat for a few minutes. Swirl the pan to allow the butter to blend with the sauce. Correct the seasoning with salt and pepper as needed. Pour over the meat and serve.

VEAL

Braised Veal Stuffed with Green Olives

A lean veal roast can be cooked by dry heat in an oven or by moist heat in a closed pot. I much prefer the latter method, especially for a shoulder cut from a mature animal. Such a cut requires careful seasoning, moist heat, and slow cooking to transform it into something special.

Mild veal is a great flavor absorber and here takes on the tastes of sherry, cinnamon, and other seasonings. I add a bed of vegetables and a veal bone to the pot to create a full-flavored base sauce. A garnish of Spanish olives flavored with more sherry and sherry wine vinegar provides a final fillip.

SERVES 6

1 boned and butterflied veal shoulder roast (about 3 pounds)

½ cup green olives, rinsed, drained, pitted, and thinly sliced lengthwise

2 ounces thickly sliced pancetta, finely chopped

3 garlic cloves, crushed with a good pinch of salt

½ teaspoon minced fresh thyme

Pinch of freshly grated nutmeg

Pinch of ground Ceylon cinnamon

Salt and freshly ground pepper

Flour, for dusting

2 tablespoons extra virgin olive oil

½ pound meaty veal bones, cut into 1-inch chunks

2 carrots, cut into 1-inch chunks

2 onions, thickly sliced

1 celery rib, cut into 1-inch slices

1 bay leaf

1 teaspoon tomato paste

¼ cup medium or dry sherry

¼ cup aged sherry wine vinegar (see Notes)

Pinch of cayenne

2 tablespoons unsalted butter

2 tablespoons chopped flat-leaf parsley

1. About 3 hours before serving, bring the veal to room temperature. Remove any netting or string from around the veal and set it on a work surface, boned side up. Put half the olives in a bowl. Add the pancetta, garlic, thyme, nutmeg, cinnamon, 1 teaspoon salt, and ½ teaspoon pepper to the olives and mash to a coarse paste. Spread the olive paste over the meat, leaving a 1-inch border. Roll up the roast and tie it with kitchen string at 1-inch intervals. Pat dry.

2. Dust the veal with flour, tapping off any excess. Heat the olive oil in a large skillet. Add the veal roast and bones and cook over moderately high heat, turning, until browned all over, about 10 minutes.

3. In a large enameled cast-iron casserole, combine the carrots, onions, celery, bay leaf, and tomato paste and spread to make an even layer. Transfer the veal roast and bones to the casserole and sprinkle with salt and pepper.

4. Return the skillet to moderate heat. Pour in the sherry and sherry wine vinegar and scrape up any brown bits from the bottom of the pan. Add ⅓ cup water and bring to a boil, then pour around the veal. (Set the skillet aside to use in Step 5.) Place a sheet of crumpled wet parchment directly over the veal in the casserole. Cover with a lid and cook the roast over low heat for 1¼ hours, or until an instant read thermometer registers between 145° and 150°F. Snip the strings and cook, covered, for 5 more minutes. Transfer the veal to a carving board and let it rest for 15 minutes before slicing.

5. Meanwhile, strain the contents of the casserole directly into the skillet, pressing hard on the vegetables to extract as much liquid as possible. Boil over high heat until reduced to about ⅔ cup, 5 to 7 minutes. Add the remaining olives, the cayenne, and the butter to the pan juices and swirl until the sauce thickens. Correct the seasoning with salt and pepper, and if necessary a dash of vinegar. Remove the skillet from the heat. Cut the veal into thin slices, discarding the cut string as you slice. Arrange the meat in overlapping slices on a warm serving platter. Spoon a little of the sauce with olives over each slice. Garnish with chopped parsley and serve.

Notes: The secret to this dish is to tie the roast in such a way that it will be evenly cooked all the way through. Less moisture is lost when a piece of meat is properly tied. About 5 minutes before you plan to remove the roast, cut away the strings, then cover the pot to let the meat slowly expand and absorb more of the pan juices.

This dish can be prepared in advance and refrigerated for up to 2 days.

If using a young and inexpensive sherry wine vinegar, reduce it by half in Step 4 before adding to the dish.

Braised Veal Shanks with Chanterelles, Carrots, Chestnuts, and Lardons

My daughter, Leila, who grew up in Morocco and is now a wine consultant, likes to cook tagines and other slow-simmered dishes from her childhood. But after a tasting trip to France, she became interested in French farmhouse dishes. I told her about a delicious dish of veal shanks smothered in carrots, chestnuts, and chanterelles.

Unfortunately, the dish didn't sound very "farmhouse" to her, and she doesn't think that veal is flavorful—or politically correct. My advice was to dispense with both the ethical and the flavor issues by buying grass-fed veal, which is tastier than the grain-fed kind. I told her that the dish was simpler than it sounded and that it would go wonderfully with her French wines.

When she prepared it for a dinner party, she found that I was right. "Plus we had a great time coaxing out the marrow—with bamboo skewers, espresso spoons, and our fingers," she said. "We even decided to name the dish The Veal Shank Redemption."

SERVES 4

2 tablespoons olive oil

2 tablespoons unsalted butter

3 to 4 pounds veal shanks, cracked at 2½-inch intervals

Salt and freshly ground pepper

4 ounces pancetta, sliced ¾ inch thick

3 medium onions, chopped

2 imported bay leaves

3 sprigs of thyme

1 star anise pod

1 pound large carrots, cut on the diagonal into pieces 1½ inches thick

Pinch of sugar

2 cups medium-dry white wine

5 garlic cloves—3 whole, 2 chopped

2 tablespoons bitter orange marmalade

1 tablespoon Champagne vinegar or white wine vinegar

1 pound chanterelle mushrooms, preferably large, halved

1 jar (8 ounces) roasted chestnuts

2 tablespoons chopped flat-leaf parsley

1. Preheat the oven to 300°F. Heat a large, heavy-bottomed skillet over medium heat for 30 seconds. Add the olive oil and 1 tablespoon of the butter. When heated to sizzling, add the veal shanks. Cook, turning carefully, until deeply browned all over, about 12 minutes. Remove the veal shanks to an ovenproof casserole, preferably stoneware or earthenware, and season with salt and pepper.

2. Add the pancetta, onions, bay leaves, thyme, and star anise to the oil remaining in the skillet. Cover, reduce the heat to moderately low, and cook until the onions are soft and glazed, about 10 minutes. Add the carrots and a pinch of sugar, return the heat to moderate, and cook, uncovered, stirring occasionally, until the carrots are glazed, about 5 more minutes. Scrape the contents of the skillet into the casserole.

3. Pour the wine into the skillet and boil, scraping up any browned bits from the bottom of the pan, until the wine is reduced by half, about 5 minutes. Pour the reduced wine into the casserole. Add the 3 whole garlic cloves, ½ cup water, and ½ teaspoon each salt and pepper. Cover with a sheet of crumpled wet parchment paper and a tight-fitting lid. Braise the veal shanks in the oven until they are very tender, about 2 hours. Use a slotted spoon to transfer the veal to a baking sheet. Set aside the carrot chunks and pancetta in a separate dish

4. Increase the oven temperature to 350°F. Skim the fat from the sauce and reserve both the fat and sauce. In a small bowl, blend the marmalade with the vinegar and ¼ teaspoon pepper. Spread the marmalade over the veal shanks and bake uncovered for 20 minutes, basting every 5 minutes with some of the sauce, until the shanks are nicely glazed. Transfer the shanks to a warm serving platter. Reserve any sauce for Step 6. Scatter the carrots and pancetta around the veal, cover everything with foil, and set in the oven with the door partly ajar.

5. Quickly wash the chanterelles; drain well and pat dry. Over medium heat in a large skillet heat 1 teaspoon of the reserved skimmed fat until hot. Add half the chanterelles and cook until they "whistle" and begin to release their liquid. Drain the mushrooms in a colander set over a bowl, reserving the liquid. Repeat with the remaining chanterelles and another 1 teaspoon fat.

6. Wipe out the skillet and set it over moderately high heat. Add the remaining 1 tablespoon butter and the chestnuts and season with salt and pepper. Add all the chanterelles and the chopped garlic to the skillet and cook, tossing, until the chanterelles are lightly browned, about 3 minutes. Scrape the contents of the skillet around the veal shanks. Add the collected mushroom juices and the remaining sauce to the skillet and quickly reduce to napping consistency, 1¼ cups, about 3 minutes. Correct the seasoning with salt and pepper. Pour over the veal shanks and carrots, sprinkle with parsley, and serve at once.

Rich Brown Veal or Poultry Stock

Roasting the bones and vegetables in the oven first until they brown adds a deeper color and richer flavor to any stock. While in a pinch, almost everyone turns to canned chicken broth upon occasion, all of the recipes in this book will benefit hugely from homemade stock, whether it be this darker version or a simple homemade chicken stock. Note: If using veal bones, ask your butcher to cut them for you.

MAKES ABOUT 4 CUPS

6 to 7 pounds meaty veal, duck, or chicken bones, cut into 1-inch pieces

2 tablespoons vegetable oil or duck fat

3 large carrots, peeled and quartered

3 medium onions, quartered

2 large shallots, sliced

2 medium leeks (white part only), thickly sliced

10 to 12 white mushrooms

Bouquet garni (10 parsley sprigs, 1 bay leaf, 2 celery tops with leaves, 2 sprigs of thyme, tied together)

1 medium tomato, coarsely chopped

4 garlic cloves—3 bruised, 1 whole

12 black peppercorns

1/4 whole nutmeg

Sea salt

1. Preheat the oven to 425°F. Place the bones in a large roasting pan greased with the oil or duck fat. Set in the oven and roast, turning once or twice, until the bones are lightly browned, about 15 minutes. Add the carrots, onions, shallots, and leeks and roast for 15 minutes longer.

2. Transfer the bones and vegetables to a stockpot. Add 4 to 5 quarts of cold water and bring to a boil over medium heat.

3. Meanwhile, pour out the fat from the roasting pan. Set the pan over high heat and pour in 1½ cups of water. Bring to a boil, scraping up any browned bits from the bottom of the pan. Pour this liquid into the stockpot.

4. Skim off any fat. Add the mushrooms, bouquet garni, tomato, bruised garlic, whole clove, peppercorns, and nutmeg. Simmer, skimming often, for 4 hours without stirring.

5. Strain the stock though several layers of dampened cheesecloth into a large bowl. Refrigerate until chilled. Scrape any congealed fat off the top.

6. Transfer the stock to a large saucepan and bring to a boil. Reduce the heat to medium-low and simmer, skimming occasionally, for 30 minutes, or until the stock is reduced to 4 cups. Season with salt to taste.

Maghrebi Veal Meatballs with Spinach and Chickpeas

*H*ere's a simple and attractive family dish from the Tunisian island of Djerba. The Tunisians have a spice mixture they call *le tabil,* which they use for soups, stews, and meatballs. These veal meatballs can be any size, though smaller is always more attractive. They are gently sautéed to enhance flavor, then placed in a simmering sauce to keep them from hardening. Brown, flavorful, and tasty, they go beautifully with chickpeas and spinach.

SERVES 4

½ cup dried chickpeas, picked over and soaked overnight in water to cover

Maghrebi Meatballs (recipe follows)

Extra virgin olive oil

1¼ cups chopped onions

2 tablespoons tomato paste

Pinch of crumbled saffron

2 pounds fresh spinach or 1½ packages frozen organic chopped spinach (10 ounces each)

½ cup chopped flat-leaf parsley

1. Drain the chickpeas, rinse well, and place in a heavy saucepan with 1½ quarts water. Cover and simmer for 30 minutes. Make the meatballs.

2. Set a 5-quart heavy casserole over medium heat, add 3 tablespoons olive oil, the onions, and ¼ cup water. Cook for 5 minutes, or until the onions are soft but not brown. Add the tomato paste and cook until it sizzles and the water has evaporated.

3. Transfer the meatballs, chickpeas, and 2 cups cooking liquid to the casserole. Add the crumbled saffron. Cover with a sheet of crumpled foil and a lid. Cook over medium heat for 30 minutes.

4. Meanwhile, prepare the spinach. If using fresh spinach, trim off any stems; wash thoroughly and gently squeeze to remove most of the water. Place the spinach in the reserved skillet and cook until wilted. Drain and coarsely chop. You should have about 2½ cups.

5. When the meatballs have simmered for 30 minutes, gently fold in the spinach and cook, uncovered, for 10 minutes. Gently stir in the parsley and cook for 5 minutes longer. Correct the seasoning and serve.

Maghrebi Meatballs

1½ slices firm-textured white bread, crust removed, diced (1 cup)

¼ cup soda water or water

1½ tablespoons crushed garlic

Le Tabil Spice Mix (recipe follows) or 4¼ teaspoons ground coriander mixed with a pinch of ground caraway

4 teaspoons sweet paprika

Salt and freshly ground pepper

¾ pound ground lean veal

2 tablespoons chopped flat-leaf parsley

1 egg yolk

3 tablespoons olive oil

1. Prepare the meatballs: Soak the bread in soda water for 10 minutes; squeeze dry. Meanwhile, in a food processor, grind the garlic, spice mix, paprika, 1 teaspoon salt, ½ teaspoon black pepper, and 2 tablespoons water to a paste. Add the veal and pulse until well combined, 20 seconds. Add the squeezed bread, parsley, and egg yolk and pulse to combine. With oiled palms, roll the mixture into 20 balls each the size of a walnut. Refrigerate for at least 20 minutes.

2. Heat the olive oil in a 9- or 10-inch nonstick skillet over medium-high heat. Add the meatballs and fry in small batches, turning several times, until golden brown on all sides, about 3 minutes. Transfer the meatballs with a slotted spoon to a colander set over a plate to catch any excess oil. Reserve the skillet and oil for Step 4 at left.

Le Tabil Spice Mix

MAKES ABOUT 1½ TABLESPOONS

1 tablespoon ground coriander seed

½ teaspoon ground caraway seed

⅛ teaspoon cayenne

⅛ teaspoon ground fennel or ground anise

⅛ teaspoon ground cumin

⅛ teaspoon ground black pepper

⅛ teaspoon ground turmeric

⅛ teaspoon ground cloves

Grind all of the ingredients together and store covered in a small jar.

Veal Tongue with Green Olives

*T*hough it hasn't been a fashionable meat for some time, I have a real soft spot for tongue. I grew up with it as a winter dish, so I always think of it as warming and "consoling." When I discovered this Tunisian tongue dish garnished with green olives, it was love at first taste.

The succulent, suave, cracked green meski olive is the one used in Tunisia; elongated, bright green picholine olives from France and Morocco may be substituted.

SERVES 6

1 fresh veal tongue

¼ cup fresh lemon juice

Coarse salt

½ cup extra virgin olive oil

2 thin slices of onion

3 sprigs of thyme

5 sprigs of flat-leaf parsley

5 teaspoons ground coriander

5 teaspoons sweet paprika

7 garlic cloves—2 crushed, 5 peeled but left whole

1 teaspoon crushed black pepper

2 tablespoons tomato paste diluted in 2 cups warm water

5 imported bay leaves

6 to 7 ounces pitted green olives

1. One day in advance, rinse the fresh tongue under cold running water; drain, rub with 2 tablespoons of the lemon juice and a handful of coarse salt, and rinse well. Place the tongue in a deep pot, cover with plenty of cold water, bring to a boil, and skim. Simmer the tongue for 40 minutes, then drain, discarding the liquid.

2. In a bowl or covered container, combine the olive oil, onion slices, thyme, parsley, ground coriander, paprika, crushed garlic, and remaining 2 tablespoons lemon juice to make a marinade.

3. When the tongue is cool enough to handle, slit around the edges and peel away the top tough skin. Cut away the gristle and fat. Put the tongue in the bowl with the marinade and rub it into the meat. Cover and refrigerate overnight

4. The following day, scrape as much of the aromatic oil as possible from the marinade off the tongue into a 5- or 6-quart flameproof casserole. Heat the aromatic oil, add the whole garlic cloves, and cook until they are golden brown, then remove and discard. Put the whole tongue, diluted tomato paste, and bay leaves in the casserole. Bring to a boil, cover with a sheet of foil or crumpled wet parchment paper, and a lid. Reduce the heat to low and cook until the tongue is very tender, about 2½ hours.

5. While the tongue is cooking, blanch the olives to remove any bitterness; drain. When the tongue is tender, remove to a wooden carving board and cut away any remaining skin. Completely degrease the cooking juices, add the olives, and bring to a boil. Correct the seasoning of the sauce. Thinly slice the tongue, nap with the sauce, and surround with the olives.

Note: The taste of a dish differs with the type of olive used, but rarely is any variety wrong when a recipe calls for green olives.

LAMB

Seven-Hour Garlic Crowned Lamb

I wish I had known the French cookbook author who called herself La Mazille, author of *La bonne cuisine du Périgord* (1929), a celebration of her native region, land of truffles, cèpes, foie gras, and confit. Her enthusiasm is infectious, and her recipes for poultry and meats cooked to delectable fork-tenderness are marvelous.

La Mazille, whose real name was Danielle Mallet-Maze, set out to preserve the simple country cooking of the Périgord, including its ingenious culinary secrets (or *trucs,* as the French like to call them). She was particularly devoted to the traditional art of slow cooking. For her, this method transformed ingredients into succulent, easy-to-digest dishes with rich, satisfying textures and robust, complex flavors. Like many of her fellow cooks in southwest France, she believed in the saying "One does not live by how one eats, but by how one digests."

The following recipe is adapted from La Mazille's Périgord-style leg of lamb with a crown of garlic. Her recipe calls for a sweet, soft, white Monbazillac wine; I use orange muscat. Either way, you end up with a thick, delicious sauce filled with garlic cloves, which somehow gives off a haunting aroma of hazelnuts. Slow-cooking a bone-in leg of lamb in a covered pot weakens the connective tissues, allowing the meat to break apart easily into rosy chunks with an incredible flavor. This is truly lamb you can eat with a spoon.

First, the choice of lamb: it should be an aged leg without the shank. To age, let it sit on a paper towel–lined rack in a dish in the refrigerator for a day or two before cooking.

Second, and most important, the meat is dropped into boiling water, then simmered for exactly 15 minutes. This firms up the outside flesh, removes unpleasant odors, and destroys all surface bacteria, thus rendering the meat perfectly safe for very low-temperature cooking.

After simmering, the lamb is drained and dried, browned on all sides in a deep pot large enough to hold the entire leg, then surrounded with dozens of peeled garlic cloves, which when cooked have the appearance of golden almonds.

Please don't be tempted to raise the heat. This will only encourage liquid to escape from the meat, making it less succulent.

How to accompany such a delectable dish? La Mazille suggests pureed favas or white beans, or, as spring approaches, a salad of young dandelion leaves.

SERVES 6

1 leg of lamb on the bone (about 5 pounds), with the shank bone removed

2 tablespoons oil, goose fat, or duck fat

5 firm heads of garlic, cloves separated and peeled (about 60)

3 tablespoons Cognac

1¼ cups sweet wine, such as orange muscat

Salt and freshly ground pepper

1. About 8 hours before serving, bring the lamb to room temperature. Fill a 6- or 7-quart enameled cast-iron casserole with 3½ quarts water and bring to a rolling boil over high heat. Carefully add the leg of lamb and boil for 15 minutes. Drain the lamb and pat dry.

2. Preheat the oven to 200°F. Heat the oil in the casserole until sizzling. Add the lamb and cook over moderate heat until it is nicely browned all over. Tilt the casserole and use a bulb baster to remove almost all of the liquid fat. Add the garlic cloves, then add the Cognac and, averting your face, carefully ignite it with a long match. When the flames subside, add the sweet wine and season the lamb generously with salt and pepper. Cover with a crumpled sheet of wet parchment paper and a tight-fitting lid. Bake the lamb for 6 to 7 hours, turning it halfway through cooking. Remove the casserole from the oven, uncover, and let the lamb stand for 30 minutes. Skim off all the fat.

3. Transfer the lamb to a platter. Remove the garlic with a slotted spoon and arrange the cloves around the lamb. You shouldn't have very much liquid in the casserole, but if you do, boil it down until it's very flavorful. Serve the lamb surrounded by the garlic, with the pan juices poured on top.

Slow-Roasted Leg of Lamb with Pomegranate Glaze and Red Onion–Parsley Relish

*H*ere is an inspired lamb dish employing the flavors of southeastern Turkey—crushed red pepper, tomato paste, and pomegranate glaze. Of course, it is not authentic to serve rare lamb in that part of the world, but by employing the method described on page 227, lamb can be slow-roasted to yield rare flesh with a wonderful silky texture.

Unlike a rack of lamb, the dense flesh of a leg requires a much longer roasting time. Yet, here again, low-temperature cooking provides meltingly tender *rare* flesh. The meat is first browned in a hot oven, then the temperature is reduced to 225°F. Roasting continues until the internal temperature of the meat reaches 130° to 135°F. In this case, you must allow the roast to rest before carving. (The temperature will slowly rise to 135° to 140°F for a rare and juicy roast.)

When carving, start at the shank end and slice perpendicular to the main bone. To obtain tender meat, always slice across the grain.

I serve this Turkish-style lamb with the same traditional Red Onion–Parsley Relish that goes so well with southeastern Turkish kebabs. Or try the baked cauliflower gratin on page 244.

SERVES 6 TO 8

1 leg of lamb (5 to 6 pounds), bone-in

2 tablespoons pomegranate concentrate or molasses (see Mail Order Sources)

1½ tablespoons extra virgin olive oil

½ cup finely chopped onion

4 large garlic cloves, mashed

2 teaspoons tomato paste

1 teaspoon crushed red pepper flakes, preferably Aleppo or Turkish

Pinch of sugar

Salt and freshly ground pepper

1 cup chicken or vegetable stock

1 to 2 tablespoons butter

Red Onion–Parsley Relish (recipe follows)

1. Five to 6 hours before you plan to serve the lamb, trim off the excess fat, leaving about a ¼-inch layer. In a large deep bowl, dilute the pomegranate concentrate or molasses with ⅓ cup water. Stir in the olive oil, onion, garlic, tomato paste, red pepper, and sugar. Add the lamb and turn to coat. Let stand for 2 to 3 hours at room temperature, turning once or twice.

2. About 3 hours before serving, place an oven rack in the lower third of the oven. Preheat the oven to 450°F.

3. Set the lamb, fattiest side up, on a rack in an oiled shallow roasting pan. Season the lamb with plenty of salt and black pepper and set in the oven. Immediately reduce the oven temperature to 250°F. Roast the lamb, basting occasionally with the pan drippings, for 1¾ hours. Turn the roast over and continue roasting and basting until the lamb reaches an internal temperature of 130° to 135°F, about 30 minutes longer.

4. Remove the lamb to a carving board, cover loosely with foil, and let rest for 15 to 20 minutes. (During this time, the temperature will rise to 135° to 140°F.) Meanwhile, defat the pan juices. Add 1 cup stock, set over medium heat, and stir to scrape up all the brown bits that cling to the pan. Boil until reduced to napping consistency. Adjust the seasoning and keep hot. Carve the lamb and serve with the sauce and the accompanying onion-parsley relish.

Red Onion—Parsley Relish

MAKES ABOUT 1 CUP

2 red onions, peeled and thinly sliced	½ cup chopped flat-leaf parsley
1 teaspoon coarse salt	1 teaspoon ground sumac (see Note)

Toss the red onions with the coarse salt. Rub the salt into the slices and let stand for 5 minutes. Rinse the onions under cold running water and drain thoroughly. Mix with the parsley and sumac. Serve within 30 minutes.

Note: Purchase sumac from a spice specialty shop such as Kalustyan's in New York (see Mail Order Sources). If you have a choice, choose the best-quality sumac, which comes from Jordan. Store in the freezer to maintain quality.

Slow-Roasted Rack of Lamb with Simple Mediterranean Flavors

Writing this recipe for an American rack of lamb weighing about 1½ pounds, I adapted the notion of chef Heston Blumenthal and Dr. Peter Barham (see box) that slow-cooked lamb need not end up falling off the bone. In fact, as in this recipe, it can end up rare and juicy, evenly cooked.

Simple Mediterranean flavors go best with the finest-quality lamb. Here I use only garlic, lemon, and fruity extra virgin olive oil. If you wish, you can marinate it overnight with an herb marinade.

The technique here is to quickly brown the rack in a skillet over medium-high heat, then let it relax while heating the oven to 300°F. (At this point a meat thermometer is essential.) The meat is slow-roasted until the desired doneness: 130°F for rare; 140°F for medium-rare. Because the roast was allowed to relax earlier, it can be carved as soon as it comes out of the oven. As it is being carved, its temperature will continue to rise another 2 degrees, creating meat that is perfectly pink. I like to serve this lamb with a sprinkling of the pan juices and a handful of fresh chopped onion and parsley.

SERVES 2

1 rack of lamb (1½ pounds), Frenched or well trimmed

¼ cup plus 3 tablespoons chopped flat-leaf parsley

1 teaspoon chopped fresh thyme

½ teaspoon finely chopped fresh rosemary

3 garlic cloves, minced

Coarse sea salt and freshly cracked black pepper

1 tablespoon plus 2 teaspoons extra virgin olive oil

2½ tablespoons fresh lemon juice

Grated zest of 1 organic lemon (about 1 teaspoon)

3 tablespoons finely diced onion

1. Put the lamb in a large plastic bag. Mix together ¼ cup parsley with the thyme, rosemary, and two-thirds of the garlic. Pat all over the meat and let stand for 2 to 3 hours at room temperature.

2. Wipe off the marinade and discard. Generously season the lamb with salt and pepper. Set a large skillet over medium-high heat, add 2 teaspoons of the olive oil, and allow to sizzle. Add the lamb, skin side down, reduce the heat to medium, and brown for 3 minutes, shaking the skillet often to keep the meat from sticking. Use tongs to turn and hold the rack while searing all the exposed flesh, 1 more minute. Remove the lamb to a side dish. Lift the skillet and pour off almost all the fat. Set aside for deglazing.

3. Place the meat in a lightly oiled shallow baking dish and let rest while heating the oven to 300°F. Insert a probe thermometer in the thickest part of the lamb. Slow roast the lamb for 35 to 45 minutes or until 130°F for rare or 140°F for medium. (A 1-pound rack roasts in 25 to 30 minutes.)

4. Reheat the skillet, add the remaining garlic, lemon juice, and ½ cup water. Bring to a boil, stirring to scrape up any browned bits. Simmer until reduced to 3 tablespoons. Off the heat, swirl in the lemon zest and the remaining 1 tablespoon olive oil, and season with salt and pepper. Spoon the pan juices onto a serving dish. Carve the rack and arrange the chops over the pan drippings. Scatter the onion and remaining 3 tablespoons parsley on top. Serve at once.

BRITISH THEORISTS IN THE KITCHEN

Dr. Peter Barham, a Reader in Physics at Bristol University in the United Kingdom and author of *The Science of Cooking*, is fascinated by food. He has worked with several chefs, trailblazing the application of science to the culinary arts. One such association has been with chef Heston Blumenthal of the famous Fat Duck restaurant in Bray, Berkshire. Blumenthal asked Barham about the pros and cons of slow-cooking tender pieces of lamb rather than applying high heat.

As the chef put it: "What you really want from a piece of meat is for it to be uniformly cooked with only modest temperature, around 122° to 140°F (50° to 60°C), inside." Blumenthal and Barham discovered that a lamb fillet "is particularly tender when the temperature is around 136°F (58°C). If it were cooler the proteins that make up the muscles would not have softened, while if it were warmer the same proteins wind up into tight balls and push moisture out."

Barham explained to Blumenthal how heat diffuses in a piece of meat. With that information, Blumenthal went back to the kitchen "and experimented until he found the perfect way to cook lamb."

The results were incredible, Barham said. The meat cooked perfectly and was pink and juicy throughout, without any overcooking except for the merest ring of crust on the outside. The only downside was that a cook had to stand and turn the meat constantly for an hour!

Fall-Apart Lamb Shanks with Almond-Chocolate Picada

*I*n this recipe I apply to large meaty lamb shanks an old-fashioned method from the Pyrenees traditionally used to prepare wild game. The shanks are marinated overnight in hearty cooked red wine (see chef Thomas Keller's note in box, page 212), then gently stewed until fork-tender.

A final addition of a *picada* of well-pounded toasted almonds and unsweetened cocoa produces an ethereal flavor. Picadas in this part of Catalonia are judged by the smoothness of the final sauce. In this dish, the cook should try for a creamy béchamel-like texture. Please marinate the lamb shanks overnight before cooking.

SERVES 6

1 bottle (750 ml) full-bodied red wine

2 carrots, coarsely chopped

1 onion, thickly sliced

1 large leek (white and tender green), halved lengthwise and thickly sliced crosswise

1 head of garlic, halved horizontally

1 lemon, quartered

½ cup drained and chopped canned plum tomatoes

1 tablespoon dried thyme

1 tablespoon dried oregano

½ teaspoon cracked black peppercorns

2 bay leaves

5 pounds lamb shanks (4 to 6 shanks)

Salt and freshly ground pepper

3 tablespoons extra virgin olive oil

Almond-Chocolate Picada (recipe follows)

Chopped flat-leaf parsley, for garnish

1. In a large saucepan, boil the wine until is reduced to 2 cups, about 10 minutes. Add the carrots, onion, leek, halved garlic head, lemon, plum tomatoes, thyme, oregano, peppercorns, and bay leaves and simmer for 5 minutes. Let the marinade cool completely.

2. Put the lamb shanks in a large glass bowl or a sealed heavy-duty plastic bag. Add the marinade. Cover and refrigerate overnight.

3. The following day, let the meat return to room temperature. Remove the lamb from the marinade and pat dry. Discard the lemon quarters and strain the marinade, reserving the vegetables and wine separately.

4. Season the lamb shanks generously with salt and pepper. Heat 2 tablespoons the olive oil in a large heavy skillet. Cook the lamb shanks in batches over moderately high heat, turning, until browned all over, about 8 minutes per batch. Transfer the browned lamb to a large enameled cast-iron casserole, preferably with about a 7-quart capacity. Preheat the oven to 250°F.

5. Add the reserved vegetables to the skillet along with the remaining 1 tablespoon olive oil and cook over moderately low heat, stirring frequently, until deep brown and tender, about 15 minutes. Press the vegetables to express the oil, tilt the skillet to remove with a spoon, and transfer to the casserole.

6. Pour off the oil in the skillet. Add ½ cup water to the skillet and bring to a boil, scraping up any browned bits that have stuck to the bottom. Boil until reduced to a syrup. Add another cup of water and bring a boil, then scrape the contents of the skillet into the casserole. Pour the wine from the marinade into the skillet and heat to a bare simmer; add to the casserole. Cover the meat and vegetables with a sheet of wet crumpled parchment paper directly on top of the meat.

7. Cover the casserole with the lid and cook the lamb in the oven for 4½ to 5 hours, or until the meat is very tender. Discard the paper. Using a slotted spoon, transfer the lamb shanks to an oiled shallow baking dish large enough to hold them in a single layer. Season the lamb shanks with salt and pepper and cover loosely with foil.

8. Strain the cooking juices through a fine sieve set over a saucepan, pressing hard on the solids to extract the liquid. Skim off as much fat as possible from the cooking juices. Boil the juices over high heat, skimming frequently, until reduced to 2 cups, about 15 minutes. *(Up to this point, the recipe can be prepared in advance. Refrigerate the meat and sauce separately.)*

9. If refrigerated, let the meat return to room temperature. Gently reheat the meat and sauce separately. Scrape the picada into the sauce and cook over moderately high heat until the sauce thickens slightly, about 2 minutes. Correct the seasoning. Pour the sauce over the lamb and bake for 30 minutes. Garnish with parsley and serve.

Almond-Chocolate Picada

24 blanched almonds

4 garlic cloves

2 tablespoons chopped flat-leaf parsley

1 slice of stale country white bread, cut 1 inch thick and toasted, crust trimmed

1 teaspoon unsweetened cocoa powder

1 tablespoon brandy

2 teaspoons cooking juices from Fall-Apart Lamb Shanks (above)

1. Toast the almonds.

2. In a mortar or mini food processor, grind the almonds and garlic to a coarse paste. Add the parsley, toast, cocoa, brandy, and 2 tablespoons of the lamb cooking juices and process or pound until smooth.

MARINATING MEAT

Marinating does not tenderize meat, and alcohol doesn't either. Only slicing, pounding, and cooking can tenderize meat. In fact, alcohol will, in effect, cook the surface, keeping the meat from absorbing the marinade. If you cook off the alcohol first, the meat will absorb the full flavor of the fruit of the wine. To get rid of the last bit of alcohol, light the simmering wine and onions.

—CHEF THOMAS KELLER OF THE FRENCH LAUNDRY, *LOS ANGELES TIMES*

Turkish-Style Lamb Smothered in Yogurt with Parsley Salad

You'll find Mediterranean people cooking lamb with milk or yogurt in a wide arc from Rome to Lebanon, including Apulia, Montenegro, Albania, Macedonia, Thrace, Kusidasi, and numerous countries in the Middle East. This Turkish version of the famous dish, *Elbasan Tavasi,* is particularly delicious, emerging golden-brown and bubbling from the oven.

Start the dish the day before, cook the lamb slowly, then chill it overnight so you can remove all the fat, gristle, and bone. Drain the yogurt for the sauce. I like to use split lamb shanks with the bone—the result is juicier and more flavorful than boned meat. The next day, assemble the dish, smother the meat in the yogurt sauce, and bake in the oven. Serve with a parsley salad or bulgur pilaf with walnuts.

If you own an electric slow-cooker, definitely use it to make this splendid dish. If not, follow the Note on page 214 for oven-braising.

SERVES 4

5 cups plain whole-milk yogurt	2 tablespoons all-purpose flour
1 bay leaf	1/3 cup milk
2 small lamb shanks, cracked (about 2½ pounds)	Pinch of ground allspice
	Salt and freshly ground pepper
3 scallions, trimmed	1 tablespoon butter
3 green garlic shoots or 2 garlic cloves	½ teaspoon crushed hot red pepper
2 whole eggs	Parsley Salad (recipe follows)
1 egg yolk	

1. Drain the yogurt in a paper towel—lined colander set over a bowl in the refrigerator for at least 4 hours or overnight. You need 2½ cups.

2. Place a small cake rack in the bottom of an electric slow-cooker. Add 1 cup water and the bay leaf. Place the lamb shanks, scallions, and garlic in the pot. Cover and cook on low until fork-tender, about 9 hours.

(continued)

Meats

3. Remove and discard all bones, gristle, and membranes. Cut the lamb into bite-sized pieces and put in a bowl or container. Season with salt and pepper. Strain the cooking juices over the lamb. Let cool, then cover and refrigerate overnight.

4. The next day, lift off and discard the congealed fat on the surface. Let the meat return to room temperature.

5. About 1 hour before serving, preheat the oven to 375°F. Arrange the lamb and meat juices in a single layer on the bottom of a greased large, shallow baking dish (9 by 12-inch or 11 by 17-inch). Bake, uncovered, for 10 minutes. In a bowl, whisk the whole eggs, egg yolk, and flour to a smooth cream. Gradually add the drained yogurt and the milk, whisking until smooth. Season with the allspice and salt and pepper. Remove the pan from the oven, pour the yogurt mixture evenly over the lamb, and return to the oven to bake until the topping has set, about 30 minutes.

6. Preheat the broiler. Broil the dish for about 2 minutes, rotating it until the topping is nicely browned. Meanwhile, in a small saucepan, melt the butter with the hot pepper until sizzling. Dribble the butter over the top and serve with the parsley salad

Note: To prepare the shanks without an electric slow-cooker, preheat the oven to 250°F. Set a cake rack in a large enameled cast-iron casserole; add 1 cup of water and the bay leaf. Set the lamb shanks on the rack and scatter the scallions and garlic over the shanks. Wet and crumple a sheet of parchment paper; place it directly over the meat, cover with a tight-fitting lid, and bring the water to a boil. Transfer the casserole to the oven and bake for about 4 to 5 hours, or until the lamb shanks are very tender. Continue with Step 3.

Parsley Salad

SERVES 4

2 cups flat-leaf parsley leaves

1 red onion, thinly sliced

1 red ripe tomato, seeded and diced

2 tablespoons verjus or rice vinegar

2 tablespoons extra virgin olive oil

Salt and freshly ground pepper

Crushed hot red pepper

Toss the parsley, red onion, and tomato with the verjus and the olive oil. Season with salt, black pepper, and a pinch of hot pepper.

TENDERIZING LAMB

Soaking meat in an acidic liquid may not tenderize it, but it does imbue the flesh with flavor. Try not to overdo it, however. Acid left on meat too long can turn the texture mushy. In the eastern Mediterranean, yogurt is used with great success as a marinade and tenderizer for meat and poultry. The milk solids bring up the flavor and gently tenderize at the same time. In Morocco, some cooks substitute *lben*, or buttermilk.

Turkish cooks like to rub grated onion and onion juice into lamb to tenderize, remove odor, and enhance flavor. You can leave meat in such a marinade without worrying about destroying its flavor or texture.

Slow-Baked Lamb with Fennel, Pecorino, and Potatoes

This one-pot recipe from the town of Montesacro in the southern Italian region of Apulia is baked in a wide, shallow terracotta dish called a *tiella,* which allows for continual slow evaporation while the meat cooks. Every Mediterranean country has a similar earthenware dish for slow-cooking: the French *tian,* the Moroccan tagine, the Corsican *tianu,* the Spanish cazuela, and the Balkan *tava.* Substitute any earthenware dish. I use a cazuela (see Mail Order Sources).

On the West Coast, wild fennel can easily be found. Crushed fennel seed is a good substitute.

SERVES 4 TO 6

2 pounds lean boneless shoulder of lamb, cut into 1½-inch chunks

2 cups whole milk

2 bay leaves

1 stalk of wild fennel, 6 inches long, or ½ teaspoon crushed fennel seed

1 sprig of rosemary

2 garlic cloves, sliced

2½ pounds boiling potatoes, such as Red Bliss

⅓ cup extra virgin olive oil

1 medium red onion, sliced

Salt and freshly ground pepper

½ cup chopped flat-leaf parsley

¾ cup grated aged sheep's milk cheese, such as pecorino sardo, manchego, or pecorino toscano

1 cup fresh bread crumbs

1. Early in the day, soak the lamb cubes in the milk mixed with the bay leaves, fennel, rosemary, and garlic. Cover with plastic wrap and refrigerate for at least 3 or up to 6 hours.

2. About 2½ hours before serving, preheat the oven to 425°F. Remove the lamb from the milk bath and pat the chunks dry with paper towels. Reserve the milk and aromatics.

3. Peel the potatoes and cut crosswise into ⅛-inch-thick slices. Add the potatoes to the reserved milk and soak for about 15 minutes.

4. Meanwhile, heat 2 tablespoons of the olive oil in a medium skillet. Add the red onion and sauté until pale golden. Add the lamb to the skillet and slowly brown on all sides, about 10 minutes.

5. Season the browned lamb with salt and pepper. Transfer the onion and lamb to a side dish. Pour the oil from the skillet. Pour in ¼ cup water and bring to a boil, scraping up any browned bits from the bottom of the pan; set aside.

6. Lightly oil a 2½-quart shallow flameproof baking dish. Scatter the onion slices over the bottom of the dish. Drain the potatoes, reserving the milk. Layer half of the potatoes on top of the onions and sprinkle with pepper. Cover with the meat in a single layer. Sprinkle on the parsley, half the cheese, and half the bread crumbs. Layer the drained potatoes on top. Pour the milk with its aromatics over all. Press down on the potatoes so there will be some room for expansion. Place the pan over low heat and slowly bring to a boil, about 15 minutes.

7. Sprinkle the remaining cheese, bread crumbs, and 3 tablespoons olive oil over the top. Set the pan on the top rack of the oven and bake for 15 minutes. Lower the oven temperature to 325°F and continue baking for 1¼ hours longer. Turn off the oven and let the dish rest another 30 minutes before removing from the oven. Serve warm.

Note: Leftovers are delicious reheated in the oven.

Lamb Tagine Smothered in Onions

Moroccan tagine pots, shallow, earthenware pots with high cone-shaped tops, glazed on only one side, are great for cooking meat stews. As the stew simmers, steam rises into the cone. The unglazed interior of the conical top absorbs some of the excess moisture, ensuring a steady, slow reduction of liquid below.

This dish of chunks of lamb slowly simmered with cinnamon, ginger, and saffron, called *quamamma,* may look like a lot of work, but it is worth it, because it is one of the very best tagines in the Moroccan repertoire.

You begin this tagine "cold," which is to say that the lamb is *not* browned, but rather, gently heated along with the spices and other ingredients, which allows the flavors to fully penetrate the meat.

Actually, in traditional Moroccan cookery, very few tagines began with browning. Instead the meat is usually browned at the end by covering the bottom half of the tagine with a flat ceramic plate, then piling hot coals on top. I simply run the meat under the broiler.

The onions create a thick, soft sauce. Note that two preparations of onions are used: grated, which disintegrate and thicken the sauce; and sliced, which impart a rich silky texture.

SERVES 6

5 pounds lamb shanks, trimmed of excess fat

Salt and freshly, finely ground pepper

1½ teaspoons ground ginger

½ teaspoon saffron threads

1 medium onion, coarsely grated (½ cup), plus 4 pounds large onions, quartered lengthwise and thickly sliced crosswise

3 whole canned Italian plum tomatoes, seeded and crushed

1 cinnamon stick, 2 inches long

2 tablespoons extra virgin olive oil

1½ teaspoons ground cinnamon

2 tablespoons plus 2 teaspoons butter

3 tablespoons sugar

1. Early in the day, place the lamb in a large, heavy casserole or tagine pot. Toss with 2 teaspoons salt, 1 teaspoon each pepper and ginger, 2 pinches of the saffron, the grated onion, tomatoes, cinnamon stick, and olive oil. Stir over low heat until the aroma of the spices is released, about 5 minutes. Do not brown the meat. Add 2 cups water, bring to a boil, reduce the heat, cover, and simmer over very low heat for 3 to 3½ hours. (The meat should be seven-eighths cooked—*almost* falling off the bone.) You can do this in a 250°F oven or in an electric slow-cooker set on high, if desired.) Remove and let cool.

2. Meanwhile, in a large heavy saucepan or flameproof casserole, combine the sliced onions with ¼ cup water, a pinch of saffron, the ground cinnamon, 1 teaspoon each salt and pepper, ½ teaspoon ginger, 2 tablespoons of the butter, and 2 tablespoons of the sugar. Cover and cook over medium-low heat for 1½ hours. Remove the cover and cook until the liquid evaporates, about 25 minutes. Reduce the heat to moderately low and cook, stirring often, until the onions are golden, about 20 more minutes. Transfer the onions to a large plate to cool.

3. When the lamb shanks are cool enough to handle, pull the meat off the bones and trim off any fat or gristle. Cut the meat into 1-inch chunks and transfer to a bowl. Discard the cinnamon stick. (*The recipe can be prepared to this point up to 2 days in advance. Let cool, then cover and refrigerate the meat, onions, and cooking liquid in separate containers.*)

4. About 1 hour before serving, preheat the oven to 400°F. Discard all the fat from the lamb juices and boil the liquid down to 1 cup. Arrange the lamb in a single layer in a shallow ovenproof serving dish. Pour the reduced lamb juices over the meat. Spread the golden onion mixture on top. Spoon any remaining onion cooking liquid over all. Sprinkle the remaining 1 tablespoon sugar on top and dot with the remaining 2 teaspoons butter. Bake for 45 minutes, or until the topping is caramelized and bubbling.

Note: As the spicing is central to the sauce of this dish, please be sure to use fresh ground spices.

Ana Sortun's Lamb Keftedes with Bibb Lettuce, Fresh Mint, and Warm Pita

I'm a big fan of the cooking of Ana Sortun, chef-owner at the Mediterranean-inspired restaurant Oleana in Cambridge, Massachusetts. Her seasoning is sophisticated and daring, her dishes warm and intense. This is one of her most tantalizing recipes: a beer-braised lamb shoulder, shredded and shaped into galettes or *keftedes,* then pan-fried until the exteriors are crisp, while the interiors remain soft and satiny.

The concept of Mediterranean people cooking with beer surprised me at first; it seemed so Nordic. But it is a fairly common practice in some Armenian communities in the Middle East. In fact, the brewing of beer was practiced thousands of years ago in Egypt. According to ancient tablets, peasants made beer using bread dough mixed with dates.

SERVES 4

1½ pounds thick lamb shoulder chops

1 tablespoon plus 1 teaspoon extra virgin olive oil

Salt and freshly ground pepper

12 ounces beer or ale

1 carrot, peeled and sliced on the bias

1 medium onion, quartered

3 garlic cloves, halved and smashed

2 teaspoons dried mint

1½ tablespoons pomegranate concentrate

Lemon juice

1 egg, beaten

1½ cups bread crumbs

1½ tablespoons butter

Fresh mint, Bibb lettuce, and 2 pita breads, halved and warmed, as accompaniment

1. Preheat the oven to 350°F. Wipe the lamb chops dry with paper towels. In a large ovenproof skillet, heat the tablespoon of olive oil until very hot but not smoking. Add the lamb and brown well on both sides, about 10 minutes. Remove the chops to a plate and season with salt and pepper.

2. Pour off all the fat from the skillet. Add ½ cup of the beer and bring to a boil, scraping up any brown bits from the bottom of the pan. Boil until the beer is reduced to a few tablespoons of glaze. Return the meat to the skillet, lower the heat, and allow the lamb to soak up the syrupy juices.

3. Add the carrot, onion, garlic, mint, and remaining beer to the pan. Pour in enough water to reach halfway up the sides of the meat. Season the liquid with salt and pepper. Bring to a boil, cover with a sheet of crumpled parchment paper and a tight-fitting lid, and transfer to the preheated oven. Braise the lamb until the meat is very tender and beginning to fall off the bone, 1½ to 2 hours.

4. Remove the lamb, reserving the juices in the skillet. Trim the lamb of all fat, gristle, and bone and finely shred. Strain the cooking juices, quickly skim off all fat, and return to the skillet. Boil until reduced by half to about 1 cup. Stir in the pomegranate concentrate and correct the seasoning with salt, pepper, and a few drops of lemon juice.

5. Fold ¾ cup of the pan juices into the shredded meat along with the egg and 1 cup of the bread crumbs. Refrigerate until firm, about 1 hour.

6. Shape the lamb mixture into 4 or 8 patties and sprinkle the remaining bread crumbs to coat. In a large skillet, heat the butter and the remaining 1 teaspoon oil. Fry the patties over medium-high heat until golden-brown on each side and warm throughout, about 4 minutes. Quickly reheat the remaining ¼ cup pan juices and drizzle over the patties. Serve with the fresh mint, lettuce, and warm pita bread.

Lamb Baked in a Clay Jar

On the Tunisian island of Djerba, an amphora-shaped unglazed terracotta pot called a *gargoulette* is stuffed with fish or meat, saffron, herbs, olive oil, and vegetables, then left in the embers that warm the water at the bathhouse to cook slowly while the women bathe. The cook brings the pot home, her husband hacks off the top and the handles, then she pours the food into a ceramic bowl to serve. The flavor of food cooked in clay is special. Of course, the pot, being broken, is discarded, which makes sense in Djerba, where pots cost about twenty cents apiece. I substitute a three-quart Chinese clay pot and don't break it open; I use it again and again for its flavor-enhancing quality.

A Romertopf brick oven can be substituted. It will provide the same fabulously moist quality—and you get to save your gargoulette for another day.

SERVES 4

1½ pounds bone-in shoulder of lamb, trimmed of excess fat and cut into 12 chunks

1 small onion, finely chopped, plus 2 tablespoons chopped onion

2 tablespoons finely chopped garlic

1 large sprig of rosemary

1 bay leaf

Salt and freshly ground pepper

Pinch of saffron threads

1 medium tomato

1 small green or red bell pepper

4 medium Yukon Gold potatoes

¼ cup extra virgin olive oil

Flour, water, and oil ribbon for sealing the clay pot, optional

Juice of 1 lemon

1 tablespoon chopped flat-leaf parsley

1. Rinse the meat; drain and mix with the small onion, garlic, rosemary, bay leaf, salt, pepper, and a good pinch of saffron. Marinate in the refrigerator for at least 5 or 6 hours.

2. Core the tomato, cut in half crosswise, and gently squeeze out the seeds. Slice the tomato. Core, seed, and thinly slice the bell pepper. Peel and halve the potatoes. Mix the vegetables with the olive oil and the marinated meat, pack into a 3-quart clay pot, and mix well. Cover with foil. Set the lid on top and seal with a ribbon of dough made with flour mixed with water and a drop of oil. Place in a cold oven, turn the temperature to 450°F, and bake for 1½ hours. Turn off the oven and leave to continue baking for 30 minutes.

3. Pour the ingredients into a deep serving plate and correct the seasoning. Sprinkle the lemon juice, chopped onion, and parsley on top and serve.

GRATING AND CHOPPING ONIONS

Moroccan cooks often use grated onions as a base for a creamy sauce, or for a jamlike salad, stuffings for vegetables, or fillings for pastry. Once grated, the onions are salted, then rinsed and squeezed dry. Very often a Moroccan cook adds chopped onions to a dish to give additional texture or heft to the sauce.

Grating is easily done in a food processor by pulsing or on the large holes of a box grater. Salting, rinsing, and draining encourages the grated onion to dissolve rapidly in a long-simmered dish. This rinsing of chopped or grated onions is done throughout the Middle East to rid the onions of a pungent aroma and taste.

Prior to hand-chopping lots of onions, sprinkle a few drops of vinegar on your cutting board to remove the pungent vapors. Rinsing your chopped onions before use will give you a more delicate dish . . . and keep your eyes dry, too.

Moroccan Lamb, Quince, and Baby Okra Tagine

Strangely, over the seven years I lived in Morocco and collected recipes, I never once tasted this tagine. Then, on a recent trip back, it was served to me twice. Turns out it's a little-known rural dish recently rediscovered, which has become hugely popular because it's so good.

The combination of okra, quince, and garlic may seem odd; but once you taste it, I think you'll be enraptured. Rabia and Fatna, the two cooks from Tangiers who taught me this recipe, believe the secret to bringing the ingredients into harmony is to use a lot of garlic. To those who think of okra simply as a thickener, eating whole okra braised to absorb other flavors may be a revelation. Here the okra pods develop a mushroom-like texture while still retaining their shape, and the cone-shaped hard stem ends pick up the flavors of the sauce. To prepare okra so that you can eat the entire vegetable, thinly peel the cones without piercing. This takes some time, but I think it's well worth the trouble.

Some Moroccan cooks rub okra with salt, hot pepper, black pepper, and a little oil, then let them rest for a few hours before frying whole in olive oil. They do this to enhance the flavor and firm up the texture before adding the okra to a couscous or tagine.

SERVES 6

$1\frac{1}{4}$ pounds fresh baby okra, trimmed top and tail (see page 227)

$1\frac{1}{2}$ tablespoons salt

Pinch of cayenne

Pinch of freshly ground black pepper

3 tablespoons plus 2 teaspoons extra virgin olive oil

2 pounds fresh quince (9 small or 3 large)

2 pounds lean bone-in lamb shoulder, trimmed and cut into 6 even chunks

1 medium red onion, grated

Pinch of saffron threads

1 teaspoon ground ginger

$\frac{1}{2}$ teaspoon hot Hungarian paprika or cayenne

2 sprigs of cilantro

2 sprigs of parsley

18 garlic cloves, coarsely chopped

$\frac{1}{4}$ cup tomato puree

$2\frac{1}{4}$ cups chopped red onion

1 jalapeño pepper, seeded and minced

$1\frac{1}{2}$ teaspoons ground cumin

2 tablespoons butter

2 tablespoons sugar

$\frac{1}{4}$ teaspoon ground cinnamon

1. Trim the okra cones: Carefully pare the cone tops of the okra pods and trim the tips if they are black, but do not cut into the pods. On a tray, toss the okra with 1 tablespoon of the salt mixed with the cayenne and black pepper and 2 teaspoons of the olive oil. Spread out and let stand for 1 hour in a warm place.

2. Meanwhile, wash, halve, and core but do not peel the quince. (If using large quince, cut each into 6 sections.) As you work, place the pieces in cold water to keep them from blackening. Let soak for at least 1 hour.

3. Put the lamb in a 4-quart casserole. Add the grated onion, remaining 3 tablespoons olive oil, saffron, ginger, paprika, cilantro, parsley, garlic, and 1½ teaspoons salt. Toss together over medium heat to release the aromas of the spices and lightly brown the onions, about 15 minutes. Add 2 cups water and the tomato puree and bring to a boil. Lower the heat and simmer, covered, for 45 minutes, adding water if necessary and turning the meat occasionally in the sauce.

4. Add the chopped onion, jalapeño pepper, and cumin and continue simmering over gentle heat for another 45 minutes.

5. Meanwhile, drain the quince. Place it in a large skillet, add 4 cups lightly salted water, cover, and cook over medium heat for about 15 minutes, or until almost tender. Carefully pour off all but a few tablespoons poaching liquid. Add the butter, sugar, and cinnamon. Raise the heat to medium-high and cook the quince, flesh side down, until tender and glazed brown, 20 minutes. Remove the pan from the heat, turn each piece over, and set aside until Step 7.

6. When the lamb has cooked for 1½ hours, quickly rinse the okra under running water, drain and thoroughly dry with paper towels. Fry in hot oil until browned on all sides; drain on paper towels. Add the okra to the meat, cover tightly, and cook until the meat is very tender and the sauce has become quite thick, 20 minutes, shaking the pan from time to time.

7. To serve, reheat the quince with a sprinkle of water and cook until the skin side is glazed, 5 minutes. Arrange the meat and okra on a large, shallow serving dish. Pour the onion sauce on top, decorate with the quinces, and serve at once with wedges of dense bread.

Greek Lamb Stew with Baby Onions and Allspice

*I*n Greece, beef, veal, venison, or rabbit would be the meat of choice here—first marinated in vinegar and then gently stewed until fork-tender. I break a cardinal rule and substitute meaty lamb shoulder, which my Greek friends have told me is incorrect. Well, it works for me. I don't marinate the meat but do brown it thoroughly before stewing. And I enhance it with plenty of allspice berries, which lend an aromatic taste to the sauce.

As with so many slow-cooked dishes, this stew is always more luscious if prepared a day in advance. Serve the dish hot, along with a big loaf of crusty bread.

SERVES 6 TO 8

4 pounds meaty lamb shoulder, cut into
    2½-inch chunks

1 can (28 ounces) Italian plum tomatoes
    packed in puree

6 tablespoons extra virgin olive oil

Coarse sea salt

2 medium onions, chopped

4 garlic cloves, crushed with a pinch of salt

2 tablespoons whole allspice berries, tied in a
    cheesecloth

2 cinnamon sticks

2 bay leaves

3 pounds small white boiling onions, trimmed
    and peeled

1 teaspoon sugar

2 tablespoons red wine vinegar

½ teaspoon freshly ground pepper

1 cup cubed feta cheese

1. Trim any excess fat from the meat and pat dry. Strain the tomatoes with their puree through a food mill to remove the seeds.

2. In a large heavy skillet, heat 2 tablespoons of the oil until hot. Add the lamb in batches without crowding and sauté over medium-high heat, turning, until browned all over, about 3 minutes. With a slotted spoon, transfer each batch to a bowl and season with salt.

3. When all the meat is browned, pour off the fat from the pan. Add 2 cups water to the skillet and bring to a boil, scraping up any browned bits from the bottom of the pan. Remove from the heat and set aside.

4. In a large flameproof casserole, heat 2 tablespoons olive oil with ¼ cup water. Add the chopped onions and stir to mix. Cook over medium-low heat, stirring occasionally, until the water has evaporated and the onions are melting and translucent, about 10 minutes.

5. Add the crushed garlic, tomatoes, allspice, cinnamon sticks, and bay leaves. Add the browned lamb along with any juices that have accumulated in the bowl. Pour in the reserved liquid from the skillet. Bring to a boil, reduce the heat to low, cover, and cook for 1 hour and 15 minutes.

6. Meanwhile, trim the boiling onions. Cut an X in the root end of each with the tip of a small knife and peel. In a large pot of boiling salted water, blanch the onions for 3 minutes. Drain, rinse under cold running water, and shake to drain well.

7. Put the onions in a large nonstick skillet with 1 tablespoon olive oil and sauté over medium-high heat, shaking the pan often, until glazed all over, about 5 minutes. Sprinkle on ½ teaspoon sugar and continue to cook until shiny and golden brown, about 3 minutes longer. Remove to a bowl and repeat with the remaining onions.

8. Add the browned onions to the stewed lamb. Continue to cook over low heat, covered, for 15 minutes. Remove from the heat, uncover, and let cool. Discard the bay leaves, cinnamon sticks, and bag of allspice.

9. When the meat is cool enough to handle, remove it from the bones and cut into 1-inch pieces. Return the pieces of meat to the onions and sauce and cover with a sheet of plastic wrap directly on top. Cover and refrigerate for up to a day.

10. About 1 hour before serving, uncover and remove the plastic wrap. Skim off all the congealed fat. Set over medium-low heat and cook, uncovered, stirring to prevent sticking, until the sauce thickens, about 30 minutes. Stir in the vinegar. Season with the pepper and salt to taste. Cover and simmer for 5 minutes longer. Let stand, covered, until ready to serve. Reheat for an instant and serve hot, with the cubes of feta sprinkled on top.

Steamed Wheat with Lamb, Winter Vegetables, and Chickpeas

*I*n this popular home dish from the southern Tunisian town of Gafsaa, coarse bulgur is steamed like couscous until tender, tossed with a savory, peppery lamb and vegetable stew, then baked like a gratin.

This dish is prepared with only the smallest amount of liquid, just the moisture exuded by its humble vegetables—cabbage, turnips, carrots, and onions—creating a sweet, burnished-onion flavor counterpointed by peppery aromatics. The pan juices are thinned a bit to moisten the steamed bulgur, then the ingredients are layered and baked in the oven with a swirl of fresh olive oil, until all the moisture has been absorbed and the top is crusty and brown. The dish is then served with a topping of chopped parsley and finely sliced marinated green chiles.

SERVES 4 AS A MAIN DISH

⅓ cup chickpeas

1 cup coarse-grain bulgur

3 tablespoons extra virgin olive oil

¾ pound boned lamb shoulder chops, divided into 12 pieces

1 tablespoon tomato paste

1 cup minced onion

3 garlic cloves, finely minced

3 to 4 teaspoons *harissa, harous,* or *harissa-harous* (pages 309 and 310), or substitute Turkish pepper paste

1 teaspoon ground coriander or *le tabil* (page 201)

4 white turnips, cut into 1-inch dice

4 small carrots, cut into 1-inch pieces

Salt and freshly ground pepper

⅓ head of green cabbage, quartered

2 pickled hot green chiles, thinly sliced

2 tablespoons chopped flat-leaf parsley

1. Soak the dried chickpeas overnight in water to cover by at least 2 inches.

2. About 2 hours before serving, moisten the bulgur in a sieve under running water; drain and toss with 1 tablespoon of the olive oil. Fill a couscous cooker or large pot with plenty of water and bring to a boil. Place the perforated couscous container or a snug-fitting colander on top, add the grain, cover, and steam for 1 hour, or until almost tender and airy. From time to time, fluff the grain with a fork for even cooking.

3. Meanwhile, in a heavy-bottomed saucepan just large enough to hold the meat, onions, and vegetables snugly, place 1 tablespoon of the olive oil, the meat, tomato paste, onion, garlic, harissa, coriander, turnips, carrots, drained chickpeas, and salt and pepper; mix well. Spread the cabbage leaves on top, lay a crumpled piece of wet parchment paper or foil over the vegetables, cover, and cook over very low heat until the meat and chickpeas are tender, about 1 hour, adding 1 to 2 tablespoons of water as necessary.

4. Preheat the oven to 375°F. Transfer the contents of the saucepan to an 8-inch shallow baking dish. Fold in the steamed bulgur and spread out evenly in the dish. Season with salt and pepper to taste. Drizzle with the remaining 1 tablespoon olive oil and bake until hot, crusty, and brown, about 20 minutes. Scatter the pickled chiles and chopped parsley on top and let stand for 5 more minutes before serving.

With thanks to Houda Mokadmi for sharing this recipe.

Lazy Lady Bulgur Pilaf with Lamb, Walnuts, and Pistachios

*F*or the past dozen years, Filiz Hösukoğlu, from Gaziantep, has been my Turkish translator and good friend. When I asked her to provide something with bulgur for this book, this delicious recipe and accompanying note arrived by e-mail: "This pilaf came about when I was having people over for dinner but didn't have the time to make what I'd intended, *icli kofte,* the Turkish version of *kibbeh.* I had made the filling. Usually my neighbors come over and help me with the molding, but that day no one could come, so I simply made a pilaf and placed the *icli kofte* filling in the center. Everyone loved it! Thus my title for this dish, Lazy Lady's Pilaf."

Serve with a bowl of Yogurt-Cucumber Salad, or storebought good-quality pickled vegetables.

SERVES 4

½ pound ground lamb with some fat, or use more olive oil

2 tablespoons olive oil

1½ teaspoons salt

1 cup chopped onion

⅓ cup pistachios, peeled

¼ cup chopped walnuts

1 teaspoon Aleppo or Turkish red pepper

½ teaspoon ground black pepper

Pinch of ground allspice

½ tablespoon tomato paste

½ tablespoon Turkish red pepper paste (see Mail Order Sources)

1 cup large-grain bulgur

1 tablespoon clarified butter, warmed

Yogurt-Cucumber Salad (recipe follows)

1. To prepare the filling: Place the lamb, olive oil, and ½ teaspoon of the salt in a heavy 3-quart saucepan. Cook, uncovered, over medium-high heat until the meat begins to exude its own moisture. Add the onion, reduce the heat to medium-low, and cook until the liquid is absorbed by the meat and onion. At this point the meat and onion should begin to sauté. Mix in the pistachios, walnuts, Aleppo pepper, black pepper, and allspice. Remove to a side dish. Do not wash out the saucepan.

2. To prepare the pilaf, place 1½ cups water in the same saucepan. Bring to a boil and stir in the tomato paste, Turkish pepper paste, and remaining 1 teaspoon salt. Stir in the bulgur. Bring to a boil, cover, and cook over medium heat for 15 to 16 minutes, or until the bulgur is tender. Stir in the warm clarified butter.

3. Make a well in the bulgur. Spoon in the lamb filling and scrape some of the bulgur on top. Cover tightly and set in a warm place for 15 minutes, or until the bulgur is completely swollen. Use a long fork to stir and fluff the bulgur and filling. Serve with the Yogurt-Cucumber Salad.

Yogurt-Cucumber Salad

MAKES ABOUT 2 CUPS

1 large cucumber, peeled and seeded	2 large garlic cloves, crushed
Salt	3 tablespoons chopped fresh mint or dill
2 cups plain yogurt	1 tablespoon extra virgin olive oil

Dice or grate the cucumber; salt lightly and leave to drain. Rinse and drain the cucumber. Fold the cucumber into the yogurt. Add the garlic and correct the seasoning with salt. Stir in the chopped herbs and dribble a little olive oil on top.

VEGETABLES

———— ✦ ————

I think one of the best things I did for my children when they were growing up was sharing the pleasure of cooking Sunday lunch. Whether it was simple food ("cabbages") or intricate dishes ("kings"), we worked together in the kitchen. They especially liked preparing vegetables—sitting on chairs around the table peeling potatoes, shelling peas, topping and tailing beans, even paring artichokes. Perhaps this is why they have always liked vegetables; I can't recall ever having to admonish them. And, of course, it didn't hurt that we were working with fresh, springy, organic vegetables in season.

The time has come, the Walrus said,
To talk of many things:
Of shoes and ships and sealing wax
Of cabbages and kings

—From Lewis Carroll's
Through the Looking Glass

Since very few vegetables in the Mediterranean repertoire are prepared al dente, slow-cooking is pretty much the norm. One of the best and easiest Mediterranean methods is to slow-simmer vegetables such as carrots, artichokes, cardoons, celery, asparagus, eggplant, leafy greens, zucchini, and tomatoes in olive oil, which produces a warm, sweet, fresh taste and a silken texture. What makes the recipes in this chapter distinctive are the flavor combinations and the textures: these vegetables are not mushy. Good examples are Glazed Carrots with Green Olives and Asparagus Baked in Parchment with Caper Mayonnaise.

Another method of cooking vegetables I particularly like, as old as Mediterranean cooking itself, is baking them in an open earthenware or clay pan, which produces a mellow-textured and true-flavored vegetable. These ceramic casseroles—shallow and either round or oval—are designed to distribute heat evenly while cooking and are beautiful enough to present at the table. They slowly produce toppings and crusts that are glazed, bubbling, or burnished with a meltingly soft interior. Among my favorites are those made with potatoes: Potato Gratin with Dried Plums; Butternut Squash and Potato Pie with Tomato, Mint, and Sheep's Milk Cheese; and Potato and Cabbage Gratin.

Pan-Grilled Asparagus and Oyster Mushrooms with Pancetta and Garlic Puree

Asparagus and mushrooms are particularly good cooked slowly on a heated iron grill, or *a la plancha*—a method that imbues these vegetables with a clean, pure taste and concentrates their flavors. For best results, I cook each vegetable in its own way, arranged side by side on a grill set over two burners, until tender and charred, then combine them just before serving.

I lightly salt half the grill before setting the asparagus on top, and I lightly oil the other half and spread out the mushrooms. When they are almost finished cooking, I add a dab of pancetta and garlic pureed with duck or goose fat to the mushrooms. This flavoring puree comes from southwest France and is best made in advance, as the flavor improves with mellowing. It will keep for up to 2 weeks in the refrigerator and can be used to enhance stews, bean or lentil soups, and any mushroom dish.

As an alternative to the garlic and pancetta puree here, pour some browned butter over the mushrooms and top the asparagus with shavings of Parmigiano-Reggiano.

SERVES 4

12 thick asparagus spears

Extra virgin olive oil

Coarse sea salt

¾ pound meaty oyster mushrooms

1 tablespoon Pancetta and Garlic Puree (recipe follows)

A few drops of lemon juice

3 tablespoons chopped flat-leaf parsley

1. Trim the thick stalk ends of each asparagus. Slowly heat a large iron plancha or skillet until very hot; sprinkle it with coarse salt. Lightly brush each asparagus spear with olive oil and cook until charred on one side. Turn each spear over and continue cooking until tender, about 12 minutes total.

2. Meanwhile, wipe the mushrooms with a damp cloth and trim off any hard parts. If there is room on the plancha, lightly brush with oil; add the mushrooms with a drop of oil and cook them, side by side with the asparagus, until nicely browned and tender. If not, separately cook the mushrooms in a heated heavy skillet.

(continued)

Vegetables

3. Add the garlic and pancetta puree to the mushrooms, toss, and cook 1 more minute. Scrape the asparagus onto a shallow serving plate and sprinkle with lemon juice to taste. Add the mushrooms and mix gently. Sprinkle the parsley on top and serve at once.

Pancetta and Garlic Puree

Use 1 to 2 tablespoons of this captivating puree to flavor pork or veal stews, soups, beans, and mushroom dishes.

MAKES ABOUT ¼ CUP

6 large garlic cloves, unpeeled

Salt and freshly ground pepper

2 tablespoons finely chopped lean pancetta

2 tablespoons duck or goose fat

1. Boil the garlic cloves in their skins for 20 minutes; drain dry, let cool, then peel.

2. In a food processor, puree the garlic cloves with a pinch of salt and pepper, the pancetta, and the duck or goose fat. Pack into a small jar with a tight lid. Keep and use within 2 weeks.

Inspired by a recipe in Jean-Paul Malaurie's Ma cuisine des quatre saisons en Périgord.

Asparagus Baked in Parchment with Caper Mayonnaise

"You can never be too thin"—we've all heard that too many times! And though it may be true applied to humans, I don't think it applies well to green asparagus. Thin spears are best for omelets, simple steaming, and dipping in coddled eggs, but I find that the fatter, purple-tipped spears, or green knobby ones, work best in more complex recipes, including this Spanish *confitado* of asparagus.

The problem with thick asparagus is that often the tips of the stalks are done while the centers are not, or, conversely, the centers are toothsome while the tips are overcooked.

Spanish chef Carlos Posadas, of the Amparo restaurant in Madrid, taught me a novel way of slow-cooking the thick spears for 1½ to 2 hours in olive oil inside an ovenproof parchment pouch. When finished, the spears are still green and evenly cooked end to end—fat, succulent, juicy, and delicious.

Chef Posadas serves his slow-cooked asparagus accompanied by mashed potatoes topped with slices of a Parmesan-like cheese. I serve my version smothered with caper-flecked mayonnaise.

SERVES 2 TO 4

18 to 24 thick asparagus spears	1 long sprig of tarragon
⅓ cup extra virgin olive oil	12 salted capers
½ teaspoon sea salt	2 tablespoons mayonnaise
¼ teaspoon sugar	2 tablespoons heavy cream

1. Preheat the oven to 175°F. Spread a 2-foot-long sheet of parchment paper on a large baking sheet. Arrange the asparagus spears in a neat, single layer on the parchment. Drizzle the olive oil over the asparagus. Season with the salt and sugar. Top with the tarragon sprig. Fold the paper over the spears and tuck the ends under themselves to form a tight package; secure the package with kitchen string.

2. Bake the asparagus for 1½ to 2 hours, or until the spears feel tender when pressed through the parchment.

3. Meanwhile, soak the capers in water for 1 to 2 hours. Pat dry and coarsely chop. In a small bowl, blend the mayonnaise, heavy cream, and chopped capers; season the sauce with salt.

4. When the asparagus is cooked, carefully cut the parchment paper open and transfer the asparagus to a platter. Mix any cooking juices into the sauce, pour over the asparagus, and serve warm.

Ragout of Artichokes with Wine and Herbs

During the 1970s, the "Queen of Artichokes" in France was a young woman chef named Dominique Versini Nahmias, known simply as Olympe. Recently, while surfing the net, I discovered that Salinas, California, celebrated its first artichoke festival in 1948. And who was the first "artichoke queen" in this country? It was Marilyn Monroe. I don't know whether MM really liked artichokes, but I think if she'd tasted this dish, she would have found it memorable and royal.

Here is Olympe's recipe for a rich, lush ragout of artichoke bottoms cooked in a combination of red and white wine and flavored with orange peel, diced pancetta, and chives. The bottoms are served in the remaining pan juices cooked down to a syrupy sauce, with a dash of olive oil added to make it shine.

What I especially like about Dominique's method of cooking artichokes is that I can leave them to cook slowly by themselves over very low heat, with a crumpled wet piece of parchment paper placed over them, and the pan covered with a tight-fitting lid. As they cook, they slowly soak in the liquid and turn plump, silky, and succulent. Over the years, this method has never let me down.

SERVES 4 AS A FIRST COURSE

16 small or 8 medium artichokes (about 1½ pounds)

1 lemon, halved

4½ tablespoons extra virgin olive oil

2 tablespoons thinly sliced scallions

½ cup chopped onion

½ cup finely diced carrot

½ cup diced pancetta (2½ to 3 ounces)

1 tablespoon chopped garlic

½ teaspoon grated orange zest

3 tablespoons coarsely chopped flat-leaf parsley

2 sprigs of thyme

1 imported bay leaf

Salt and freshly ground pepper

½ teaspoon sugar

1 cup dry red wine

½ cup dry white wine

2 tablespoons minced fresh chives

1. Break off and discard the tough outer leaves of each artichoke, then break off the stems. This will remove the stringy parts of the bottom, which are tough. Rub the cut surfaces with the lemon halves. Trim away the rough areas around the stem and any tough, fibrous parts of the leaves. Cut larger artichokes in half; scoop out and discard the fuzzy chokes. Squeeze lemon juice into a bowl of water and add the artichoke pieces.

2. In a medium nonreactive skillet, heat 4 tablespoons of the olive oil over medium heat. Add the scallions, onion, and carrot and cook until glazed, about 1 minute. Add the pancetta and cook for 1 minute longer, or until lightly brown. Drain the artichokes, pat dry, and add them to the skillet along with the garlic, orange zest, parsley, thyme, bay leaf, and salt and pepper, tossing to coat the ingredients with the fat in the pan. Bring to a boil, cover, and cook for 5 minutes.

3. Add the sugar, red wine, and white wine and reduce the heat to a slow simmer. Cover and cook for about 20 minutes, or until the artichokes are tender. Remove from the heat and without uncovering the lid, let the artichokes cool down slowly.

4. Transfer the artichokes and aromatics to a serving dish. Remove and discard the bay leaf. Boil the pan juices until reduced to a thick syrupy sauce, about 3 tablespoons. Correct the seasoning with salt and pepper and add the remaining ½ tablespoon olive oil. Pour the sauce over the artichokes. Sprinkle with the chives and serve warm or cool.

DOMINIQUE, THE QUEEN OF ARTICHOKES

In 1978 I had the pleasure of working with Dominique Nahmias in Paris, Boston, and New York. We shared a great love for "women's cooking"—slow, easy, and traditional.

Short, with jet black hair cut straight across her forehead in bangs, Dominique had an oriental look about her eyes. Her kitchen garb at the time was extraordinary: white T-shirt, white slacks and apron, and, to my astonishment, black high-heeled shoes.

Dominique was open, refreshing, and direct. "I cook by instinct," she told me. "I don't make stocks; they're just restraints. Without a stock I force myself to face my food without a crutch. Difficult dishes are devised by chefs to justify their importance. If a dish takes four hours to cook, I want it to cook on its own. I'd rather use the time to take a walk than to have to tend a dish standing at the stove."

Artichoke Bottoms Stuffed with Oeufs Mollets

I collect cookbooks in all languages. (As for how I'm going to read them, I worry about that afterward!) Some years ago, I bought a midcentury French cookbook at a secondhand bookstore in Bordeaux. It was larded with clippings, recipes from old newspapers. One, dated 1948, was this recipe for artichoke bottoms stuffed with eggs, cooked so that the yolks are runny and the whites completely surrounding them are firm, topped with a flowing mayonnaise scented with tarragon and dotted with capers. The writer described it as "exquisite for summer." Here is my version. It makes a marvelous lunch or brunch dish or a substantial first course.

SERVES 4

4 eggs

⅓ cup plus 1 tablespoon extra virgin olive oil

1 large bunch of flat-leaf parsley

Coarse salt

4 globe artichokes

½ cup mayonnaise

⅓ cup milk

2 teaspoons small Spanish capers, rinsed and drained

1 tablespoon chopped fresh tarragon

Salt and freshly ground pepper

1. Bring the eggs to room temperature. Meanwhile, combine 1 quart water, ⅓ cup of the olive oil, all the parsley, and 1 tablespoon coarse salt in a deep saucepan. Slowly heat to simmering.

2. One at a time, clean the artichokes: Break off the stem and trim to make a flat bottom. Switch to a melon baller to scoop out the choke, then scrape along the inside walls of the vegetable. Remove the hard leaves by snapping them back, trimming the leaves straight across, then smoothing out the whole bottom with a small knife. Drop into the simmering water. Repeat with the remaining artichokes. Cover and simmer until the artichoke bottoms are *almost* tender. Remove the pan from the heat; let the artichokes finish cooking in the receding heat.

3. Prepare the mayonnaise dressing. Thin the mayonnaise with milk, stirring until smooth. Add the capers and tarragon and let stand until ready to serve. Taste for salt and pepper.

4. Make the *oeufs mollets* as directed on page 242.

5. To serve, gently reheat the artichoke bottoms in the cooking liquid; drain. Pat the artichokes dry with paper towels. Place each one on an individual serving plate and season with salt and pepper. Reheat the eggs for an instant in hot water, remove the shells or the plastic wrappings, and place 1 egg in each artichoke hollow. Spoon some of the mayonnaise on top of each egg. Serve at once.

Note: Artichokes are a nuisance to clean; there's really no easy way. I did, however, recently learn a new way to cook them: poaching them in heavily "parsleyed" water along with olive oil and a pinch of salt, but *no* lemon juice. The artichoke bottoms maintain color and flavor, without that peculiar tinny taste they acquire when soaked and rubbed with lemon juice. (This cooking method also works for cardoons.) The artichokes are stored in the cooking liquid until ready to serve. (Cooked artichoke bottoms won't keep long, so it's best to consume them within a few hours.)

OEUFS MOLLETS

An ideal medium-cooked egg or *oeuf mollet* should have a runny yolk with firm white completely surrounding it. An oeuf mollet is not the same as a poached egg. Here are two methods, both of which work perfectly. Be sure to use very fresh large eggs.

1. Allow the eggs to attain room temperature. Gently slip them in their shells, one by one, into slowly boiling, lightly vinegared water. Immediately remove from the heat, cover, and let stand 5 or 6 minutes. Transfer the eggs to ice water to quickly cool down. One by one, drain, gently roll on a hard surface to crackle the shell, then peel, beginning at the larger side of the egg. Dip occasionally into cool water to facilitate peeling.

2. I learned the second method from Basque chef Carlos Posadas of the Madrid restaurant Amparo. Carlos lines a small ramekin with plastic wrap, then drops in a bit of olive oil. He cracks a large egg into the lined ramekin and seasons it with a pinch each of salt and pepper. Then he pulls up the plastic wrap around the egg so that the white encloses the yolk. After removing as much air as possible, he fastens it shut with a plastic tie, creating a hobo-shaped package. The plastic-wrapped eggs are poached in simmering water for 7 minutes, after which he drops them into a bowl of ice water to firm them up. When ready to serve, he reheats the egg for an instant in hot water, removes the plastic wrap, and sets the egg on the plate, or artichoke bottom, as detailed in the preceding recipe on page 240.

Glazed Carrots with Green Olives

*I*nspired by a homey recipe in Guy Gedda's wonderful Provençal cookbook, *La table d'un Provençal,* I decided to create a slow-cooker version. Here winter carrots, cut into thick strips, are slow-cooked in their own moisture until swollen, succulent, and flavorful. The vivid taste of the carrots, the aroma of the olives, and the pungency of the thyme makes this a great accompaniment to meat or poultry.

SERVES 4

1 pound large organic carrots

2 tablespoons butter or olive oil

3 ounces picholine olives (about 24)

1 large garlic clove, sliced

1 tablespoon chopped flat-leaf parsley

2 sprigs of thyme

Salt and freshly ground pepper

3 tablespoons heavy cream

1. Peel the carrots, cut in half crosswise, quarter the thicker ends lengthwise, and halve the thinner ends. Place in an electric slow-cooker or a heavy skillet wide enough to hold the carrots in one layer.

2. Add half the butter, cover the slow-cooker, set the heat to high, and cook, stirring once, for 2 to 3 hours, or until very tender. If substituting a skillet on top of the stove, set on a heat diffuser over very low heat. Add a few tablespoons water, cover with a round of parchment paper and a tight-fitting lid, and cook until very tender, about 1 hour.

3. Drain the carrots on paper towels and let rest. Meanwhile, pit the olives by gently tapping each one with a wooden mallet, halve, remove the pit, rinse, and drain.

4. About 10 minutes before serving, melt the remaining butter in a medium skillet over moderate heat. Add the garlic and parsley and cook, stirring, for 1 minute. Add the carrots, thyme, olives, and salt and pepper. Cook, stirring, until glazed. Pour in the cream, cover, and reduce the heat to low. Cook for 5 minutes and serve.

Oven-Baked Cauliflower with Yogurt-Garlic Sauce

*H*ere is my own personal version of the Turkish classic *yogurtlu kanibahar,* traditionally made by frying thickly battered cauliflowerets in lots of olive oil, then serving them with a yogurt-garlic sauce as a dip. In my version, the cauliflower is first blanched, then chilled, and finally baked in just enough batter to adhere until sufficiently crisp to hold in one's fingers. Dipping hot cauliflorets in a cool sauce is a real treat.

Try this dish as a side with the pomegranate-glazed leg of lamb on page 206.

SERVES 4

1 cauliflower

2 tablespoons white vinegar

1 cup plain yogurt

½ teaspoon crushed garlic

Salt

3 large eggs

6 ounces aged sheep's milk cheese such as kasseri or manchego, coarsely grated (about 1½ cups)

Juice of ½ lemon

Freshly ground pepper

1 tablespoon chopped flat-leaf parsley

1 tablespoon bread crumbs

2 tablespoons extra virgin olive oil

1. Soak the cauliflower in vinegared water for 5 minutes; rinse and drain. Steam whole until barely tender, 7 to 9 minutes. Drain well on kitchen towels. Chill in the refrigerator, then cut into florets with ½ inch of the stem attached. Arrange in a single layer in an oiled shallow baking dish.

2. At least 1 hour before serving, combine the yogurt, garlic, and salt to taste in a small bowl: mix well. Let the yogurt sauce stand at room temperature.

3. About 35 minutes before serving, transfer an oven rack to the upper shelf and preheat the oven to 425°F.

4. In a mixing bowl, beat the eggs until well combined. Whisk in the cheese, lemon juice, pepper, and parsley. Spread the cheese mixture over each caulifloweret; sprinkle with the bread crumbs and drizzle of the olive oil on top. Bake until golden brown, about 20 minutes. Serve hot with the yogurt-garlic sauce.

Casserole of Black-Eyed Peas with Fennel and Tomatoes

This rustic, earthy dish comes from the island of Crete, where the combination of black-eyed peas and fennel is as popular as apple pie and Cheddar cheese in the United States. It's one of those wonderful culinary marriages in which each ingredient makes the other taste better.

Fennel benefits greatly from slow-cooking, developing flavor as it loses moisture. To simulate the flavor of wild fennel (which is what the Greeks use), add a pinch of bruised fennel seeds to the cultivated market fennel.

SERVES 4

1 package (10 ounces) frozen black-eyed peas, thawed

2 tablespoons extra virgin olive oil, plus a few teaspoons for garnish

1 medium fennel bulb, halved, cored, and sliced paper thin (about 1½ cups)

½ cup finely chopped onion

Tiny pinch of fennel seeds, bruised

4 Swiss chard leaves, stemmed and finely shredded

½ cup diced tomatoes

Salt and freshly ground pepper

1. In a large, heavy saucepan of boiling water, cook the black-eyed peas until just tender, about 10 minutes. Drain, shaking out any excess water.

2. Wipe out the saucepan and heat the 2 tablespoons olive oil with the fennel, onion, and bruised fennel seeds. Cook until soft and pale golden, about 15 minutes. Stir in the chard, black-eyed peas, tomatoes, and ¾ cup water. Season with salt and pepper. Cook, uncovered, over medium-low heat for 20 more minutes. Serve warm or cool with a drizzle of olive oil.

Note: To substitute dried black-eyed peas: Soak the peas according to package directions. Drain and cook in fresh water to cover until almost tender, just under 1 hour. Drain the peas and add them to the saucepan about 10 minutes after adding the chard and tomatoes.

Eggplant Sautéed with Zucchini and Quince Tarhana

*H*ere's a savory vegetable sauté followed by a slow gentle simmering that develops late summer vegetables such as zucchini, eggplant, and squash into a meltingly tender mélange that is irresistible and delicious. It doesn't look like much because the colors wash out, but the vitality of the dish comes from the flavor of the very special quince-flavored *tarhana,* a kind of Turkish pasta.

SERVES 4

2 thin Italian eggplants, 1¼ pounds

Coarse salt

¾ cup Quince-Flavored Tarhana (page 318)

½ cup extra virgin olive oil

1 medium onion, chopped

1 small butternut squash, peeled and cut into 1½-inch chunks, or 1 large Yukon Gold potato, peeled and quartered

2 pale green zucchini, about ½ pound, trimmed and cut into 1½-inch lengths

1 red ripe tomato, grated

½ cup chopped flat-leaf parsley

1 imported bay leaf

1 small dried hot red pepper

Freshly ground black pepper

Brined sheep's milk cheese, such as Turkish peynir beyaz or feta, crumbled, as accompaniment

1. Peel the eggplants and cut into 1-inch lengths. Soak them for 30 minutes in salted water to remove any bitterness.

2. Meanwhile, soak the tarhana in 1½ cups water to soften, 10 minutes. Drain, squeeze out the moisture, and place in a small saucepan. Add fresh water to cover and simmer for 15 minutes. Drain and set aside.

3. Drain the eggplant, squeeze gently to remove as much moisture as possible, and pat dry. Heat the olive oil in a large sauté pan over medium heat. Add the onion and cook until golden and softened. Add the eggplant and sauté until golden on both sides, about 3 minutes. Add the squash and maintain sufficient heat to seal all sides and create some caramelization around the edges, about 5 more minutes. Tilt the pan and remove the excess oil. Reduce the heat, add ½ cup water, and cook, stirring occasionally, for 5 minutes.

4. Add the zucchini, grated tomato, parsley, bay leaf, hot pepper, and, if dry, ¼ cup water. Cook over medium heat, stirring now and then, for 10 more minutes.

5. Reduce the heat to low, sprinkle the cooked tarhana evenly on top, cover, and continue cooking for 15 minutes without stirring. Discard the hot pepper and bay leaf. Season with salt to taste. Remove the skillet from the heat and let stand, covered, for 30 minutes. Serve warm or cold with a sprinkling of freshly ground black pepper. Pass a bowl of brined white cheese on the side.

With thanks to Mirsini Lambraki for inspiring this recipe.

Skillet-Braised Endives

When I lived in Paris, I used to market on Rue Monge. A vegetable vendor, who insisted upon calling me "mademoiselle" despite my obvious state of pregnancy, gave me a litany of advice on perfect endive cookery. I've always followed his rules and added to them over the years:

◆ Never soak endives in water. In fact, you don't even need to wash them if they've been sold in individual blue paper wrappers. Simply remove all damaged leaves, then rinse quickly.

◆ Never leave raw endives sitting in a sunny spot lest their leaves oxidize (turn greenish). Remove all green leaves before using.

◆ Don't add liquid to the pan unless absolutely necessary. Endives have sufficient moisture, which they will slowly release as they cook.

◆ The slower the cooking, the sweeter the endives. Slow-cooking allows endives to produce their own steam, then cook in it. In fact, you can cook endives over the warm electric stove setting for up to three hours, and they will be even more delicious than usual.

◆ Always remove the little hard center in the core. (I do this with the tip of a swivel-bladed vegetable peeler.)

◆ Endives should be browned ever so slightly at the end as they begin to caramelize. This dish goes well with grilled or braised chicken or duck and with roast pork.

SERVES 4

8 plump Belgian endives

2 tablespoons unsalted butter

Pinch of salt

Pinch of sugar

1 to 2 teaspoons strained lemon juice or Banyuls wine vinegar (see Mail Order Sources)

Salt and freshly ground pepper

1. With a vegetable peeler or a small paring knife shave the root end of each endive. Hollow out the hard center, drilling up about ¼ inch. Rinse under running water; drain and pat dry. Put the butter in a heavy saucepan or deep skillet *almost* large enough to accommodate the endives in a single layer. Add the salt and sugar and the endives. Wet a sheet of parchment paper and place directly over the endives. Cover the pan and cook over very low heat for 15 minutes. (Steaming will make the endives shrink to one layer.) Rearrange the endives, cover, and cook for 30 more minutes.

2. Carefully turn each endive over with a small spatula to avoid spoiling its shape. Continue cooking, covered, for another 30 minutes. Be careful not to burn the endives; if necessary, add spoonfuls of water or stock from time to time. The endives are done when they are very soft and lightly caramelized on all sides.

3. About 5 minutes before serving, sprinkle the endives with lemon juice or vinegar. If necessary, increase the heat to reduce the pan juices to a syrupy sauce, taste for salt and pepper, and pour over the endives. Serve hot.

Note: The same method may be applied to artichokes, cardoons, celery stalks, celery root, fat green beans, and leeks (see page 54), all of which will taste delicious when slow-cooked.

Swiss Chard with Lentils and Preserved Spiced Meat

*H*ere's a humble home winter dish you'll never find in a tourist-oriented Moroccan restaurant, though you might find it in a Moroccan workingman's café, or sold off a stand in the Djemaa el Fna in Marrakech.

It employs *khelea,* a form of preserved meat used throughout the Maghreb as a condiment. Cubes of preserved lamb or beef add bursts of flavor to numerous North African winter dishes.

Velvet-textured cooked Swiss chard goes beautifully with the spicy meat and brown lentils. This trio makes for a delicious rendition of lentils and greens, a dish you'll find prepared in numerous ways around the Mediterranean.

Khelea can be salty, so be sure to wash it well. In some parts of northern Morocco, especially in the Rif mountains where they prefer it salty, a handful of young borage leaves, believed to have diuretic properties, is added to this dish.

MAKES ABOUT 6 CUPS

10 pieces preserved meat (½ recipe khelea; page 316)

1½ cups (½ pound) small brown lentils, preferably Spanish pardina (see Mail Order Sources)

¾ pound large Swiss chard leaves, leaves shredded, ribs peeled and diced

3 medium red onions, diced

2 large garlic cloves, crushed

Sea salt

1 tablespoon Moroccan Mixed Spices (page 313)

½ cup chopped tomatoes

½ cup chopped cilantro

¼ cup chopped flat-leaf parsley

Freshly ground pepper

Fresh lemon juice

1. Remove the preserved meat from the refrigerator. Scrape off the fat and reserve 2 tablespoons. (Save the remaining khelea and fat for Moroccan couscous, dried bean dishes, or sautéed potatoes.) Rinse the meat under running water to remove the excess salt; shred coarsely and soak in fresh water until ready to use.

2. Pick over and wash the lentils. Put them in a 3- or 4-quart saucepan, cover with water, and bring them slowly to a full boil, skimming; drain. Cover the lentils with 1 quart of cold fresh water and return to a boil. Add the chard leaves and ribs to the lentils. Reduce the heat and simmer for 20 minutes.

3. Meanwhile, heat the reserved 2 tablespoons fat in a large straight-sided skillet over medium heat. Add the red onions and cook until golden brown, about 10 minutes. Add the garlic, a pinch of salt, and the Moroccan spices and cook for 2 minutes longer. Drain the meat and add to the skillet. Stir in the chopped tomatoes and half the chopped cilantro and parsley. Continue to cook, covered, until the lentils are tender, about 20 minutes. (If necessary, add a few tablespoons water to keep the mixture moist.)

4. Add the contents of the skillet to the saucepan; bring to a boil, cover, and cook over medium-low heat until the lentils are tender, 10 to 20 minutes, depending upon the quality of the lentils. Remove from the heat and let the lentils rest, covered, for 15 minutes. Adjust the seasoning with salt, pepper, and lemon juice. Garnish with the remaining cilantro and parsley.

Slow-Baked Treviso-Style Radicchio

*H*ere's a simple bitter vegetable to serve alongside the sweet wine-cooked leg of lamb on page 204.

Avoid any radicchio that is turning green, a sure sign of oxidation. Store treviso wrapped in paper towels in the refrigerator until ready to cook. Like most winter vegetables, freshly harvested treviso will keep well in the crisper for up to two weeks.

Nibble on a leaf—if it seems too bitter, try soaking the heads in fresh cold water for 10 minutes.

SERVES 3 TO 6

6 heads of radicchio, preferably treviso

Extra virgin olive oil

Herbes de Provence, for sprinkling

Salt and freshly ground pepper

Balsamic vinegar, for drizzling

1. Preheat the oven to 300°F. Cut the radicchio lengthwise into halves or quarters, depending on their thickness. Brush lightly with oil and fry quickly on both sides until very dark and crisp on the outside and wilting and tender within, about 3 minutes.

2. Place the radicchio in a baking pan and sprinkle with herbs and salt and pepper. Cover and bake for 30 minutes longer. Transfer to a platter, drizzle very lightly with balsamic vinegar, and serve.

Slow-Roasted Stuffed Tomatoes

We've all seen lots of recipes for slow-roasted stuffed and unstuffed tomatoes. This one, based on an old way of preparing stuffed tomatoes in the receding heat of the baker's oven, is a little different and results in an especially sensual texture. Once again, slow-cooking increases flavor intensity. Here the stuffed tomatoes are left to finish cooking in the receding heat of a turned-off oven, ensuring that any remaining moisture is fully absorbed by the stuffing and that the tomatoes do not collapse.

SERVES 4

8 medium red ripe tomatoes

Coarse sea salt

2 teaspoons minced garlic

½ cup coarsely chopped flat-leaf parsley

¼ cup coarse fresh bread crumbs

Extra virgin olive oil

1. Core the tomatoes, cut in half horizontally, and squeeze each half gently over the sink to extract as many seeds as possible. Cut out the insides and reserve for Step 3. Sprinkle about ¼ teaspoon salt over each tomato half, turn them upside down on paper towels on a rack, and leave to drain for 30 minutes.

2. Preheat the oven to 300°F. Gently squeeze the tomatoes again to rid them of any excess moisture. Lightly oil a shallow baking dish large enough to hold all the tomato halves in one layer. Add the tomatoes, cut sides up, and bake, uncovered, for 2½ hours.

3. Chop the reserved insides of the tomatoes. Mix with the garlic, parsley, and bread crumbs. Divide into 8 equal parts. Remove the tomatoes from the oven and place one portion into each tomato, pressing down lightly with the back of spoon.

4. Drizzle about 1 teaspoon olive oil over each tomato and return to the oven for 20 more minutes. Turn off the heat but leave the tomatoes in the oven until serving time.

Inspired by a recipe in Bernard Loubat and Jeannette Bertrandy's La bonne cuisine Provençale.

Spaghetti with Oven-Roasted Tomatoes and Bottarga Shavings

*H*ere's a truly outstanding sauce for spaghetti. Slow-roasting halved cherry tomatoes brings out their sweetness and intensifies their flavor. The resulting sweetened, blistered, and charred tomatoes are especially delicious when combined with pungent shavings of Sardinian caviar.

SERVES 4 AS A FIRST COURSE

1 pint cherry tomatoes (about 10 ounces)

Extra virgin olive oil

2 garlic cloves, sliced

Pinch of sugar

1 bay leaf

Salt and freshly ground pepper

2 ounces Sardinian caviar (*bottarga di muggine*; page 7)

¼ teaspoon grated lemon zest

¾ pound spaghetti

1. Preheat the oven to 300°F. While the oven is heating, cut each tomato in half and arrange cut side up in an oiled 10-inch flameproof baking dish, preferably a cazuela. Add the garlic, sugar, and bay leaf and season lightly with salt and pepper. Bake for 1 hour, or until the tomatoes are lightly caramelized.

2. Grate the bottarga on the coarsest side of a four-sided grater or on a flat shredder. Toss with the lemon zest and ½ teaspoon freshly ground pepper. Soak the bottarga in a few tablespoons olive oil to keep it moist and soft.

3. Cook the spaghetti in boiling salted water until *almost* tender. Drain, reserving 2 tablespoons of the pasta cooking water.

4. Place a flameproof baking dish with the tomatoes over medium heat. Add the reserved pasta water and the spaghetti to the dish. Fold in the bottarga and continue cooking over medium heat for 1 minute. Divide among 4 warmed serving plates and serve at once with more olive oil.

Mallorquín Casserole of Eggplant, Peppers, Sardines, and Potatoes with Caramelized Tomatoes

*L*ate last summer I finally tasted the famous Majorcan dish *tumbet*. Tumbet, which literally means "flattened," is an uncomplicated, oven-baked casserole of fried eggplant, peppers, and potatoes, topped with a thick, delicious sauce of fried ripe caramelized tomatoes and sometimes garnished with pieces of fish. It's a bit like a Provençal ratatouille without the herbs, a Tunisian *chachouka* without the harissa, Sicilian caponata without the capers and olives, despite which it isn't missing anything. For me it's just about perfect!

Tumbet travels well, meaning you can make it just about anywhere in the world provided you use vegetables in peak seasonal condition. First and foremost, you need a good extra virgin olive oil for frying, as it's this component that coaxes flavor from the vegetables. The secret of a good tumbet is to cook the ingredients separately, then combine them at the end for baking.

Some food writers say you don't need to salt eggplant before frying. I disagree. I will never stop salting Mediterranean eggplants. Many of the new eggplant hybrids that don't require salting to remove bitterness have very little taste: ironically, they still need salting, not to rid them of bitterness but to bring out some flavor. Also, salting tightens the flesh of eggplant so it won't absorb as much oil during frying. Finally, salting helps to create a good creamy texture.

The peppers used in tumbet should be sweet rather than hot, and, preferably, thin-skinned, the kind you find at farmers' markets in late summer. I use late-summer New Mexican chile peppers that have turned red, sweet, and delicious. Another choice would be pale green frying peppers sold in late summer at farmstands.

The potatoes are only partially cooked to avoid hardening, then finished off in the final baking. The tomatoes are fried until their natural sugars create caramelization.

Tumbet often accompanies grilled or roasted meat or fish, but I also serve it warm or at room temperature as a course unto itself, with the addition of fried fish baked right into the layering.

(continued)

A final note: Back in the 1980s, Juan Martinez Rivas, a well-known landscape painter and gourmet from Mallorca, was interviewed on Spanish television about tumbet, his favorite dish. He made the astonishing comment that the very best rendition he had ever tasted was served in the home of a Basque friend who lived in California, where it was prepared by a Chinese chef. As I said, this is a dish that can really travel.

SERVES 4 TO 6

2 Italian eggplants, 1¼ pounds each

Coarse salt

1½ pounds New Mexican sweet red peppers, or sweet pale-green frying peppers, cored, seeded, and thinly sliced into rings

Extra virgin olive oil

1 pound ripe fresh tomatoes, cored and quartered

¼ cup garlic cloves, left unpeeled, rinsed and drained, plus 1 garlic clove, minced

1½ pounds red potatoes, peeled and sliced ¼ inch thick

2 cans (4 ounces each) top-quality oil-packed whole sardines

2 teaspoons finely chopped flat-leaf parsley

2 tablespoons flour, for dusting

Salt and freshly ground pepper

¼ teaspoon sugar

1. Peel the eggplant and cut into ½-inch slices. Salt each slice, placing the layers in a nonreactive colander or on a plate. Cover and let drain as long as possible, anywhere from 30 minutes to overnight.

2. Preheat the oven to 375°F. Put the peppers on a baking sheet lined with parchment paper. Sprinkle with a little oil, toss to coat, then spread them out on half the baking sheet. Pile the tomatoes and whole garlic cloves in their skins on the other half of the baking sheet and lightly sprinkle them with olive oil. Bake for 15 minutes.

3. While the peppers are baking, put the potatoes on a second baking sheet lined with parchment paper and toss with a little olive oil; spread the slices in a single layer. Bake the potatoes along with the peppers for another 30 minutes, until almost tender but not brown.

4. Meanwhile, drain the sardines and divide them into fillets, removing the bones. Arrange in a 5- to 6-cup shallow ovenproof dish. Sprinkle with 1 to 2 tablespoons fresh olive oil, the chopped garlic, and half the parsley. Let marinate while you fry the eggplant.

5. Rinse the eggplant slices, squeeze gently to remove the moisture, and pat dry with paper towels. Heat enough oil to cover the bottom of a large skillet over medium-high heat until it quickly browns a piece of bread. Working in small batches, and reheating the oil between batches, fry the eggplant slices on both sides until golden brown. Drain on paper towels.

6. Remove the sardines from the baking dish, leaving the marinade behind. Dust the fillets with flour and fry in the remaining oil until crispy. Drain on paper towels.

7. Remove the vegetables from the oven. Leave the heat on. Rub the oily sardine marinade all over the inside of the baking dish. Place the cooked potatoes on the bottom and season with salt and pepper. Top with the eggplant and peppers and season lightly with salt and pepper. Scatter the crispy sardine fillets on top.

8. Add a tablespoon of oil to the skillet and set over medium-high heat. Squeeze the garlic out of the skins and, using a food mill, press the tomatoes and garlic cloves directly into the skillet, add the sugar, salt, and pepper and cook, stirring, until the tomatoes lightly char and reduce to about ½ cup. Dilute with ⅓ cup water, bring to a boil, spread the tomato sauce over the vegetables, scatter the remaining chopped parsley on top, and bake in the oven for 30 minutes.

OKRA

Since I personally adore okra, I've spent years collecting methods of ridding it of the slimy texture a lot of people don't like. Since okra is fairly fragile and breaks easily during cooking, Mediterranean cooks have devised all sorts of ways of handling and preparing it.

One thing all Mediterranean cooks do is use a very sharp, small knife to peel away the thin ring between the cone-shaped stem end and the pointed pod. They also peel the top cone and remove the bottom tip *without piercing the pod itself.* If this is done properly, none of the interior gluey substance will be released. A second tip: whenever you wash okra, be sure to dry it immediately.

In the great gastronomic city of Aleppo in northern Syria, I watched my hostess prepare a dish of stewed okra and meat. She had sliced her okra into ½-inch lengths the day before, then set the pieces out to dry on a towel. Overnight the cut sides had developed a thin seal, which allowed her to stew the vegetable pieces without having to worry about seepage from their interiors.

In other parts of the Levant, I learned other approaches to the problem, including washing okra, drying thoroughly, then leaving the vegetables in a warm place for an hour prior to peeling. I also met cooks who did the reverse—peeled the vegetables, then washed and dried them. Still other cooks stiffened them in a bath of vinegar and water (3 to 4 tablespoons to 2 cups water per pound okra), or dipped the trimmed okra cones in coarse salt before placing them in the sun to dry out for an hour before cooking. Ten minutes in a low oven (not hot enough to cook) will dry okra out equally well.

In northern Morocco, I watched cooks use a needle and thread to tie okra together into a necklace. This way, whenever the cook wanted to stir her sauce, she simply lifted out the necklace, set it carefully aside, then returned it to the pot after stirring, thus relieving herself of the need to stir slowly for fear the okra would break up.

From Patience Gray's *Honey from a Weed,* I learned a method of dealing with large mature okra. "It is best to top and tail them," she writes, "season with salt, pour a little oil over them and leave to marinate for a day; this removes a certain viscosity in older fruits. Then rinse . . ." To which I would add: *dry well before cooking.*

My own preferred method: wash, trim, toss with vinegar (3 tablespoons per pound), let stand for at least half an hour, then rinse and towel dry thoroughly before using.

Stewed Tomatoes with Okra and Potatoes

*I*n this Greek island dish, which makes a very nice accompaniment to grilled fish fillets or shrimp, I fry the okra in olive oil to enhance its flavor and texture

SERVES 2 TO 3

½ pound small, firm whole okra

3 tablespoons white vinegar

⅓ cup extra virgin olive oil

½ cup minced onion

1 teaspoon finely chopped garlic

2 red ripe tomatoes, seeded and grated on a shredder (about 1 cup; see Note)

2 teaspoons tomato paste

½ teaspoon sugar

2 tablespoons chopped flat-leaf parsley or coriander leaves

Salt and freshly ground pepper

3 waxy medium potatoes (¾ pound), peeled and cut into 6 wedges

Lemon wedges

1. Rinse the okra and carefully peel the cone-shaped caps, taking care not to cut into the pod. Toss with the vinegar and let stand for at least 30 minutes. Rinse again and dry on kitchen towels.

2. In a large nonstick skillet, heat the olive oil, add the okra, and quickly brown on all sides. Tilt the skillet to keep the oil while removing the okra to a side dish.

3. In the remaining oil, sauté the onion over moderate heat until soft and golden. Add the garlic, grated tomato, tomato paste, sugar, parsley, ½ cup water, and salt and pepper. Bring to a boil, add the potatoes, and spread the fried okra on top. Cover tightly, lower the heat, and cook until the potatoes are tender and the sauce is thickened, about 30 minutes. Serve with lemon wedges.

Note: To grate tomatoes: Halve and gently squeeze the tomatoes to remove the seeds. Grate the tomato halves, cut side facing the coarsest side of a four-sided grater, or on a flat shredder. You will be left with just the tomato skin in your hand; discard.

Stewed Eggplant Stuffed with Cheese

*I*n summer, southern Italians feast on eggplant. Early in the season, they have the large and small black-skinned varieties, which they sauté, braise, bake, fry, stuff, and gratinée. In August, when the smaller, lavender-colored Tunisian variety, *rosa bianca,* comes into the market, it's time for *mulanciane muttunate*—literally "small eggplants that have been massaged"—rolled on the counter until their interiors are softened. They are stuffed with cheese, garlic, and herbs inserted through slits in their surfaces, then simmered in a rich tomato sauce. It's an earthy dish of the countryside, colorful and highly seasoned, based on great, simple ingredients. And *mulanciane muttunate* is extremely forgiving; even if the cheese spurts out, or the eggplant and the cheese don't totally meld, the dish is still delicious.

Anna Tasca Lanza, owner of the Regaleali Cooking School in Sicily, told me that in her family, this dish was called "eggplant with buttons" and was only served on Thursdays, "because that was our *monzu's* day off." A monzu, she explained, was the Sicilian word for the family chef, a corruption of the French *monsieur.* Monzus were men trained in the tradition of French haute cuisine, integral to Sicilian aristocratic life since the time of Bourbon rule.

"Our monzu cooked everything from game pâtés to elaborate timbales," Anna told me, "but never anything so plain as an eggplant. On Thursday, our maid, Angelina, prepared the meals using local in-season ingredients. The main element of Sicilian cooking has always been the sun. Its energy gives Sicilian foods their richness and flavor. You'll find all that in eggplant with buttons. It's my most nostalgic dish."

SERVES 4

2 black or pink, plump or round eggplants
    (¾ pound each)

Coarse salt

1 pound red ripe tomatoes

3 tablespoons extra virgin olive oil

1 medium onion, chopped

8 large garlic cloves, thinly sliced

Fine salt and freshly ground pepper

Pinch of sugar

1 small piece of dried peperoncino or
    ½ teaspoon hot red pepper flakes

5 ounces sharp caciocavallo or provolone
    cheese, sliced ¼ inch thick and cut into
    2-inch pieces

2 tablespoons shredded fresh mint leaves

2 tablespoons shredded fresh basil leaves

2 tablespoons shredded flat-leaf parsley

1. Gently roll each eggplant back and forth on a work surface several times, applying light pressure, to soften the flesh. Cut off the stems. Using a sharp paring knife, make 8 deep 2-inch-long slits in each eggplant, making sure the slits do not meet at any point. Soak the eggplants in cold salted water for at least 1 hour.

2. Halve the tomatoes, squeeze out the seeds, and coarsely chop the flesh. In a large, heavy casserole, gently heat the olive oil. Add the onion, 3 tablespoons water, and half the sliced garlic. Cover and cook over medium heat until the onion is wilted and golden, about 5 minutes. Add the chopped tomatoes, salt, pepper, sugar, and peperoncino, cover, and simmer the sauce for 5 minutes.

3. Meanwhile, drain the eggplants and pat dry. Stuff the cheese and the remaining sliced garlic deep into the slits. Press the eggplants back to their original shape and nestle them into the sauce in the casserole.

4. Sprinkle with half the herbs, lay a sheet of foil or wet parchment paper directly on the eggplant, and cover the pan with a tight-fitting lid. Cook slowly for 30 minutes, then turn each eggplant over; cover and continue cooking over low heat until the eggplants are meltingly tender, about 30 minutes.

5. Carefully transfer the eggplants to a serving dish. If the sauce is too thin, boil rapidly to reduce it to a jammy consistency. Adjust the seasoning with salt, black pepper, and sugar to taste. If desired, strain the sauce. Halve the eggplants crosswise and spoon the sauce on top. Sprinkle with the remaining herbs and serve warm.

Zucchini Stuffed with Lamb and Toasted Chickpeas in Yogurt-Tahini Sauce

This dish, served to me in a home in the small, southern Anatolian town of Kilis on the Turkish-Syrian border, is a quintessential slow-cooked Mediterranean dish: juicy, unctuous, delicious.

When I first ate it, I was especially intrigued by the fact that the outside of the vegetable was soft, while its stuffing remained slightly crunchy. Toasted chickpeas endow the stuffing with a warm, nutty flavor. Toasted chickpeas are available from Middle Eastern and Indian grocers.

This recipe may be prepared in advance, then reheated just before serving.

SERVES 4

½ cup unsalted toasted chickpeas (see Mail Order Sources)

8 small zucchini, about 2½ pounds

Salt and freshly ground pepper

2 tablespoons extra virgin olive oil

1 medium onion, finely chopped

8 ounces lean lamb shoulder, coarsely ground

½ teaspoon ground Middle Eastern Spice Mixture (page 312), or use pinches of ground cinnamon, cloves, and allspice

½ cup finely chopped flat-leaf parsley

2 tablespoons finely chopped jalapeño or other mildly hot green pepper

2 tablespoons tomato paste

3 garlic cloves, sliced

Pinch of sugar

2 to 3 tablespoons fresh lemon juice

Yogurt-Tahini Sauce (recipe follows)

Turkish red pepper or Aleppo pepper

1. Wash the chickpeas and soak in hot water for at least 2 hours. Drain before using.

2. Meanwhile, gently scrub each zucchini. Cut off and reserve ½ inch from the rounded end. Gently roll each zucchini back and forth 4 or 5 times on a work surface to soften. Hollow out the zucchini with a vegetable reamer or an apple corer. Put a pinch of salt and pepper in each zucchini and let stand for at least 1 hour to remove the excess moisture.

3. Wipe the zucchini with paper towels. In a large heavy skillet, fry the zucchini shells in the hot olive oil until lightly browned all over. Drain on paper towels and allow to cool. Set the skillet aside.

4. Reheat the oil in the skillet, add the onion, and cook over medium heat, stirring occasionally, until soft but not brown, about 3 minutes. Increase the heat, add the lamb, and cook until it is no longer pink, about 3 minutes longer. Add ½ teaspoon salt, the spice mixture, and the chickpeas. Cook, stirring, until the chickpeas are nicely glazed, 2 to 3 minutes. Stir in the parsley and jalapeño pepper. Remove the stuffing to a dish. Pour ¼ cup water into the pan and bring to a boil, stirring up any browned bits from the bottom of the pan. Pour over the stuffing. Correct the seasoning and set aside to cool.

5. Stuff the zucchini, using your fingers or a funnel or small spoon. Trim the reserved zucchini ends so they just fit the openings and use them to plug the stuffing in. Pack the stuffed zucchini into a 4- or 5-quart casserole. Dilute the tomato paste with ⅔ cup water and stir until creamy. Pour over the zucchini. Scatter the garlic slices on top and dust with pinches of sugar, salt, and pepper. Place a heavy, inverted plate on top of the zucchini and cover with a lid. Bring to a boil, reduce the heat to low, and simmer gently for 30 minutes. Turn off the heat and let rest for 15 minutes before removing the cover.

6. Add a few tablespoons lemon juice to the pan juices. Serve the zucchini with the yogurt-tahini sauce and a sprinkling of hot pepper.

Yogurt-Tahini Sauce

MAKES ABOUT 2½ CUPS

1 large garlic clove
¼ teaspoon coarse sea salt
1 teaspoon lemon juice

1 tablespoon tahini
3 cups whole-milk yogurt, drained to 2½ cups

Crush the garlic with the salt in a wide heavy bowl. Add the lemon juice, tahini, and a few tablespoons yogurt; crush until smooth. Add the remaining yogurt, stirring well. Wait for 1 hour and correct the salt.

Potato Gratin with Dried Plums

*T*he famous prunes from Agen in southwestern France are large, soft, and moist. American prunes are the same as the Agen variety and can easily be substituted to make this incredibly delicious dish. Prunes are now sold as "dried plums" as part of a campaign to give a "sexier image" to this much maligned, wrinkled fruit. The California Dried Plum Board, which has started off with lots of success, kindly gave me a recipe, which I adapted for this collection.

SERVES 6

2 teaspoons butter or duck fat

3 large garlic cloves, left unpeeled

1 cup whole milk

1 cup pitted prunes (dried plums; about 6 ounces)

3 tablespoons port or sweet red wine

¾ cup heavy cream

½ teaspoon freshly grated nutmeg

2 pounds Yukon Gold potatoes (about 6 medium)

Salt and freshly ground pepper

1. Use a quarter of the butter or duck fat to grease an 2-quart round baking dish. Add the garlic cloves and bake in the oven until soft, about 15 minutes. Set the baking dish aside. Skin and crush the garlic to a paste; blend with the remaining butter or duck fat. Stir in the milk and set aside.

2. Cut the dried plums into small pieces. Place in a food processor, add the port, and process until a paste forms. Add the heavy cream and nutmeg and grind to a saucelike consistency.

3. Preheat the oven to 350°F. Peel and slice the potatoes. Arrange a layer of potatoes in the bottom of the greased baking dish. Season lightly with salt and pepper, spoon a thin layer of the dried plum mixture on top of the potatoes, and continue to build layers, finishing with a layer of potatoes. Season with salt and pepper. Pour the garlic-flavored milk over the potatoes.

4. Bake for 1½ hours, or until the potatoes are tender and most of the liquid has been absorbed. Let stand for 10 minutes before serving.

Golden Potato Gratin

*H*ere is a wonderful French gratin of thin slices of potato smothered with melted cheese. Be sure to use a shallow earthenware pan or cazuela so that the potatoes will cook and brown evenly.

SERVES 4

1 tablespoon unsalted butter

1 pound Yukon Gold or red potatoes

¾ cup milk

1 whole egg

1 egg yolk

2 tablespoons flour

½ teaspoon salt

¼ teaspoon freshly ground pepper

2 to 3 ounces French Chaource, with rind removed, or California teleme, or mozzarella cheese, cut up

1. Preheat the oven to 375°F. Butter a 10- or 12-inch baking-serving dish.

2. Peel the potatoes and cut them into paper-thin (1mm) slices. Rinse the slices in cold water; shake dry. Arrange the potato slices in overlapping rows and cover the dish with foil or a lid. Bake until the potatoes are tender and steamy, about 30 minutes.

3. In a food processor, blend the milk, whole egg, egg yolk, flour, salt, pepper, and cheese until smooth and creamy, about 1 minute. Pour the cheese mixture over the potatoes and bake, uncovered, on the top rack of the oven for 30 minutes. Serve hot.

Potato and Cabbage Gratin

*I*n this superb southwestern French gratin, a base of silky soft leaves of green cabbage are topped with a layer of crusty potatoes plus a second super-thin layer of cheese custard. The whole is baked to a golden brown crust.

SERVES 6

2 pounds green cabbage, quartered

Salt

1 tablespoon plus 1 teaspoon extra virgin olive oil

1 tablespoon unsalted butter or duck fat

2 garlic cloves, thinly sliced

3 juniper berries, gently bruised

3 sprigs of thyme

1 bay leaf

½ cup poultry, pork, or vegetable stock

2 ounces dry-cured ham, such as Bayonne or serrano, finely diced (½ cup)

1 to 1¼ pounds red potatoes (about 3 medium), sliced ¼ inch thick

¾ cup milk

1 whole egg

1 egg yolk

2 tablespoons flour

Pinch of freshly grated nutmeg

Salt and freshly ground pepper

2 ounces imported Cantal, aged gouda, or Swiss Gruyère, shredded

1. About 3 hours before serving, preheat the oven to 325°F. Slip the cabbage wedges into a large pot of boiling salted water until tender but still green, about 12 minutes. Drain the cabbage and rinse under cold running water. When cool enough to handle, squeeze out the excess water. Cut the cabbage into 3-inch pieces, discarding the core.

2. Meanwhile, put 1 tablespoon olive oil and the butter or duck fat in the center of a 10-inch (9-cup capacity) baking-serving dish. Add the garlic, juniper berries, thyme, and bay leaf, cover with a lid or foil, and set on the lowest oven rack. Bake for 10 minutes.

3. Add the cabbage, stock, and ham to the baking dish and stir to mix; then spread evenly in the dish. Arrange the potatoes in overlapping circles over the cabbage. Cover with foil and bake for 1 hour.

4. Remove the foil and lightly sprinkle the remaining 1 teaspoon olive oil over the potatoes. Increase the oven temperature to 400°F, transfer the dish to the upper rack, and bake for 35 minutes, or until the potatoes are lightly browned.

5. Heat the milk in a small saucepan. In a medium bowl, whisk together the whole egg, egg yolk, flour, and nutmeg, Whisk in the hot milk and season with salt and pepper. Pour over the potatoes, sprinkle the cheese on top, and bake on the upper rack of the oven for 30 minutes, or until browned. Serve hot.

Fennel and Potato Gratin

*H*ere is a wonderful gratin of thin slices of potato and fennel smothered with melted cheese. Be sure to use an earthenware cazuela or a shallow, round baking pan so that potatoes will cook and brown evenly.

SERVES 4

4 large red potatoes

2 medium fresh fennel, trimmed

1 tablespoon butter, softened

2 tablespoons flour

½ teaspoon salt

½ teaspoon freshly ground pepper

2 cups milk

2 to 3 ounces French chabichou du Poitou, Italian mozzarella, California teleme, or Cypriot haloumi cheese, coarsely diced

1 egg

1. About 2 hours before serving, preheat the oven to 350° F. Peel the potatoes and cut them into paper-thin slices, preferably on a mandoline. Rinse them in cold water; drain well. Slice the fennel paper-thin.

2. Use the 1 tablespoon butter to grease a 10-inch round cazuela or shallow baking-serving dish. Toss together the potato and fennel slices with the flour, salt, and pepper. Arrange in the dish in an even layer. Pour 1¾ cups of the milk over all. Bake until the potatoes and fennel are tender and steamy, about 1 hour.

3. In a food processor, puree the cheese and egg with the remaining ¼ cup milk until smooth. Pour this mixture over the top of the gratin. Raise the oven temperature to 400°F and continue baking, uncovered, until the gratin is golden-brown and glazed, 25 to 35 minutes.

Spicy Potato Tagine with Preserved Lemon and Olives

This Moroccan, main-course vegetable dish integrates marvelous components: preserved lemons, juicy tan olives, and well-spiced potatoes.

SERVES 4 TO 6

2 pounds red potatoes

1 small onion, grated and squeezed dry (see Note), plus 1 medium onion, thinly sliced

3 tablespoons extra virgin olive oil

⅓ cup grated tomato (see page 259)

¼ teaspoon ground ginger

¼ teaspoon hot Hungarian paprika

Pinch of ground cumin

1 teaspoon crushed garlic

1 bay leaf

¼ fresh lemon

2 tablespoons chopped flat-leaf parsley

2 tablespoons chopped fresh cilantro

Salt

4 to 5 dry saffron threads, crumbled

24 juicy purple or tan olives

½ preserved lemon (see page 303)

1. Peel the potatoes and thickly slice into a bowl of cold water.

2. In heavy saucepan set over moderate heat, cook the grated onion in olive oil until melting, 3 to 4 minutes. Add the tomato, ginger, paprika, cumin, and garlic. Cook, stirring, for 2 more minutes.

3. Drain the potatoes and add to the pan with the thinly sliced onion, the bay leaf, and the fresh lemon quarter. Toss to coat the potatoes, onion, and lemon quarter with the parsley, cilantro, and salt to taste. Add the saffron and 1½ cups hot water and bring to a boil. Reduce the heat to very low and simmer until the potatoes are tender, about 40 minutes.

4. Use a slotted spatula to transfer to a covered serving dish to keep warm. Discard the lemon. Add the olives to the liquid and boil until the pan juices are reduced to a thick sauce. Correct the seasoning, pour over the potatoes, and garnish with the preserved lemon.

Note: Use a four-sided box grater to grate the onion, then squeeze to remove excess moisture.

Adapted from a recipe shared by Fatima Hal.

Butternut Squash and Potato Pie with Tomato, Mint, and Sheep's Milk Cheese

*T*his very rustic "pie" from the Island of Crete is a cinch to prepare and will fill your house with a wonderful aroma.

The word *pie* implies some sort of pastry. This one will be the easiest you'll ever make! Simply sprinkle a handful of flour over the contents of the baking dish. The juices will mingle with the flour during the baking period, forming a thin "pastry" crust.

SERVES 4 AS A SIDE DISH

2 heaping tablespoons shredded fresh mint leaves

2 tablespoons finely chopped flat-leaf parsley

1 teaspoon chopped garlic

Salt

1/2 teaspoon freshly ground black pepper

1 1/4 pounds butternut squash, quartered, peeled, seeded, and thinly sliced crosswise

1 large red ripe tomato, halved, seeded, and grated

2/3 cup (3 ounces) grated hard sheep's milk cheese, such as Spanish manchego, Italian *fiore sardo*, or Greek dried *mizithra*

1/4 cup fresh white cheese, such as ricotta or small-curd cottage cheese

1 1/2 pounds red or Yukon Gold potatoes, peeled and thinly sliced

1 cup milk

3 tablespoons flour

1 tablespoon extra virgin olive oil

1. Preheat the oven to 350°F. In a large bowl, combine the mint, parsley, garlic, and salt and pepper. Remove and reserve half the mixture. Add the squash to the bowl and mix well. Add the grated tomato and the hard and fresh cheeses and toss to combine.

2. Toss the potatoes with the reserved garlic-herb mixture. Place half the sliced potatoes on the bottom of a generously oiled 2 1/2-quart earthenware baking dish. Spread the squash-tomato-cheese mixture on top and cover with the remaining potatoes. Pour the milk over all, dust with the flour, and drizzle the olive oil on top.

3. Bake for 40 minutes. Raise the oven temperature to 400°F and continue to bake for 30 minutes, or until the gratin is brown and the liquid is nearly absorbed. Allow to rest for 15 minutes before serving.

Moroccan Spring Couscous with Barley, Fresh Fava Beans, and Buttermilk

*H*ere's a delicious rural couscous dish for spring made with young fresh fava beans. Steam the favas in their skins and pods for maximum flavor.

SERVES 6

2½ cups (1 pound) barley grits, medium-cracked barley, or Scotch barley

3½ tablespoons extra virgin olive oil

1½ teaspoons minced garlic

½ cup thinly sliced scallions

⅔ cup coarsely chopped cilantro leaves

2 cups shelled and peeled fava beans (see Step 1 on page 15)

1 teaspoon sugar

3 tablespoons butter

1 teaspoon salt

½ teaspoon freshly ground pepper

¼ teaspoon ground cumin

¾ cup buttermilk

2 tablespoons plain yogurt

1. Put the barley grits in just enough salted hot water to cover and leave for 15 minutes. Under water, knead the grains with your hands to soften them.

2. Fill the bottom part of a couscous pot with water and bring to a boil. If you don't own a couscous pot, a deep kettle and a snug-fitting vegetable steamer or colander will do. If the latter doesn't fit perfectly, use padding: Dampen a cheesecloth, twist it into a strip the length of the circumference of the kettle top, and tuck it between the two parts, to make sure the steam rises only through the perforated holes. Lightly oil the inside of the steamer. Don't let the perforated top touch the boiling water below.

3. Drain the barley, toss with 1½ tablespoons of the olive oil, pile into the perforated top, cover tightly, and steam until tender, about 15 minutes.

4. Tip the barley into a wide dish; sprinkle with 1 cup cold water and fluff with a fork. Pile the barley back into the perforated top, cover, and continue steaming for 15 minutes.

Rhubarb
Custard Tart
(page 280)

ABOVE: *Pastis with Apples (page 284)*

OPPOSITE: *Sweet Pumpkin Dessert with Walnuts (page 291)*

BELOW: *Braised Veal Shanks with Chanterelles, Carrots, Chestnuts, and Lardons* (page 196)

OPPOSITE: *Steamed and Crisped Duck Legs with Umbrian Lentils* (page 151)

ABOVE: *Fall-Apart Lamb Shanks with Almond-Chocolate Picada (page 210)*

OPPOSITE: *Fresh Tuna with Green Olives, Capers, Celery, and Mint (page 118)*

Canelés de
Bordeaux (page 286)

5. Meanwhile, make the fava bean–buttermilk sauce. Heat the remaining olive oil in a medium skillet and sauté the garlic, scallions, and half the cilantro for 2 minutes over moderate heat. Add the fava beans, sugar, butter, and 2 tablespoons water. Cook over medium-low heat for a few minutes longer. Season with the salt, pepper, and cumin. Remove from the heat and add the buttermilk and yogurt. Scoop out 2 tablespoons favas and toss with the remaining chopped cilantro; set aside for garnish.

6. Dump the steamed barley into a large serving dish. Fluff it up with a fork and fold in the fava bean–buttermilk sauce. Shape into a mound and place the reserved fava bean and cilantro garnish on top. Serve hot.

Note. If cracked barley, fine hulled barley, or grits are not available, you can pulse whole hulled barley to the size of coarse bulgur in a spice mill or electric blender—but not in a food processor.

DESSERTS

"*I* wanted to do it the hard way, which is also the most pleasurable," wrote feminist author Germaine Greer, explaining why she makes her own marmalade with hard-to-find Seville oranges.

I, too, take great pleasure in preparing sweets from scratch. But I hope Ms. Greer won't mind if I change her phrase "the hard way" to "the slow way."

The Mediterranean is graced with wonderful fruits bulging with flavor in every season. And the women of the region often employ slow-cooking methods to turn these fruits into "spoon-sweets," syrupy preserves, pies, or dried fruit "leathers." The metamorphosis of orange and grapefruit rinds into candied sweets (such as Armenian *turunc*) by the simple addition of sugar, water, and slow-cooking, has always struck me as . . . well . . . magical.

Most Mediterranean cakes and pastries, consumed midday with coffee or tea, are not usually made in the home; the custom is to purchase them from a local pastry shop. But I have gotten so much pleasure from making these types of dishes at home that I offer here foolproof recipes for simple phyllo confections, slowly baked cheesecake, and the *pièce de résistance* of southwest French confections, one of my favorite dessert pastry recipes in the world: canelés de Bordeaux.

When I make fruit desserts (such as the following exemplary rhubarb pie), I control the quality and preparation by choosing the best-quality fruits or nuts that I can find, then carefully preparing them without shortcuts.

Fig, Fennel, and Lemon Tart

*T*his southern Italian–inspired tart is made especially aromatic with just a touch of fennel seed. But it's the figs, standing between the two contrasting flavors—lemon and anise—that bring this dessert together. Be sure to macerate the lemon slices and make the pastry a day in advance.

Though figs come in a rainbow of colors ranging from black to purple to brown to green to tan, for me black ones work best here. Whatever type you choose, please be sure they're ripe and bulging, without soft spots or broken skins.

Note: This tart calls for half a recipe of Flaky Pastry. Do not halve the recipe itself. Rather, make the full amount of dough, which is divided into two rounds. Use one round for this dessert and the other for another use. It can be frozen for up to 6 weeks.

SERVES 6

1 large (6 ounces) organic lemon, washed

½ cup plus 1 tablespoon sugar

Pinch of salt

½ recipe Flaky Pastry (recipe follows)

1 large whole egg

1 egg yolk

1½ tablespoons unsalted butter, at room temperature

2 tablespoons almond meal or 1½ tablespoons flour

1½ pounds (about 24) fresh black figs

2 teaspoons lightly bruised fennel seeds

1. A day in advance, to prepare the lemon: use a 1mm slicing blade fitted on a food processor or a mandoline to make paper-thin slices. Remove all the seeds and put the slices in a bowl. Mix with the sugar and salt; cover and let stand for 24 hours at room temperature.

2. Also a day ahead, make the pastry as directed in the following recipe and refrigerate overnight.

3. The following day, butter a 9-inch shallow tart pan with a removable bottom. Remove the pastry round from the refrigerator and let soften for 10 minutes. On a lightly floured work surface, roll out the dough to an 11-inch thin round. Fit the pastry into the prepared pan; press

(continued)

the dough gently into the bottom and up the sides of the pan without stretching. Chill in the coldest part of the refrigerator for at least 30 minutes.

4. Preheat the oven to 350°F. Prick the bottom of the pastry shell in several places with a fork. Line with foil or parchment paper and fill with pie weights, rice, or dried beans. Put the pastry shell on a baking tile or the bottom rack of the oven and bake for 12 minutes. Remove to a wire rack and let cool for about 15 minutes.

5. While the pastry is cooling, drain the lemon slices, reserving the juices. In a food processor, combine the whole egg, egg yolk, butter, drained lemon slices, and almond meal or flour. Pulse until well blended.

6. Raise the oven temperature to 400°F. Spread the lemon filling over the cooled tart shell. Cover with the halved figs; sprinkle the fennel seeds on top. Bake for 40 minutes.

7. Meanwhile, in a small nonreactive saucepan, bring the reserved lemon juices to a boil. Cook until reduced to 2 tablespoons glaze. Let cool until just warm to the touch.

8. Remove the tart from the oven. Brush with the lemon glaze. This tart is best served at room temperature.

Flaky Pastry

For the best crust, use one of the following: King Arthur's Italian-style; Arrowhead's whole-wheat pastry flour; White Lily unbleached all-purpose flour.

9 tablespoons unsalted butter, frozen

⅓ cup sugar

2 teaspoons finely crushed fennel or anise seeds

Pinch of salt

1 egg

8 ounces (about 2 cups) sifted pastry or all-purpose flour

1. Grate the frozen butter in a food processor. Add the sugar, fennel seeds, and a pinch of salt and pulse 4 or 5 times. Add the egg and pulse 2 to 3 times to combine.

2. Add the flour and pulse until crumbly, 3 or 4 times. Dump into a plastic bag, seal, and press the mixture to form a dough, adding 1 tablespoon water if necessary. Chill for 1 hour; form into a flattened round. Wrap up and chill overnight. The pastry can be refrigerated for up to 3 days or frozen for up to 6 weeks.

MACERATING LEMONS

Those who believe that macerating lemon slices with their rinds in sugar is of Shaker origin may be surprised to learn it's a Mediterranean method, too—used to soften lemon slices for desserts, drinks, and syrups. In fact, it was a Tunisian cook who first showed me how to macerate the small Egyptian limes (a green lemon) with sugar, then leave them overnight to be used as a base for an incredibly rich-flavored lemonade.

Green Grape Tart

I must thank French chef-owner Jean-Charles Baron of the restaurant Toile à Beurre in Ancenis for sharing his method of reducing green grapes to a thick syrup and using it in place of sugar to endow the creamy custard with a subtle grapey flavor.

Additional green grapes are sautéed to bring up their flavor by light caramelization, then cooled and tumbled into a partially baked tart shell. I like to use fruity Thompson seedless, light Chasselas, or aromatic Muscat grapes. All these varieties are available at one time or another during the year, which means you can make this delicious tart right up to Christmas.

SERVES 6

Flaky Pastry, prepared as on page 277, but fennel seeds omitted

3 pounds seedless green grapes (preferably organic)

1 tablespoon unsalted butter

3 large whole eggs

1 egg yolk

¾ cup heavy cream

Pinch of fine salt

½ teaspoon grated lemon zest, or more to taste

1. Make the pastry crust. Use three-quarters of the dough. Save the remainder for some other purpose. (Scraps can be frozen for up to 6 weeks.)

2. Butter a 10½- or 11-inch tart pan with a removable bottom. On a lightly floured work surface, roll out the dough to a 15-inch thin round. Fit the dough into the prepared pan; press the dough gently into the bottom and up the sides of the pan without stretching and trim off the overhang. Refrigerate the prepared shell for at least 30 minutes.

3. Meanwhile, prepare the filling. Puree two-thirds of the grapes in a food processor and press through a sieve to remove their skins. In a 9-inch nonstick skillet, sauté the remaining grapes in 1 tablespoon butter over medium heat until glazed and light brown around the edges, 2 to 3 minutes. Use a slotted spoon to transfer the grapes to a plate and let cool. Add the sieved grape juice to the skillet juices and boil down to ⅓ cup. Let cool.

4. Preheat the oven to 350°F. Prick the bottom of the pastry shell in several places with a fork. Line with foil or parchment paper and fill with pie weights, rice, or dried beans. Place on a baking tile or the bottom rack of the oven to bake for 12 minutes. Remove to a wire rack and let cool.

5. Raise the oven temperature to 400°F. In a food processor, whirl the whole eggs, egg yolk, cream, salt, grated lemon zest, and cold reduced grape juice until well blended; pour into a pint measuring cup or other container with a lip.

6. Arrange the grapes in the prebaked tart shell in a single layer and place on a baking sheet. Set in the oven on a baking stone or the lowest rack. Slowly and carefully pour the custard mixture over the grapes. Bake for 30 minutes. Let the tart cool on a wire rack and serve at room temperature.

Note: Do not refrigerate this tart before serving.

Rhubarb Custard Tart

People who love making rhubarb tarts tend to fall into two groups, each battling the other with the vigor of hockey players. The first group insists on simmering the rhubarb before baking it in a tart shell. Members of the second group are appalled. "Cooking rhubarb twice? For the most vibrant flavor, just sugar it, juice it, then add it raw to the filling."

It's true that sugar will temper raw rhubarb. The late British food writer Jane Grigson, who wasn't all that fond of rhubarb, described a pleasant memory of the fruit: "Sitting with my sister on a doorstep, each with a stick of rhubarb, and a saucer of sugar between us. We dipped and chewed, dipped and chewed in the warm sun, with clucking hens stepping round us."

Learning of the raw rhubarb theory, I decided to test it myself. Last year, early in the rhubarb season, when the stalks were at their most tender and least stringy, I sprinkled one with sugar, let it stand for a while, then tasted it. It was an exciting, lively eating experience. I decided then to join the only-cook-the-rhubarb-once group when making my rhubarb tarts. I now sprinkle the raw stalks with sugar, let them stand, then reduce the extracted juices, which are later added to the fruit and custard. I now declare that this rhubarb tart, containing as it does both the raw and the cooked, is the best, purest-tasting, most exciting tart for spring!

A good wine match would be a Muscat de Beaumes-de-Venise.

Make the pastry crust ahead and macerate the rhubarb overnight.

SERVES 6 TO 8

Flaky Pastry, prepared as on page 277, but fennel seeds omitted

1½ pounds crisp, tender rhubarb stalks

⅔ cup sugar

2 teaspoons anise-flavored liquor such as Pernod, ouzo, anisette, sambuca, or Ricard

1½ teaspoons finely grated orange zest

3 large whole eggs

1 large egg yolk

¾ cup heavy cream

Pinch of salt

1. Make the pastry crust. Use three-quarters of the dough. Save the remainder for some other purpose. (Scraps can be frozen for up to 6 weeks.)

2. Make the filling: Wash the rhubarb, discard any leaves, and trim the ends. (Pull off the strings if the rhubarb is late season, old, or thick). With a very sharp knife, cut each stalk into 1- by ½-inch pieces. In a glass or ceramic bowl, toss the rhubarb with ⅓ cup of the sugar. Cover and refrigerate overnight.

3. The following day, preheat the oven to 375°F. Butter a deep, 10½-inch tart pan with a removable bottom, or a fluted porcelain quiche pan, preferably 1 inch deep. Remove the dough from the refrigerator and let soften slightly. On a lightly floured work surface, roll out the dough to a 14-inch thin round. Fit the dough into the prepared pan; press the dough gently into the bottom and up the sides of the pan without stretching. Prick the bottom of the shell all over with a fork and refrigerate the shell for at least 20 minutes, or until thoroughly chilled and firm.

4. Meanwhile, drain the rhubarb in a colander set over a large skillet. Press firmly on the rhubarb to extract as much juice as possible. Boil the rhubarb juice over high heat until it is syrupy and reduced to 3 tablespoons, about 5 minutes. Remove the skillet from the heat. Add the rhubarb to the pan and toss it in the syrup until coated. Stir in the anise-flavored liquor and orange zest. Let the rhubarb cool to room temperature.

5. Line the tart with foil and fill it with pie weights or dried beans. Bake on a baking tile or the bottom rack of the oven for 10 minutes. Remove the liner and weights and return the pie shell to bake for 5 more minutes, or until just golden. Let cool to room temperature.

6. Raise the oven temperature to 400°F. In a medium bowl, whisk the whole eggs with the egg yolk, cream, salt, and remaining ⅓ cup sugar. If using a tart pan with a removable bottom, set it on a jellyroll pan. Distribute the rhubarb evenly in the tart shell and pour half of the custard over it; let the custard settle, then pour on the rest.

7. Bake the tart until the custard is golden brown and bubbling, about 30 minutes. Transfer the rhubarb tart to a rack and let cool completely. Serve the tart at room temperature directly from the porcelain quiche pan, or unmold before cutting into wedges. Do not refrigerate this tart.

Sweet Bisteeya with Almonds

*T*he word *bisteeya* needn't necessarily refer to the famous Moroccan *pièce de résistance*—a pigeon pie with almonds and an eggy sauce all wrapped in a flaky pastry pie and topped with sugar and almonds. It can also refer to the following simple, crackling, crunchy almond dessert, a specialty of Marrakech.

This is an easy dessert to make, as almost all of it can be prepared in advance: bake the pastry early in the day, then prepare the vanilla and rose-scented milk sauce a few hours before serving. At serving time, simply assemble the dish by placing some reheated sauce on individual plates and topping each with a crisp, almond-filled triangle.

SERVES 6 TO 8

5 tablespoons unsalted butter

1 cup whole blanched almonds

2 tablespoons confectioners' sugar

½ teaspoon ground cinnamon

6 to 8 sheets of phyllo (about ¼ pound, plus extra in case of tearing, thawed overnight in the refrigerator if frozen

Vanilla and Rose-Scented Milk Sauce (recipe follows)

1. Melt 1 tablespoon of the butter in a skillet. Add the almonds and cook over medium-low heat, stirring, until golden, about 5 minutes. Drain on paper towels and let cool. Chop the almonds. Transfer them to a bowl and toss with the confectioners' sugar and cinnamon.

2. Preheat the oven to 350°F. Melt the remaining 4 tablespoons butter. Set the stacked sheets of phyllo dough on a work surface. Using a 10-inch plate as a template, cut out 6 to 8 rounds. Brush 1 phyllo round with melted butter, fold it in half, and brush it again. Fold it in half again, forming a triangle. Sprinkle 1 rounded tablespoon of the almonds on half the phyllo triangle and fold again, covering the almonds. Brush the triangle with butter and place on a parchment-lined baking sheet. Repeat with the remaining phyllo rounds and butter, using half the almond mixture.

3. Bake the bisteeya triangles for 20 minutes, or until golden and crisp. Immediately sprinkle each with a scant tablespoon of the remaining almond mixture. Let cool.

4. To serve, spoon the milk sauce into shallow bowls and top with the baked phyllo.

Vanilla and Rose-Scented Milk Sauce

The quality of the rose water determines the amount needed here to perfume the sauce. I use the Lebanese Cortas brand.

MAKES ABOUT 3 CUPS

3 cups milk

3½ tablespoons superfine sugar

Pinch of salt

3 tablespoons cornstarch

1 tablespoon rose water, or more to taste

¼ teaspoon vanilla extract

1. In a medium saucepan, combine 2½ cups of the milk with the superfine sugar and salt and bring to a simmer. In a small glass, stir the cornstarch into the remaining ½ cup milk until smooth.

2. Pour the cornstarch mixture into the simmering milk, whisking constantly, and cook until the custard thickens and is just beginning to boil, 2 to 3 minutes. Remove from the heat and cool slightly, then stir in the rose water and vanilla.

Note: The milk custard can stand at room temperature for up to 3 hours. Refrigerate for longer storage. Cover the custard directly with plastic wrap to avoid a skin forming on the surface.

Pastis with Apples

*T*he dessert called *pastis,* a specialty of the Landes, a region in France not far from the Pyrenees and Spain, is closely related to the *tourtière,* another regional dessert from Quercy. Both desserts are made with a version of phyllo dough baked up crisp and paper thin. The filling for this pastis is made of apples deeply flavored with vanilla, rum, Armagnac, and grated lemon zest, a wonderful combination very typical of the region.

The dessert is especially delicious when served with vanilla ice cream.

SERVES 8

1 pound Granny Smith apples

¾ cup superfine or baker's sugar

1 tablespoon vanilla extract

¼ teaspoon grated lemon zest

3 tablespoons Armagnac

2 tablespoons dark rum

½ pound phyllo leaves, about 10 sheets

⅓ cup clarified butter, melted and warm

Confectioners' sugar, for garnish

Vanilla ice cream or crème fraîche, as accompaniment

1. Peel, core, and thinly slice the apples. Combine the apple slices with ½ cup of the superfine sugar, the vanilla, lemon zest, Armagnac, and rum in a saucepan. Cover and cook over medium-low heat until the apples are soft, 5 to 6 minutes. Drain the apples, reserving the juices.

2. Return the aromatic juices to the saucepan and boil until reduced to about ½ cup syrup, 3 to 5 minutes. Mix with the apples and leave to cool. (*The apples can be cooked a day ahead.*)

3. A few hours before serving, preheat the oven to 400°F. Place 3 of the phyllo sheets in a buttered 12-inch pizza pan, brushing or spraying each sheet with clarified butter, and allowing the phyllo to extend over the sides of pan. Spread half the cold apple slices evenly over the phyllo. Fold the overhanging phyllo over the filling and brush or spray with butter. Cover with 2 more sheets of phyllo and repeat, then cover with 3 buttered phyllo sheets. Trim off the extended leaves of phyllo, cut into strips, and scatter attractively over the top of the pie. Sprinkle with any remaining butter and a few drops of cold water.

4. Bake the pastis for 12 minutes. Reduce the oven temperature to 350°F and bake for 30 minutes longer.

5. Sprinkle the remaining superfine sugar over the top of the pastry. Run under the broiler just long enough to caramelize the top here and there, 1 to 2 minutes.

6. Slide the pastis onto a wire rack and let cool to lukewarm. Just before serving, dust with confectioners' sugar. Serve with vanilla ice cream or dollops of crème fraîche.

Canelés de Bordeaux

The *canelé de Bordeaux* (a.k.a. *cannelé bordelais*) is a magical bakery confection, a cake with a rich custardy interior enclosed by a thin caramelized shell. It's a brilliant construction, developed long ago by an anonymous Bordeaux cook whose innovation has been subjected to three hundred years of refinements.

Nearly black at first sight, bittersweet at first bite, the crunchy burnt sugar canelé shell makes an exquisite complement to its smooth, sweet filling, fragrant with vanilla and rum. Small enough to eat out of hand, these little cakes have recently gained cachet after years of neglect to the extent that they may one day rival the popularity of *crême brûlée* in the category of caramelized French sweets.

Canelé de Bordeaux is the "politically correct" name for this recipe. Additions or alterations to the recipe will run afoul of the canelés *gendarmes*, transforming the baked product into cannelés bordelais.

Canelé batter must be prepared ahead two or three days before baking. If you prefer, you can make it two weeks in advance and freeze it; thaw in the refrigerator. Both the batter and the molds must be very cold before baking. While this recipe is long, it is not difficult.

MAKES 10 CANELÉS

2 cups whole milk

2 tablespoons unsalted butter, chilled and diced

¾ cup cake flour

Pinch of salt

¾ cup plus 2 tablespoons superfine or baker's sugar

4 extra-large egg yolks

1 tablespoon dark rum

1 teaspoon vanilla extract

"White Oil" (see box, page 290, on seasoning the molds)

1. Rinse a saucepan with cold water. Add the milk and set over low heat. Heat to 183°F on a candy thermometer, about 8 minutes.

2. Meanwhile, place the butter, cake flour, and salt in a food processor; pulse until combined. Scatter the sugar on top; pulse until mixed.

3. Add the egg yolks; pulse until the mixture begins to tighten.

4. With the machine on, quickly and steadily pour the hot milk into the mixture in the food processor. Strain the batter through a very fine sieve into a clean container, pressing any congealed yolk through. Stir in the rum and vanilla and let cool to room temperature; then cover and refrigerate for 24 to 48 hours.

5. About 6 hours before serving, lightly brush the interior of each canelé mold with "white oil" (see page 290.) Set crown side up on paper towels to avoid pooling of the oil in crevices. Place the molds in the freezer for at least 30 minutes before baking.

6. Preheat the oven to 400°F. Place the chilled molds 1½ inches apart on a baking sheet. Gently stir or shake the batter, then fill each mold almost to the top. Place on the lower oven rack. Bake until the canelés are deep, deep brown in color, or, if desired, almost black, about 2 hours. Remove from the oven. (If using a convection oven, bake at 375°F for 1 hour and 15 minutes for deep, deep brown canelés.)

7. One by one, use an oven mitt to grasp each hot mold, firmly rap the crown against a hard surface to loosen the cake, and tip out onto a rack. Let cool to room temperature before serving, about 1 hour. If any canelés resist unmolding, bake 5 to 10 minutes longer; if necessary, use a toothpick to loosen. For a shiny exterior, lightly brush the sides of cooled, baked canelés with a little flavorless oil.

Notes: After baking, don't wash or scrub the interiors of the molds. To remove baked debris, place the molds in a moderate oven; heat until the debris burns; remove the debris with paper towels.

Canelés turn spongy and heavy after 4 to 5 hours. To refresh, heat the unmolded pastries in a 450°F oven for 5 minutes; remove from the oven; let cool until the exteriors harden.

Leftover baked canelés can be frozen for up to 1 month; to freeze, wrap individually in plastic wrap. To serve, remove from the freezer and while still frozen, bake unwrapped at 500°F for 5 minutes. Remove from the oven, and let rest for 30 minutes; bake again for 5 minutes. Remove from the oven; cool until the exteriors harden.

The Story of Caneles

Many recipes don't carry a tale; the canelé carries many. One of the oldest refers to a convent in Bordeaux, where, before the French Revolution, the nuns prepared cakes called *canalize* made with egg yolks donated by local winemakers, who used only the whites to clarify their wines. Any records that might verify this were lost in the turbulent revolution, thus relegating the convent story to legend.

But the alternative tale may be even better: residents of Bordeaux who lived along the docks gleaned spilled low-protein flour from the loading areas, then used it to make sweets for poor children. The small canelé molds, fluted and made of copper or brass, were nestled in embers to be baked.

Whatever the actual derivation, the popularity of canelés has risen and fallen numerous times over the years. Twenty-five years ago, when I first started working in Bordeaux, I never heard of these little cakes. No local guide or notable cookbook published since the start of the twentieth century even mentioned them. Later, I heard that a few Bordeaux bakers were working to revive their local specialty.

Soon, the little cakes, described by a local culinary historian as shaped like "a Doric column without a base," began cropping up in all sizes and flavorings throughout France. In 1985, stunned by this surge in popularity, eighty-eight Bordeaux pâtissiers formed a *confrérie,* or brotherhood, to protect the integrity of their canelés. They staged a "linguistic coup d'etat" by removing one of the n's from the old spelling (cannelé) to differentiate their cake, with its secret method of preparation, from bastardized versions. Today, *canelé de Bordeaux* is the official cake of the city, while *cannelé bordelais* is a generic name used in Paris, New York City, Osaka, Los Angeles, etc.

"Our canelé de Bordeaux had to be protected and promoted as our own," says Daniel Antoine, a jolly, stocky pâtissier who operates Pâtisserie Antoine in Bordeaux. "Recently, chocolate and orange cannelés have appeared," he tells me. "We don't want them confused with the real thing."

The official recipe, he told me, has been written down and locked in his vault. All eighty-eight pâtissiers have sworn to protect its secrets. This much is known: the general recipe calls for a cold batter to be poured into an ice-cold, fluted tin-lined copper mold, then placed in a hot oven and baked for a very long time. After baking, the canelés are firmly tapped out onto a grill while still hot, then left to cool until their exteriors harden. They're at their most glorious one hour out of the oven; within five or six hours they begin to turn spongy. Pâtissiers have all sorts of tricks to revive them, ranging from putting them back in a hot oven for a few minutes, to flaming them with quality rum to crisp the shells. I believe they're so delicious that they're worth the expense of buying the special copper molds. Silicone-coated Gastroflex molds are also available, although I don't think they produce as good a result. Only the Cannele Silicon Flex molds available at Bridge's Kitchenware are an acceptable substitute for copper molds.

"The canelé is an artisanal product, so sometimes it doesn't come out perfectly," Antoine says. When I tell him that my canelés sometimes have pale yellow spots on their tops, he replies, "Oh, sure, I know that problem well. It's due to the puddling of oil in the crevices of the molds. When they come out that way, we say they have 'a white ass!'"

Antoine then compliments me on having figured out one of the major secrets, the special method of combining flour and butter. I had based my findings on a letter I received from him several years back. He smiles as I tell him how I finally succeeded in making delicious canelés with a custardy center. "Yes, I see you understand," he says unbegrudgingly.

Many pâtissiers line their molds with a film of "white oil" containing beeswax, a messy and highly flammable substance that may deter home cooks. In my opinion, this step is helpful if you want to make canelés successfully.

To fully understand the fabulous quality of a true canelé de Bordeaux, eat it out of hand as a snack, with a glass of wine or a cup of coffee.

HOW TO SEASON NEW CANELE MOLDS

To make this dessert, you will need ten large copper canelé molds. These can be ordered through the mail or over the Internet (see Mail Order Sources). To prevent sticking, new canelé molds must be seasoned.

Canelé Molds

To season new molds, preheat the oven to 350°F. Wash the molds in soapy water; rinse and dry thoroughly. Heavily grease the interiors with vegetable oil. Set on a baking sheet and place in the oven for 1 hour. Remove from the oven and place the molds upside down on a wire rack set in a rimmed baking sheet; return to the oven and heat for 5 minutes. Turn off the heat; leave the molds in the oven until cooled to room temperature. Store lightly oiled molds in a cool, covered place.

"White Oil"

Before using the seasoned molds, coat them with a small amount of the following mixture: 1 ounce beeswax (see Mail Order Sources) and 1 cup safflower oil. Put the beeswax in a heatproof 2-cup glass jar. Melt in a pot of simmering water. Slowly stir in the oil. Store at room temperature.

Brush the interiors of the molds with "white oil." To remove any excess, preheat the oven to 350°F; invert the molds onto a rack set atop a foil-lined baking sheet; bake for 1 minute to allow excess oil to run out (only the finest film of oil should remain). Remove the molds from the oven and let cool to room temperature. Pour the expressed oil back into the jar to use another time. Freeze the molds before filling with batter and baking. "White oil" needs to be applied in this manner every time the molds are used.

Canelé de Bordeaux Molds and Beeswax

The copper, tin-lined canelé molds can be ordered from J. B. Prince in New York City (800-473-0577, www.jbprince.com), which carries three sizes $1\frac{1}{2}$ inches round by 1 inch high, 1-ounce capacity; $1\frac{1}{2}$ inches round by $1\frac{1}{2}$ inches high, $1\frac{1}{2}$-ounce capacity; $2\frac{1}{4}$ inches round by 2 inches high, 3-ounce capacity, or from the Parisian culinary equipment store Culinarion (011-33-141-90-09-11, www.culinarion.com). Culinarion carries only one size, the 3-ounce capacity mold, because it is the only one that is "politically correct."

You can substitute 8 Cannele Silicon Flex molds (size 2.2 x 1.9) available at Bridge Kitchenware. I brush the insides with a thin coating of "white oil."

Beeswax can be ordered from J&N Sales (765-459-4589, e-mail: info@jandnsales.com).

Sweet Pumpkin Dessert with Walnuts

*H*ere's a striking, easy-to-make Turkish sweet called *kabak tatlisi*. The cooking method is fascinating: you macerate cubes of squash in sugar until they weep, cook the cubes at a low temperature, then gently cool, allowing the squash cubes to swell with the syrupy juices. It goes beautifully with walnuts and a cultured cream such as crème fraîche.

I suggest you use a tasty orange winter squash, such as butternut or hubbard, dense enough to hold its shape through the unique cooking process. Either variety will produce a sweet with an intense flavor and creamy texture.

SERVES 4

1⅓ pounds butternut squash

1 cup superfine or baker's sugar

⅓ cup shelled walnuts

1 teaspoon unsalted butter

1 cup cultured cream, such as crème fraîche, optional

1. Peel and trim the squash. You should have 1 pound. Cut the squash into 1-inch cubes. Mix with the sugar in a shallow ceramic baking dish and let stand for at least 30 minutes, or until the squash weeps and the sugar melts.

2. Preheat the oven to 300°F. Use a wooden spoon to mix the squash and sugar. Cover with a crumpled sheet of wet parchment paper, place in the oven, and bake for 1½ hours, or until the juices boil and the squash is tender. Turn off the oven and leave the dish inside until completely cool. (The squash will continue to re-absorb their syrupy juices.) Store in a cool place or in the refrigerator. Let return to room temperature before serving.

3. Sauté the walnuts in the butter until glistening. Serve the squash and a few teaspoons of the syrup in individual serving bowls. Garnish with a sprinkling of toasted walnuts. If desired, garnish with dollops of cultured cream.

Corsican Cheesecake with Orange Marmalade

Corsicans make a glorious version of cheesecake using their favorite fresh cheese, *brocciu,* a goat or ewe's milk cheese: white, light, and soft when fresh. If you drain ricotta and push it through a sieve, you will obtain an excellent substitute.

I first tasted this Corsican cheesecake (*fiadone*) in Ajaccio in early June, when the local brocciu cheese season was nearly over. The cake was a revelation: simple, wobbly, delicate, and creamy throughout, with a thin black topping. The man who sold it told me he made his fiadone just the way his mother had, searing it in a hot wood-burning oven until it was almost set, then moving it to a cooler part of the oven to finish baking slowly on its own.

As it happens, this is basically the same method used to make the famous New York Lindy's cheesecake. Food writer James Villas told me his father so admired Lindy's version that back in 1954, he asked his waiter for the recipe, slipping him a twenty-dollar bill while telling him that his wife simply "had to have it." The waiter dutifully returned with the details handwritten on a paper napkin. According to these notes, at Lindy's the cake is first blasted with high heat to set the outside, then baked slowly at a very low temperature to avoid curdling the eggy cheese mixture, and finally finished in the receding heat of a turned-off oven.

Many baking books warn you not to overbake, but slow-baking is not only forgiving, it will actually produce a better cake with a fragile texture and a subtle flavor. And the burnt topping resulting from the final broiling makes it especially delicious. For best flavor, drain the cheese two days before using.

SERVES 8

1 container (15 ounces) whole-milk ricotta, preferably fresh

¼ cup milk

Pinch of salt

2 whole large eggs

1 large egg yolk

½ cup confectioners' sugar

1¾ teaspoons orange liqueur, such as triple sec

Zest of 1 lemon

¼ teaspoon vanilla extract

1 tablespoon unsalted butter

1 tablespoon granulated sugar

¼ cup bitter orange marmalade

1. In a food processor, blend the ricotta, milk, and salt until smooth. Dump into a wet cheesecloth–lined sieve set over a bowl and refrigerate for up to 2 days. You should have about ¾ pound drained cheese.

2. Place the oven rack in the bottom third of the oven. Preheat the oven to 400°F.

3. In the food processor, combine the whole eggs, egg yolk, confectioners' sugar, 1¼ teaspoons of the orange liqueur, the lemon zest, and the vanilla. Process until thick and lemon colored. Add the drained ricotta and process until smooth.

4. Use the butter to grease an 8-inch nonstick square or round baking pan. Dust with half the granulated sugar. Spread ⅔ cup of the batter in the prepared dish and bake until golden brown, about 3 minutes. Remove from the oven and let cool for 5 minutes. Leave the oven on.

5. Gently heat the marmalade in a microwave or over low heat until syrupy. Drizzle half the marmalade over the baked cheese batter in an even layer. Pour the remaining batter on top, and spread evenly. Set the cake in the oven. Immediately reduce the temperature to 185°F and bake until the cake is set around the edges but still a bit wobbly in the center, about 2 hours.

6. Scatter the remaining granulated sugar over the hot cake and set under the broiler until the top browns. Turn off the oven and leave the cake on the rack with the door ajar for about 1 hour. Remove the cake, cover with plastic wrap, and refrigerate for at least 4 hours, or preferably overnight.

7. Cut the cake into 8 squares. Thin the remaining orange marmalade with 1 tablespoon water and the remaining ½ teaspoon orange liqueur. Spoon around the cheesecake and serve.

Sweet Couscous with Fresh Pomegranates

Moroccan fine-grain couscous, called *msfouf*, is freshly steamed, then very simply served—anointed with melted butter, mixed with orange-flavored pomegranates, then sprinkled with some crushed pistachios and delicate cinnamon. I know of no other dessert quite like it.

SERVES 6 TO 8

2 large very red pomegranates

2 tablespoons orange juice

1 tablespoon orange flower water

Pinch of freshly ground pepper

Pinch of ground dried orange peel, optional

¼ cup plus 1 tablespoon superfine or baker's sugar

1 cup fine-grain or medium-grain packaged couscous

Salt

1 tablespoon extra virgin olive oil

1 tablespoon unsalted butter, melted

Ground Ceylon cinnamon

2 tablespoons crushed, peeled pistachios

Confectioners' sugar

1. Roll the pomegranates around on your kitchen counter to soften them, then break up in a bowl of water to keep the juice from spurting. Drain, place skin side up in the bowl, and give each section a good bang with the back of a heavy knife to loosen the seeds.

2. Combine the pomegranate seeds with the orange juice, orange flower water, pepper, dried orange peel, if using, and ¼ cup superfine sugar. Cover and refrigerate for at least 2 hours.

3. Put the couscous in a fine sieve and rinse under cold running water. Turn into a bowl; let soak for a minute or two, break up any clumps, and let stand until ready to steam.

4. Meanwhile, fill the bottom part of a couscous pot with water and bring to a boil. If you don't own a couscous pot, a deep kettle and a snug-fitting vegetable steamer or colander will do. (If the latter doesn't fit perfectly, use padding: Dampen a cheesecloth, twist it into a strip the length of the circumference of the kettle top, and tuck it between the two parts, to make sure the steam rises only through the perforated holes.) Lightly oil the inside of the steamer. Don't let the perforated top touch the boiling water below.

5. Break up the couscous with a fork. Pile into the perforated container, cover tightly, and steam for 30 minutes.

6. Dump the couscous onto a tray. Sprinkle with ½ cup lightly salted cold water and rake the grains to keep them separate. Gradually add another ½ cup water while raking the couscous. When the couscous has absorbed all the water, toss with the olive oil and fluff with a long whisk. Pile the couscous back into the container and repeat the steaming for 30 minutes.

7. Dump the couscous onto a tray, gradually work in another cup cold water, and rake the grains to keep them separate. Gently mix in the remaining 1 tablespoon superfine sugar. Loosely cover with a damp towel and let stand in a cool place until ready to serve.

8. Fluff up the couscous and add the melted butter and the prepared pomegranate seeds with their soaking liquid. Gently fluff the couscous again; pile in a mound, decorate with lines of cinnamon and pistachios, and dust the top with confectioners' sugar.

Slow-Baked Quince with Apple, Clotted Cream, and Toasted Almonds

Quince cooked leisurely like this as it is in Turkey becomes a seductive compote. Once baked and covered with its own syrup, it will keep for weeks in the refrigerator.

SERVES 8

1⅓ cups superfine or baker's sugar

2 whole cloves

3 tablespoons fresh lemon juice

4 medium quinces, about 2 pounds

Clotted Cream (recipe follows) or 1 cup drained yogurt or crème fraîche

2 tablespoons chopped toasted almonds

Ground dried orange peel and ground rosebuds (see Note), optional

1. In an electric slow-cooker or a shallow 3-quart baking dish, combine the sugar, cloves, and lemon juice with 1⅓ cups water. Stir to dissolve the sugar.

2. Wash the quinces; peel, halve, and remove the cores, reserving all trimmings. Place the peels, cores, and quince halves in the slow cooker or baking dish. Cover and cook on low or bake in a 250°F oven for 5 to 7 hours, until the fruit turns creamy pink. Turn off the heat and let cool before uncovering. (This allows the quince to re-absorb more of the syrup.)

3. Use a slotted spoon to transfer the quince halves to a wide container. Strain the cooking liquid and boil it down to 1 cup. Pour over the quince. Store covered in the refrigerator. (Discard the peels and cores.)

4. Serve the quince well chilled, with dollops of clotted cream, drained yogurt, or crème fraîche. Decorate with chopped toasted almonds. If desired, dust lightly with ground dried orange peel and rosebuds.

Notes: Some American varieties of quince may never turn the beautiful red you see in Turkish sweet shops. In fact, some of our quinces seem to take forever to turn pink. Though some cooks slip a little coloring in the cooking liquid for extra glow, I don't go that route.

Turkish cooks spread grated apple over the exposed halves during baking so the surfaces won't dry out.

You can tell your quinces are fully cooked when they're firm to the touch yet meltingly tender within.

Dried orange peel and rosebuds ground to a fine powder can be lightly sprinkled on top for a subtle extra taste. To make this mixture, use a blender to grind equal amounts of dried rosebuds and dried orange peels to a fine powder. Add a small amount of ground coriander to taste. Keep stored in a tightly closed jar to be used on any type of poached fruit or savory food. Tunisian cooks even use this powder and quince to flavor fish couscous.

Clotted Cream

Samira Yago Cholagh, a Chaldean Christian born in Iraq now living in the States told me: "Once a year, perhaps on Christmas morning, I treat myself to this luxury for breakfast, spreading the cream on bread and topping it with honey or fig jam."

Samira's clotted cream can be cut into squares to use over desserts, or used in place of butter with marmalade. Making your own clotted cream takes some time, but since there is little actual work involved, it's definitely worth the trouble.

MAKES 1 CUP

1 quart milk
1 quart heavy cream

1. Place the milk in a heavy enameled pot. Bring to a boil and reduce the heat. Add the cream in a steady stream from as far above the pot as possible. Simmer, partially covered, over very low heat for 2 hours. Remove from the heat and let stand at room temperature for 7 hours.

2. Return the cream in the pot to very low heat. Simmer for 30 minutes; let cool again. Place the pot in the refrigerator for 2 days before cutting. Loosen the edges of cream that form around the pan with a knife. Cut and carefully transfer pieces to a flat plate. Refrigerate, tightly covered, for up to 4 days.

Armenian Candied Bitter Orange Rind

A couple of years ago, I drove with my Turkish friend Ayfer to a town called Vakif in the foothills of the Musa Dagh, a gorgeous, old-world citrus growing region just a few miles from the Mediterranean. No signs showed us the way. Ayfer had to stop frequently to ask directions. But when we finally arrived she became enormously excited, for Vakif is a pure Armenian Christian village, one of the very few still remaining in Turkey.

Our hostess was Surpuhi Karfun, a strong, slim, shy young woman in her early thirties, wife of the village leader. Her stucco house was comfortable—no telephone or running water, but everything was immaculate and beautifully kept. The kitchen was incredibly simple: a two-burner stove and a few aluminum pans and copper pots plated and lined with tin.

But such food! It was different from anything I'd ever eaten in Turkey: a blend of meat and bulgur (such as *kibbeh*) poached in a delicious stock enriched with an addition of cooked preserved yogurt; baby eggplant stuffed with bulgur and lamb flavored by mint and pomegranate molasses; a stew of lamb, chickpeas, and taro root; a green bean pilaf topped with fried onions; and tea served with delicious twirls of preserved bitter orange peels, called *turunc*.

After lunch we took a walk to the center of town, a square with benches sheltered by poplar trees. Here Ayfer talked politics with the men, while Surpuhi joined the women's sewing circle.

The sky began to darken. It was getting time for us to leave. We made a quick visit to the stark stone church, center of village life, distributed our gifts, said our farewells, then drove back down through the hills.

Before leaving, Surpuhi gave me the recipe for the candied orange peel I so admired. Candied in a curled state, they'd been served on a piece of candy paper with a toothpick. She used the rinds of bitter oranges. I've substituted grapefruit peel, adding a little grapefruit and orange juice to the syrup. This confection isn't quick to make, but is definitely worth the trouble and especially good with Turkish coffee or tea.

7 organic bitter oranges or 3 or 4 grapefruits, washed and dried

2 cups sugar

Juice of ½ lemon

⅔ cup bitter orange juice, or ⅓ cup grapefruit juice and ⅓ cup orange juice

1. Using a microplane zester or the fine side of a grater, remove all the colored zest from the bitter oranges or grapefruit; reserve for some other purpose.

2. Cut the oranges into quarters or grapefruits into 6 sections. Remove the flesh and crush for juice. Use a thin-bladed knife to remove any excess white pith.

3. Place the peels in a large saucepan and cover with cold water. Bring to a boil. Reduce the heat to medium and cook until soft enough for a finger to penetrate the skin, about 40 minutes for the orange, and 1 hour for the grapefruit. Drain and cut the peel into long strips about ¼ inch wide. Soak the strips in a bowl of cold water for 3 days, changing the water once or twice each day. (This helps to remove the bitter taste.)

4. Drain the peels, roll each into a tight curl, and use a long needle and thread to string the curls to make a garland. Press the curls close together to avoid unraveling and maintain the shape Press the prepared curls between kitchen towels to express the moisture. Let dry on towels, covered with another towel, until very dry, about 2 hours.

5. Put the sugar, lemon juice, and 2⅓ cups cold water in a medium saucepan; bring to a boil. Cook until a light syrup is formed. Add the garland of peels and boil slowly, uncovered, until the syrup is thick enough to drop in a steady stream from a wooden spoon. Snip the thread and allow the rinds to float in the syrup.

6. Remove from the heat; use a slotted spoon to transfer the peels to hot, dry, sterilized jars and pour the syrup over, leaving a ½-inch headspace. Seal with an airtight lid. Turn the jars upside down and allow to cool. Store in a dry, dark place until ready to serve. Keep the preserves in the refrigerator after opening. Serve each curl with a toothpick on an individual candy paper with a dribble of syrup.

Strawberries with Orange-Flavored Wine

Maceration, soaking food in a syrup or liquid to infuse flavor, is a wonderful old French cooking method. It's especially useful in strawberry season when so often the berries don't have the aroma and flavor you expect. I won't guarantee this old French *truc* will transform tasteless strawberries, but it will definitely improve them. And if your strawberries are at their prime, the results will be glorious.

SERVES 6 TO 8

2 pounds strawberries

3 tablespoons sugar, or more to taste

²/₃ cup fresh orange juice

2 tablespoons fresh lemon juice

¹/₃ cup orange muscat or rosé wine

Vanilla ice cream, for serving

1. Clean and hull the strawberries. In a food processor, puree 5 of the largest berries. Add the sugar, the orange juice, lemon juice, and wine. Puree and strain through a fine sieve. Add more sugar to taste.

2. Pour the puree over the remaining strawberries and let them macerate for at least 3 hours, stirring occasionally. Serve with vanilla ice cream.

Note: Italians have a similar trick: cooks dribble a few drops of balsamic vinegar over prime sweet strawberries. When they aren't perfect, they sprinkle them with sugar and leave them to exude some of their juices, then add balsamic vinegar, stir the juices and vinegar together, and serve chilled.

THE
MEDITERRANEAN
LARDER

———— ❖ ————

When you walk through an open-air Mediterranean market, you often see little old ladies carrying string shopping bags with just a few beautiful fresh vegetables and a tiny package of meat or fish or a small chicken. If you were to follow them home, you might see a dozen people sitting around waiting for lunch, and you'd think: How will they ever feed twelve with so few provisions?

The answer, of course, is the Mediterranean larder: grains, nuts, salt-preserved meats, oil-preserved vegetables, dried fruits, and all kinds of condiments to add to meat, fish, poultry, and vegetables to expand their flavor and liven them up. Most items in a Mediterranean larder are not difficult to make, and since they are preserved, benefit from the passing of time. Preparing special foods for another day will teach you something new about slow Mediterranean cooking. Think of stocking your larder as a gift to yourself.

In my Mediterranean larder there are preserved lemons, spice mixtures, homemade cereals, spiced meats, and bottles of interesting sauces and condiments. To begin your larder, I suggest starting with *harissa,* Tunisian hot red pepper paste (page 309). It's easy to make and a boon to have on hand, useful for embellishing couscous, kebabs, and olives. It brightens and enriches all kinds of fish dishes, meat stews, and vegetable ragouts. And when you don't feel like cooking but need something to serve right away, simply blend some harissa with a little water and olive oil, and use it as a dip for bread.

Preserved Lemons

10 ripe organic lemons   Extra virgin olive oil

½ cup coarse salt

1. Scrub 6 of the lemons and dry well. Quarter the 6 lemons, cutting from the top to within ½ inch of the bottom, sprinkle salt on the exposed flesh, then reshape the fruit. Toss with the remaining salt and pack the lemons into a 3- or 4-cup dry, sterile Mason jar with a glass or plastic-coated lid.

2. With a wooden spoon, gently push down on the lemons. Squeeze the juice from the remaining 4 lemons and pour into the jar. Close the jar tightly and let the lemons ripen at room temperature for 30 days, shaking the jar each day to redistribute the salt and juice. (Within a few days the salt will draw out enough juice to completely cover the lemons.)

3. For longer storage, add olive oil to cover and refrigerate for up to 1 year. Rinse the lemons before using.

Variation 7-Day Preserved Lemons

Scrub 2 ripe lemons and dry well. Cut each into 8 wedges. Toss them with ⅓ cup coarse sea salt and place in a ½-pint glass jar with a glass or plastic-coated lid. Pour in ½ cup fresh lemon juice. Close the jar tightly and let the lemons ripen at room temperature for 7 days, shaking the jar each day to distribute the salt and juice. To store for up to 1 week, add olive oil to cover and refrigerate.

North African Cooking with Lemons and Oranges

In their cuisines, North Africans use every variety of orange and lemon that grows in their region. They preserve lemons in salt for use in salads, tagines, and stuffings and to flavor olives. They steam bitter and sweet orange flowers to make aromatic waters for flavoring sweets, meat dishes, and couscous. They crush bitter oranges to use as an acidic brine for olives; crush sweet lemons with sugar to make a refreshing lemonade; and, in season, add a bitter orange flower to their favorite mint tea.

Preserved lemons are an indispensable ingredient in North African food, raising fish, poultry, fruits, and vegetables up a notch for exciting eating. Although you can find these lemons in specialty food markets, it's very easy to make your own. When you preserve lemons in salt, you can enjoy their tangy zest all year long. They only get better as they mature. The bitterness of the pith changes and mellows, while the flavor acquires a piquancy unlike any other condiment I know.

In Morocco, many types of lemons are put up in salt. Some are used in cooking while others are best in salads. The mildly aromatic, thick-skinned *limun buserra,* a shiny lemon with a nipple at each end, is similar to our California Eureka lemon. Every winter, I put up a batch of Eurekas in coarse salt to be used in cooking. They take about a month to ripen and soften.

The fragrant, thin-skinned *lim doqq,* the crème de la crème of Moroccan lemons, is similar to the American hybrid Meyer lemon in appearance but not in flavor. Both are small lemons with a greenish yellow pulp, very juicy and aromatic. Preserved Meyer lemons can be used to flavor olives, salads, and vegetables in brine.

In Fez, there is yet another sweet lemon, called *lim lamsayyar.* It, too, is thin-skinned and small with a sweet flavor. Fassis (citizens of Fez) consider it the finest lemon in Morocco to preserve. It is also known as *lime,* Mediterranean sweet lemon, and *limetta.* If you visit Fez, you can buy this lemon already preserved in salt in jars.

When using preserved lemons, please follow these rules: Always rinse the lemons before using to remove any excess salt and use sparingly in cooking—the flavor of preserved lemons is very intense, and a little goes a long way.

Salt-Cured Green Olives

*P*ick only those that are unblemished and firm. You will need a 2-gallon crock.

5 pounds firm green or purple olives

Sea salt

1 egg

Pinches of thyme, oregano, and savory

1. Pick over the olives and remove any that are heavily bruised.

2. If the olives are green, place a handful on a clean kitchen towel, fold to cover, and gently tap each olive with a rolling pin, pestle, or smooth stone. (The cloth will absorb the olive juices and soften the impact from the cracking.)

3. If the olives are tan to purple or green to purple, place a handful of olives on a clean kitchen towel and slit each one on one side with a small sharp knife.

4. Place the cracked or slit olives in a large plastic bucket or a deep earthenware crock and cover completely with cold water and a loose-fitting lid. Store in a dark cool place and change the water twice a day until the olives no longer taste bitter, about 1 week. (Bitterness varies with the variety and ripeness of the olive.) Use a wooden spoon to remove an olive for testing. Discard any mushy olives.

5. When the olives no longer taste bitter, make a saltwater brine. It should be strong enough to float an egg: mix 3 quarts water with ¾ cup sea salt. Wash and dry an egg. Place it in the solution. It should just float—that is, a small part of the egg's surface about the size of a half dollar should rise above the liquid. If the egg doesn't float, add more salt.

6. Rinse the olives in a colander under cool running water, drain, and slip into the prepared brine. Place a clean cloth over the brine and olives. Cover with a lid and store in a cool dark place for 6 months. If scum appears, remove and discard. The olives are now ready to eat.

7. If you wish to keep the olives longer, drain them. Repeat with a fresh salty mixture and keep for up to another 6 months. About 3 to 4 days before serving, remove the amount of olives you wish to use. Place in a clean bowl, cover with fresh water, and soak for 1 day, changing the water 2 or 3 times. Season the olives with dried herbs or the quince dressing (page 306) and store in the refrigerator for up to 2 days. Serve at room temperature.

Brine-Cured Green Olives with Quince Dressing

*H*ere's an unusual and delicious olive marinade from the Alicante region in Spain. Green olives are flavored with the quince paste called *membrillo,* along with a local, pungent, dried herb called *pebrella* and some cut-up lemon pulp. The result: a perfect balance between sweet and herbal.

Wild pebrella *(Thymus pebrella)* is the herb of choice. As it is now a protected species in southern Spain, I use the "politically correct" grown-under-glass pebrella imported by The Spanish Table (see Mail Order Sources). You may, of course, substitute a pungent mixture of dried savory, thyme, and oregano.

SERVES 6

2 tablespoons quince paste (Spanish mem-
     brillo)

½ large lemon, diced

Pinches of pebrella, or substitute a mixture of
     thyme, oregano, and savory

¼ cup fruity extra virgin olive oil

2 cups green olives (about ¾ pound),
     preferably brine-cured or Salt-Cured
     Green Olives (page 305)

1. In a small saucepan, melt the quince paste in 1½ cups water over low heat, stirring to dissolve. Remove from the heat and let cool. Add the lemon, a few pinches of pebrella, and the olive oil. Set the quince dressing aside.

2. Rinse the olives and drain. If the olives have not been cracked or slit, use a thin-bladed knife to make a cut on one side of each olive. This will help them to absorb the marinade.

3. Pack the olives into a ¾-quart jar. Pour the cooled quince dressing over them, cover, and leave the olives to marinate in a cool dark place *at least* 2 days and up to 4 days before serving. Drain and serve with a fresh sprinkling of pebrella and olive oil.

OLIVES

In the Middle East there is a saying: "Wheat and oil are pillars of the house, and olives are the Sultan of the table." Olives were served in almost every Mediterranean home I have ever visited. In some countries, they are served for breakfast, in others just before the main meal, and sometimes both.

Olives end up black, pink-purple, or green, depending on when they are picked. They are manipulated by various methods of curing, then preserved in oil or in vinegar, or salt brine, or simply dried. Type, texture, seasoning, and degree of oiliness give each type of olive its distinct taste. Olives can be bitter, pungent, juicy, meaty, or tangy. The texture of a good olive should be firm, not pulpy or mushy, and its flavor should not be overwhelmed by brine or curing. It should be neither too salty nor too bitter. Above all, it should capture and impart the great fresh aroma of its tree. And it is best when seasoned.

The earliest written recipes for seasoning olives date back to the first century. Olives were crushed; heavily seasoned with minced leeks, pungent rue, young celery, and mint; and sweetened with honey to counter any bitterness.

There are ancient Roman recipes in which green olives are flavored with wild fennel and a particular variety of fragrant, thin-skinned lemon. Fruits are used to flavor olives: thin and thick-skinned sweet or bitter oranges; thin- and thick-skinned lemons, fresh or preserved; and even the tart quince after it is cooked down to a paste called *membrillo* (see Mail Order Sources).

You don't have to do much to a shriveled sun-dried black olive—its flavor has already been concentrated. Still, Greeks often season their crinkly black Thasos olives with garlic, oregano, and lemon, and Turks do the same with their delicious *gemliks*.

A rustic and glamorous olive presentation is the much photographed pile of black North African olives, topped with a vivid red pepper sauce. You can make this sauce, Tunisia's famous explosively hot harissa, following the directions on page 309, or you can use spoonfuls of commercial *sambal oelek* from Indonesia, or Turkish red pepper paste (see Mail Order Sources).

Castagna's Marinated Olives

Chef Kevin Gibson, at the Restaurant Castagna in Portland, Oregon, is working with Mediterranean recipes in wondrous and creative ways, as in this delicious and interesting mixed olive marinade.

It's difficult to obtain perfect culinary pitch when marinating mixed olives. Kevin's recipe is as good as any I've encountered. He mixes earthy French picholines and crunchy Spanish manzanillas in a toasted, spiced, and "seedy" dressing that reflects Mediterranean seasoning at its best.

SERVES 10

1½ cups manzanilla olives

1½ cups picholine olives

¾ teaspoon coriander seed

¾ teaspoon cumin seed

¾ teaspoon fennel seed, plus ½ teaspoon whole toasted fennel seeds

2 bay leaves

¾ teaspoon crushed hot red pepper

¼ teaspoon freshly ground black pepper

2 sprigs of thyme

Zest of ½ orange

Zest of ½ lemon

Extra virgin olive oil

1. If the olives have been packed in brine, drain, rinse, and drain well. Taste for salt; if necessary, soak in fresh water for 10 minutes and drain. Roll dry in paper towels.

2. Lightly toast the coriander and cumin seeds in a dry skillet. Combine in a blender with the ¾ teaspoon fennel seed and 1 of the bay leaves and grind to a powder.

3. Mix together the hot red pepper, black pepper, thyme, orange, and lemon. Add the olives and stir with a fork to mix. Scrape into a washed and dried clean 1½-quart glass container. Pour in enough olive oil to cover. Let stand for 1 week in a cool place before serving. If desired, garnish with an additional pinch of hot pepper when serving.

Three Tunisian Harissas

*T*unisia is the only Mediterranean country whose hot sauces can be measured on a seismic counter! When the Ottoman Turks returned from the East, they brought back Goan red pepper, which they distributed throughout their empire. From the Balkans to North Africa, wherever pepper seeds grew well, the resulting red pepper powders—both hot and sweet— became famous: the paprika of Hungary; the *bouhka* of northern Greece; the flavorful red pepper of Aleppo in Syria; the Maras of southeastern Turkey; the hot and hotter peppers of Nabeul and Gabes in Tunisia. These Tunisian hot red peppers are not unlike our easily available New Mexican and dried guajillo chile peppers. The chile sauces prepared from Tunisian peppers are important ingredients in Tunisian cuisine, packed and kept under olive oil so as to be always close at hand.

Here are recipes for three excellent Tunisian hot red chile sauces, which can be diluted by the addition of water, olive oil, and a drop of lemon juice.

Harissa # 1

MAKES 2½ TABLESPOONS

1 garlic clove

2 dried New Mexican chiles, stemmed, seeded, and torn into 2-inch pieces, softened in warm water and squeezed dry

1 sun-dried tomato half, softened in warm water and squeezed dry

1 teaspoon salt

½ teaspoon Tunisian *le tabîl* (page 201) or ground coriander

⅛ teaspoon ground caraway

Extra virgin olive oil

Lemon juice, optional

1. In a stone mortar or food processor, combine the garlic, chiles, sun-dried tomato, salt, le tabil or ground coriander, and ground caraway; pulse until pasty. Pulse in the oil by the teaspoon until thick and spreadable.

2. To serve as a dip, thin 2½ tablespoons harissa with warm water and olive oil to a dipping consistency. Correct the seasoning and, if necessary, add a few drops of lemon juice to round out the flavor.

Harissa # 2

More often called *harous,* this harissa is the preferred sauce in Southern Tunisia for soups, couscous, salads, and meat dishes. It is far more complicated to make than the harissa above but is worth the effort as it is more complex in flavor. It will keep under olive oil for a year in the refrigerator.

MAKES ½ CUP

¼ pound juicy onions, peeled and thinly sliced

Pinch of turmeric

2 tablespoons coarse salt

7 dried Nabeul peppers or a mixture of chipotle and New Mexican dried chiles

½ teaspoon *le tabil* (page 201) or ground coriander

½ teaspoon ground caraway

½ teaspoon freshly ground pepper

1 good pinch of ground cinnamon

1 good mixture of ground dried rosebuds, optional

3 tablespoons extra virgin olive oil

1. In a wide shallow bowl, mix the onions, turmeric, and salt. Let stand until soft and very wet, from 1 to 3 days.

2. Place a handful of the onions in cheesecloth and squeeze until very dry. Repeat with the remaining onions.

3. Stem, seed, and break up the dried chile peppers. Carefully toast them in an ungreased skillet over low heat until they give off their aroma. Remove at once to avoid burning. Grind to a powder in a blender or spice mill. Add the spices and the onions, blending well. Pack into a 1-cup dry jar, cover with oil, and tightly close. Keep refrigerated.

Harissa # 3 (Harissa-Harous)

My friend chef Haouari Abderrazak taught me to combine harous and harissa fifty/fifty to make the most magnificent of all Tunisian red pepper sauces. The flavor of harissa-harous is one of the most exciting in the world of red hot pepper sauces, and if you have the temperament to prepare both you will not be disappointed. Use harissa-harous to provide a glowingly delicious, smoky flavor to any savory dish.

CHEESES

Feta and other brine-ripened white cheeses are the cheeses of choice in the Middle East, whether made from buffalo, cow, goat, or sheep's milk. According to the FAO handbook on traditional foods, this cheese is believed to have originated in Egypt 2,400 years ago. Middle Easterners serve brined white cheese with watermelon for breakfast, cream it with olive oil and hot paprika for a dip with pita bread, bake it in a phyllo-type pastry for a *meze,* and crumble it to sprinkle on all sorts of salads. In Turkey it's called *peynir beyaz;* in Egypt, *domiati;* in Jordan, *nabulsi;* and in Greece, feta.

Some fetas have strong flavors that can be adjusted simply by changing the brine. My friend Greek-born Daphne Zepos, a highly knowledgeable cheese expert, suggests: "If it's too salty, store it in plain water; if the salt level is perfect, keep it in the brine it came in; and if you want it creamier, then cut the liquid with 1 to 2 tablespoons of milk per pint of brine. A large chunk of feta kept in brine should last almost a month."

Mozzarella is favored not only by Italians, but also by cooks in southern Turkey and parts of Syria where its oozy, wobbly texture is perfect for filling pastries. To avoid stringiness, freeze mozzarella, grate it, then use right away in pastry.

Ricotta is a soft, rich, and moist by-product of mozzarella. You can now find good sweet, slightly grainy ricotta at most cheese counters. Ricotta is called *lor* in Turkey and *mizithra* in Greece, where it turns up in pastries, casseroles, and stews. In Turkey it's also used in pastries, and even as a binder in vegetable purees in place of yogurt. (See the Roast Eggplant and Walnut Dip on page 22.) On Crete, mizithra or ricotta is baked with squash and tomatoes for a delicious gratin (page 269). I use top-quality ricotta to replace Corsican *brocciu* in the recipe for my cheesecake called *fiadone* (page 292). Though it's easy enough to make your own ricotta, it's widely available and so not necessary. Please remember to drain before using in the recipes in this book.

Try to find a good local source for quality cheese. Most large cities have cheese shops and upscale supermarkets with good cheese departments. An alternative is to order cheeses by mail through the Internet:

American teleme, crescenza, and crème fraîche are available at www.cowgirlcreamery.com and www.mozzco.com (The Mozzarella Company). Spanish manchego, cabarales, Mahon, and Idiazabal are available at www.tablespan.com and www.tienda.com.

Italian Parmigiano-Reggiano, Gorgonzola, Taleggio, pecorino, Fontina from Valle d'Aosta, and Occelli butter from the Piedmont are available at www.esperya.com.

Middle Eastern Spice Mixture

This popular spice blend called *bharat* is used in many Turkish dishes. See the stuffed zucchini on page 262.

MAKES ¼ CUP

1 tablespoon ground allspice

1½ teaspoons freshly ground black pepper

1½ teaspoons ground cinnamon

1½ teaspoons freshly grated nutmeg

1 teaspoon ground coriander

½ teaspoon turmeric

½ teaspoon cardamom seeds

12 whole cloves

½ teaspoon ground ginger

½ teaspoon dried rose blossoms

Whirl all the spices in a grinder to a powder. Pass through a fine sieve and store in a closed jar in a cool cupboard.

Moroccan Mixed Spices

I always smile when I think of the variety of spice mixtures a Moroccan cook has at her disposal—more than in any other Mediterranean country. This particular blend is used for lentils, beans, and potatoes in the city of Tangier.

MAKES 3½ TABLESPOONS

2 teaspoons sweet paprika

2 teaspoons ground cumin

2 teaspoons freshly ground pepper

½ teaspoon ground ginger

¼ teaspoon ground turmeric

½ teaspoon ground cinnamon

¼ teaspoon cayenne

Mix well. Store in a tightly closed jar.

Quick Duck and Pork Confit

Duck and pork can cook together in duck fat. They will each enhance the flavor of the other. Begin this recipe two days or up to a week before you want to use the confit.

SERVES 12

6 fatty duck legs (about 1 pound)

2 pounds boneless pork shoulder or butt

⅓ cup coarse salt

2 tablespoons lightly crushed juniper berries

2 tablespoons lightly cracked black peppercorns

2 teaspoons lightly cracked coriander seeds

2 tablespoons coarsely chopped garlic

2 imported bay leaves

¼ cup chopped fresh thyme leaves

¼ cup chopped flat-leaf parsley

⅜ teaspoon freshly grated nutmeg

1 whole clove, slightly crushed

1. Trim off and reserve as much duck fat as you can but leave as much skin intact as possible. Render the duck fat; cool, cover, and refrigerate. Cut the pork into 6 equal portions.

2. Make a dry marinade by mixing together all the remaining ingredients. Rub the duck and pork with the dry marinade. Place them in a glass, earthenware, or glazed dish, cover, and refrigerate for 24 hours.

3. The following day, wipe away all the marinade and exuded juices. Place the pork pieces and duck legs in a deep baking dish; add the rendered duck fat. (The fat should almost cover the meat.) Place the dish in a cold oven; turn the heat to 275°F and leave the duck and pork to cook about 3 hours, or until the pieces are very tender. Remove from the oven and allow the duck and pork to cool in the fat.

4. Transfer the duck and pork to a deep container. Ladle fat over the pieces to cover. When cold, cover with plastic wrap and refrigerate. (The confit keeps for up to 6 days, submerged in its cooking fat in the refrigerator. Scrape off all fat before using.)

Notes: Fatty duck legs can be ordered through your butcher or by mail.

Quality rendered duck or goose fat can be purchased in many German and Hungarian butcher shops during the winter months. You can purchase it in cans or packets through mail order.

You can freeze any unused pieces of fresh duck fat and skin whenever you cook a duck, and then, when you have accumulated several cups' worth, render the fat and use as directed. Avoid using poultry or pork fat that has reached its smoke point or burned (e.g., drippings gathered from a roasting duck). If you do not have enough fat, the duck and pork can be cooked in batches. Fat used to make confit can be used again. Keep the fat refrigerated for up to 3 months or freeze.

Moroccan Preserved Meat

Known as *khelea,* this Moroccan preserved meat is a lovingly produced, hand-crafted, slow-motion product of the North African kitchen and can be made with either lamb or beef. It is used to flavor stews, lentils, beans, couscous, soups, and even scrambled eggs. Moroccans also add it to their famous onion-spice jam confection, *mezgueldi,* which is served on top of couscous, or as a substitute for meat in Swiss Chard with Lentils and Preserved Spiced Meat (page 250).

The cook carefully salts chunks of meat to add flavor and extract moisture, seasons the meat with various spices and herbs, then allows it to dry on the bone. (In Morocco, I have actually seen meat hanging on a clothesline to dry!) After drying, the meat is simmered in olive oil, then packed in crocks with oil and lamb or beef fat to cover, much like French confit. To serve khelea, remove from the oil and soak in water to remove salt and restore softness. Use as directed in the recipe.

To make this recipe, you will need a 3-cup sterile and dry Mason jar, enough to hold 20 meat strips.

$1\frac{1}{4}$ pounds boneless lamb shoulder or beef, cut into 1 long slice $\frac{1}{2}$ inch thick, or 2 smaller slices of the same thickness

3 tablespoons coarse sea salt

1 small head of garlic, crushed

$1\frac{1}{2}$ teaspoons crushed hot red pepper

$1\frac{1}{2}$ teaspoons ground coriander

1 teaspoon ground cumin

$\frac{1}{2}$ teaspoon cider vinegar

Extra virgin olive oil

2 tablespoons chopped hard meat fat, preferably trimmed from lamb kidneys, optional (but necessary if you intend to store the meat for more than a few weeks)

1. Divide the meat into 20 strips, each about 3- by 1- by ½-inch. Combine the salt and garlic and rub into the meat. Stack in a bowl, cover, and refrigerate overnight.

2. The following day, preheat the oven to 175°F. Dry the meat with paper towels. Combine the spices and vinegar; rub into the meat and set out on a wire rack over a baking sheet to catch the drip. Cook the strips in the oven until dry but still supple, 4 to 8 hours, depending on the density of the flesh.

3. In a large skillet, heat 3 to 4 tablespoons olive oil and the meat fat, if using. When hot, add the meat and fry until crisp on all sides, about 3 minutes. Remove the skillet from the heat and allow the fat and meat to cool to room temperature. Have ready a sterile, dry jar. Place the meat and strained frying fat into the jar; top with plenty of fresh oil and store in the refrigerator.

Quince-Flavored Tarhana

Turkish *tarhana* is one of the oldest forms of preserved wheat and dairy food in the eastern Mediterranean, and it hasn't evolved much over the centuries. Its gentle, sour flavor comes from yogurt, soured milk, or yeast. The one I offer here, made with a combination of yogurt, semolina flour, and quince has a unique flavor and complex aroma and is a personal favorite from the Black Sea town of Amasra. It is used to flavor vegetable dishes such as Eggplant Sautéed with Zucchini and Quince Tarhana (page 246) and Quince-Flavored Tarhana Soup (page 92).

To make this quince-flavored tarhana, onion, tomatoes, and fresh red pepper are pureed in a food processor, then blended with baked quince, yogurt, salt, and dill. The mixture is left to lightly ferment for three days. A mixture of flour and semolina, fenugreek, and salt is worked in to make a firm dough. The mixture is dumped into a cloth bag and left to drain. The hard dough is formed into flat small balls and left to dry in the sun. (I use a home dehydrator, but you can use a slow oven to dry them completely.) The dried pieces are then crushed to a coarse powder. If well dried, the tarhana will keep up to two years.

This is a "commitment recipe," but well worth the trouble. It takes about a week to make, but less than twenty minutes of actual hard work. Here is the recipe in the style of the town of Amasra.

MAKES ABOUT 4 CUPS

1 medium quince

1 large red bell pepper

2 large plum tomatoes, grated (see page 259)

1 small onion, grated

8 ounces plain yogurt, drained (1 cup)

Handful of dill sprigs

¼ teaspoon active dry yeast, optional

1 cup pasta (semolina) flour

1½ teaspoons fine sea salt

1 teaspoon ground fenugreek

1 pound bread flour

1. Preheat the oven to 350°F. In a heatproof glass dish, bake the quince and bell pepper for 1 hour. When cool enough to handle, discard the skin, seeds, and core.

2. With a potato masher, crush the quince and pepper into a puree and scrape into a large bowl. Add the tomatoes, onion, and yogurt and mix well. Wrap the sprigs of dill in cheesecloth and push them into the center of the mixture. Cover the bowl and let stand at room temperature for 3 days, or until the surface is bubbling and there is a nice clean but sour aroma. Discard the dill. (If fermentation does not occur, dissolve the yeast in 2 tablespoons warm water, stir into the mixture, and let stand until bubbly.)

3. Add the pasta flour, salt, fenugreek, and enough bread flour to make a medium-soft dough. Knead until smooth. (You can do this in a food processor, processing for about 35 seconds.) Set the dough aside, loosely covered with a cloth, for 1 more day.

4. The following day, place heaping spoonfuls of the mixture on a baking sheet lined with parchment paper. Flatten each dollop to ⅛ inch thick. Place in a dehydrator heated to 145°F and dry for 30 minutes, then reduce the temperature to 105°F and leave until bone dry on both sides, 2 to 3 days, turning the pieces from time to time. The tarhana is ready when each piece is as hard as a walnut. (Alternatively, you can dry the pieces in a 150°F oven for 24 hours.) Crush the tarhana to a coarse powder in a food processor, then press through a coarse sieve. Store in a jar in a dry, dark cool place.

With thanks to Maviye Kayakiran of Amasra, Turkey, for sharing this recipe.

APPENDICES

MAIL ORDER SOURCES FOR SPECIALTY INGREDIENTS

Ingredients

Aleppo pepper: Adriana's Caravan; Kalustyan's; Zingerman's

Almonds, fuzzy green: Big Valley Farms

Almonds, marcona: The Spanish Table

Anchovies from Spain: Rogers International; The Spanish Table; Tienda

Apricots, dried: Adriana's Caravan; Kalustyan's; Turkish Taste

Argan oil: Berber Sources, Exotica Oils

Barley grits: Guisto's Flour Mills

Basturma: Haig's Delicacies; Kalustyan's

Borage plants, live: Richter's; Well-Sweep Herb Farm

Borage stems in a jar: The Spanish Table

Bottarga di Muggine (cake): Manicaretti-Market Hall Foods (The Pasta Shop); Corti Brothers

Bulgur: Kalustyan's

Capers in sea salt: Adriana's Caravan; Balducci's; Corti Brothers; Manicaretti-Market Hall Foods (The Pasta Shop); Zingerman's

Chestnuts, roasted and vacuum packed: Williams-Sonoma; Zingerman's

Chickpeas, toasted and unsalted: Kalustyan's

Chile peppers (dried anchos, guajillos, etc.): Kalustyan's; Mo Hotta Mo Betta

Couscous, fine grain: Kalustyan's

Ducks, duck fat, and game birds: D'Artagnan

Fava beans (large dried): Kalustyan's

Fig leaves; Lone Star Organics

Flour, durum and fine semolina: King Arthur Flour; Kalustyan's; Todaro Bros.

Flour, Italian-style: King Arthur Flour

Green walnut preserves: Haig's Delicacies; Kalustyan's

Honey, chestnut, acacia: Zingerman's

Ham, serrano: The Spanish Table; Tienda

Ham, Bayonne: D'Artagnan

Lentils

    Umbrian lentils: Esperya USA

    Pardina lentils: The Spanish Table

Mastic: Kalustyan's

Membrillo (quince paste): Adriana's Caravan; Tienda; The Spanish Table

Mint leaves (dried): Haig's Delicacies; Kalustyan's, The Spice House; Turkish Taste

Olive oils

ITALIAN top-quality extra virgin olive oils, such as Capezzana: Formaggio Kitchen; Corti Brothers; Zingerman's; Manicaretti/Market Food Hall; Esperya USA; Rogers International

SPANISH top-quality extra virgin olive oils, such as Nunez de Prado: The Spanish Table; Tienda; Rogers International

TUNISIAN top-quality extra virgin olive oils, such as Majoub Moulins: Rogers International; Strictly Olive Oil

FRENCH top-quality extra virgin olive oils, such as *Les Moulins Dorés*: Zabar's; Zingerman's

GREEK top-quality extra virgin olive oils, such as Morea: Strictly Olive Oil

WORLDWIDE: Strictly Olive Oil

MILD top-quality extra virgin olive oils, such as *La Bella Dolci Moliture*: Strictly Olive Oil

Olives, picholines, lucques, niçoise: Adriana's Caravan; Formaggio Kitchen; Zingerman's

Orange flower water: Berber Sources; Haig's Delicacies; Kalustyan's; The Spice House

Paprika and pepper sauces

Moroccan *felfla hloua* for *m'hammer*: Berber Sources

Pepper paste, Turkish sweet and hot: Adriana's Caravan; Haig's Delicacies; Kalustyan's

Pepper sauce from Indonesia *(sambal oelek)*: Haig's Delicacies; Kalustyan's

Peppers, piquillos: The Spanish Table; Tienda; Zingerman's

Piment d'Espelette: Corti Brothers; The Spanish Table

Pimentón de la Vera (smoky paprika): The Spanish Table; Tienda; The Spice House

Turkish red pepper flakes (Maras): Formaggio Kitchen; Turkish Taste; Zingerman's

Pebrella (Spanish wild thyme): The Spanish Table

Pomegranate concentrate (pomegranate molasses): Haig's Delicacies; Kalustyan's; Turkish Taste

Porcini, dried: Plantin America

Rice, Spanish bomba: The Spanish Table; Tienda

Rosebuds, dried for cooking: Kalustyan's

Rose water: Kalustyan's; Turkish Taste

Saba: Corti Brothers; Esperya USA; Mani-caretti/Market Hall Foods; Zingerman's

Sausage, black morcilla (blood sausage) and semi-cured chorizo: The Spanish Table; Tienda

Semolina, coarse: Kalustyan's; Todaro Bros.

Spices and sea salts: Formaggio Kitchen; Kalustyan's; The Spice House

Turkish bay leaves: Kalustyan's; The Spice House; Turkish Taste

Truffle oil: Plantin America; Strictly Olive Oil; Zingerman's

Verjus: Fusion Foods

Vinegar

Spanish aged sherry vinegar: (*Gran Capirete* sherry vinegar): The Spanish Table

Spanish wine vinegar (*Toro Albala Reserva*): The Spanish Table

French Banyuls: Zingerman's

Italian balsamic: Roger's International; Formaggio Kitchen; Zingerman's

Italian Lucini's Pinot Grigio white wine vinegar: for nearest grocery: 1-885 LUCINI

Walnut oil: Williams-Sonoma; Zingerman's

Mail Order Sources

Adriana's Caravan
321 Grand Central Terminal
New York, NY 10017
212-972-8804
www.adrianascaravan.com

Berber Sources
247 Valley Road, Suite 111
Ithaca, NY 14850
607-273-0002
www.berbersources.com
info@berbersources.com

Big Valley Farms
4888 Faith Home Road
Ceres, CA 95307
www.goodnut.com

Bridge Kitchenware
(Cannele Silicon Flex molds)
214 East 52nd Street
New York, NY 10022
212-688-4220
www.bridgekitchenware.com

Corti Brothers
5810 Folsom Boulevard
P.O. Box 191358
Sacramento, CA 95819

D'Artagnan
280 Wilson Avenue
Newark, NJ 07105
800-327-8246
www.dartagnan.com
info@dartagnan.com

Esperya USA
1715 West Farms Road
Bronx, NY 10460
718-860-2949
ww.esperya.com

Exotica Oils
Kimberly Ouhirra
727-786-6213
www.exoticaoils.com
kouhirra@exoticaoils.com

Formaggio Kitchen
244 Huron Avenue
Cambridge, MA 02138
888-212-3224
www.formaggiokitchen.com

Fusion Foods:
Napa Valley Verjus
If a specialty foods store
in your area doesn't carry it,
call 707-963-0206 to order by mail.

Guisto's Flour Mills
344 Littlefield Avenue
South San Francisco, CA 99080
650-873-6566

Haig's Delicacies
642 Clement Street
San Francisco, CA 94118
415-752-6283
www.haigsdelicacies.com
rita@haigsdelicacies.com

Kalustyan's
123 Lexington Avenue
New York, NY 10016
212-685-3451
www.kalustyans.com

King Arthur Flour
Box 876
Norwich, VT 05055-0876
800-827-6836
www.kingarthurflour.com

Lodge Manufacturing Company
(Cast-iron skillets and pots)
P.O. Box 380
South Pittsburg, TN 37380
www.lodgemfg.com

Lone Star Organics
367 Spain Street East
Sonoma, CA 95476

Manicaretti/Market Hall Foods
(The Pasta Shop)
Rockridge Market Hall
5655 College Avenue
Oakland, CA 94618

Mo Hotta Mo Betta
P.O. Box 4136
San Luis Obispo, CA 93403
800-462-3220
www.mohotta.com

The Oriental Pantry
(Peking Pan for cooking polenta
and Chinese sand pots)
423 Great Road
Acton, MA 01720
800-828-0368
www.orientalpantry.com

Pacific Rim Gourmet
(Chinese sand pots)
I-clipse, Inc.
4905 Morena Boulevard, Suite 1313
San Diego, CA 92117
800-910-WOKS
www.pacificrim-gourmet.com

Plantin America, Inc.
518 Gregory Avenue, Suite B208
Weehawken, NJ 07087
201-867-4590
www.plantin.com

Richter's Herbs
Goodwood, Ontario, Canada
905-640-6677
www.richters.com

Rival
The Holmes Group
(Crock-Pots and electric skillet
slow-cookers)
32-B Spur Drive
El Paso, TX 79906
800-557-4825
www.rivalproducts.com

Rogers International Ltd.
58 Fore Street
Portland, ME 04101
207-828-2000
www.rogersintl.com

The Spanish Table
1427 Western Avenue
Seattle, WA 98101
202-682-2827
www.tablespan.com

The Spice House
1941 Central Street
Evanston, IL 60201
847-328-3711
www.thespicehouse.com

Strictly Olive Oil
Betty Pustarfi
831-372-6682
strictlybetty@aol.com

Sur La Table
1765 Sixth Avenue South
Seattle, WA 98134-1608
866-328-5412
www.surlatable.com

Tagines.com by Berber Trading Co.
9467 Main Street, Suite 120
Woodstock, GA 30188
877-277-7227
www.tagines.com
custcare@tagines.com

Tienda
4514 John Tyler Highway
Williamsburg, VA 23188
757-220-1143
www.tienda.com

Todaro Bros. Specialty Foods
Web Department
555 Second Avenue
New York, NY 10016
877-472-2767
eat@todarobros.com

Turkish Taste
31 Downs Avenue
Greenland, NH 03840
603-661-5460
www.turkishtaste.com

Well-Sweep Herb Farm
205 Mount Bethel Road
Port Murray, NJ 07865
908-852-5390
www.wellsweep.com

Zabar's
2245 Broadway (at 80th St.)
New York, NY 10024
212-787-2000
www.zabars.com
info@zabars.com

Zingerman's
422 Detroit Street
Ann Arbor, MI 48194
www.zingermans.com

EQUIPMENT

I wasn't born a pots and pans junkie, I became one—which isn't hard if you love to cook and try out new recipes. For slow-cooking, some pots are better than others. So the question is: How to choose?

The phrase "you get what you pay for" is generally true in regard to pots and pans. Much modern cooking gear will give you long durability and steady, even cooking. There are wonderful pots and pans constructed of assorted alloys such as stainless steel, aluminum, and copper bonded in sheets, then shaped, and covered in anodized or copper exteriors. There are great pans slicked with nonstick coatings. Sides are flared, sloped, or turned inward. All are easy to clean.

Of course you can cook all the dishes in this book with any good pot or pan so long as it's the right size and hefty enough to hold and distribute slow even heat. But since my recipes are rooted in the Mediterranean, where iron and clay pots have traditionally been preferred, I generally go that route, using shallow cazuelas, clay pots, tagines, and, one of my favorites, a *fait tout* made of a type of clay found only in the French region of Burgundy.

When I try to explain why food tastes better when cooked in clay or seasoned iron, I fall back on the word *coddling*. These pots, in effect, coddle the food as if wrapping it in a warm blanket, then slowly bring out unctuous tenderness and a particular taste and aroma that food writers like to call *"gout de terroir."*

I also do a lot of my slow-cooking in electric slow-cookers and in a five-quart skillet slow-cooker fitted with a removable stoneware crock. The latter is especially useful as a substitute for a tagine. Electric appliances don't create the same sense of personal bonding as do clay or iron, but the food itself doesn't seem to suffer.

Asian clay pots, clay roasters, cazuelas, and tagines are now readily available. Though fragile (a hot pot can break if you put it on a cold surface or over high heat without a flame-tamer), they are relatively inexpensive. (To test ceramic pots for any lead escaping from the glaze, you can buy Lead Check from www.doitbest.com.) Cast-iron pots are also inexpensive, and the more you use them the better they get. You need to season them (see below), but if cared for they will serve you for decades. On the other hand, I know many housewives in the Middle East who prepare stews and soups during the week in that champion of "faux slow," the pressure cooker. But on weekends, to show love and give pleasure to their family, they switch right back to glazed cookware, convinced that food cooked in it tastes better.

Recently I purchased a HearthKit, a chamber much like a beehive oven that fits right into your oven. It is made of earthen materials and has great conductive properties. It is fantastic for baking bread, roasting chicken, and baking gratins and casseroles. You can buy the Emile Henry *fatt tout* at Sur La Table; earthen cazuelas at The Spanish Table; authentic Moroccan tagines at Tagines.com; Chinese sand pots at The Oriental Pantry; an electric skillet slow-cooker at Rival; the HearthKit Insert at Sur La Table (see Mail Order Sources).

Seasoning a Black Iron Pot

I love my heavy black pots from Lodge. Though very heavy, they control the heat perfectly. To season a cast-iron skillet or pot such as one from Lodge: wash, dry, and rub with oil; set in a cold oven; heat to 350°F and let the pot or skillet bake for 2 hours. Turn off the heat and leave to cool in the oven.

Lodge black pots are available for sale in many housewares stores, or through their website: www.lodgemfg.com.

Curing a Clay Pot such as a Cazuela or Tagine

Clay pots are fragile—they inevitably do break—but proper curing will harden them to the point that they can be used with a flame-tamer over direct heat.

Soak the entire dish in water to cover for 12 hours. Drain and wipe dry. Rub the unglazed bottom with a cut clove of garlic. Fill the dish with water to ½ inch below the rim, then add ½ cup of vinegar. Place the dish on a flame-tamer over low heat and slowly bring the water to a boil. Let the liquid boil down until only about ½ cup remains. Cool slowly and wash. Your pan is ready for use—the garlic has created a seal.

Alternatively, after soaking, rub the inside of the base and lid with olive oil and put into a preheated 300°F oven for 1½ hours. Turn off the heat and let cool. Either method will strengthen your tagine or cazuela.

To clean, soak in sudsy water and scrub with a soft brush to remove any hardened food.

Curing an Asian Clay Pot or Chinese Sand Pot

I like to cook beans in a clay pot. I have an assortment purchased at Asian markets. Soak your pot overnight in cool water, then use it in the oven or on top of the stove with a flame-tamer beneath. Repeat only if you haven't used your pot in a long time.

BIBLIOGRAPHY

Aidells, Bruce, and Denis Kelly. *The Complete Meat Cookbook.* New York: Houghton Mifflin, 1998.

Al-Jabri, Lamya. *Shahiyaya Tayyiba* (Delicious Good-Tasting), in Arabic. Damascus: Tlas, n.d.

Alexander, Stephanie. *Cooking and Traveling in South West France.* Victoria, Australia: Viking, 2002.

Aris, Pepita. *The Spanishwoman's Kitchen.* United Kingdom: Seven Dials, 1999.

Barham, Peter. "Kitchen Cornucopia," Radio 4, transcript. London: BBC, 5 August, 2001.

Beers, Maggie. *Maggie's Farm.* Sydney, Australia: Allen & Unwin, 1993.

Bellakhdar, Jamal. *La pharmocopée Marocaine traditionnelle: Médicine Arabe ancienne et savoirs populaires.* Paris: Ibis Press, 1997.

Bittman, Mark. "Poached, Not Parched." *New York Times,* 17 October, 2001.

Blumenthal, Heston. "Sunday Best." *Guardian Unlimited* (London), 9 February, 2002.

Chiche-Yana, Martine. *La table Juive recettes et traditions de fêtes.* Aix en Provence: Self published, 1992.

Cholagh, Samira Yako. *Treasured Middle Eastern Cookbook.* Saline, Michigan: Self published, 1998.

Claiborne, Craig, and Pierre Franey. *Cooking with Craig Claiborne and Pierre Franey.* New York: Times Books, 1983.

Combret, Henri. *Saveurs et traditions gourmandes.* Biarritz: Atlantica, 1998.

Corriher, Shirley O. *CookWise: The Hows and Whys of Successful Cooking with Nearly 150 Great-Tasting Recipes.* New York: William Morrow, 1997.

Davidson, Alan. *The Oxford Companion to Food.* Oxford: Oxford University Press, 1999.

Davis, Adelle. *Let's Cook It Right.* New York: Harcourt Brace Jovanovich, 1970.

Durack, Terry. "Eating Out: Your Starter for 10 at Mezedopolios." *Independent on Sunday* (London), 18 November, 2001.

Fabricant, Florence. "Tenderizing Octopus." *Nation's Restaurant News,* 17 July, 2000.

Fletcher, Janet. "Ready for Brine Time." *San Francisco Chronicle,* 25 March, 1998.

Food and Agricultural Organization of the United Nations. *Traditional Foods in the Near East.* Rome, 1991.

Gedda, Guy. *La table d'un Provençal.* Paris: Editions Roland Escaig, 1987.

Gray, Patience. *Honey from a Weed.* New York: Harper & Row, 1985.

Grigson, Jane. *Jane Grigson's Fruit Book.* London: Michael Joseph, 1982.

Hamlin, Suzanne, and Fran McCullough. *The Best American Recipes 2000.* New York: Houghton Mifflin, 2000.

Hodgson, Moira. "Cruising the Tribeca Riviera for Purely Shellfish Reasons." *The New York Observer,* 25 June, 2001.

Jenkins, Nancy Harmon. *Flavors of Puglia.* New York: Broadway Books, 1997.

Judd, Terri. "Celebrity Chefs." *London Independent,* 14 December, 2001.

Keller, Thomas. "Marinating." *Los Angeles Times,* 3 May, 2000.

Kimball, Christopher. *The Cook's Bible.* Boston: Little, Brown, 1996.

———. "Roasting Chicken 14 Ways." *Cook's Illustrated,* January/February 1996.

Kochilis, Diane. *The Glorious Foods of Greece.* New York: HarperCollins, 2001.

Kremezi, Aglaia. *The Foods of the Greeks Islands.* New York: Houghton Mifflin, 2000.

Kummer, Corby. "Tuscan Tomatoes." *The Atlantic Monthly,* September 1998.

Kurti, Nicholas, and Giana Kurti. *But the Crackling Is Superb.* Bristol and Philadelphia: Institute of Physics Publishing, 1988.

Lalli, Carole. *Yesterday's Bread.* New York: HarperCollins, 1999.

La Mazille. *La bonne cuisine du Périgord.* Paris: Flammarion, 1929.

Loubat, Bernard, and Jeannette Bertrandy. *La bonne cuisine provençale.* Paris: Solar, 1994.

Malaurie, Jean-Paul. *Ma cuisine des quatre saisons en Périgord.* Perigueux: Editions Fanlac, 1998.

Malouf, Greg, and Lucy Malouf. *Moorish Flavours from Mecca to Marrakech.* South Yarra: Hardie Grant Books, 2001.

March, Lourdes, and Alicia Rios. *El Libro del Aceite y la Aceituna.* Madrid: Alianza Editorial, 1989.

McGee, Harold. *On Food and Cooking: The Science and Lore of the Kitchen.* New York: Charles Scribner's Sons, 1984.

Music Dance Group of Paros. *Delicacies of Paros.* Naoussa, n.d.

Olney, Richard. *Simple French Food.* New York: Atheneum, 1974.

Parsons, Russ. "For the Love of Lamb." *Los Angeles Times,* 28 March, 1999.

———. *How to Read a French Fry*. New York: Houghton Mifflin, 2001.

Perry, Charles. "Crazy for Milk Scum." *Los Angeles Times,* 7 July, 1999.

———. "Coddled Pie." *Los Angeles Times,* 12 July, 2000.

Peterson, Joan, and David Peterson. *Eat Smart in Turkey*. Madison, Wisc.: Ginkgo Press, 1996.

Pezzini, Wilma. *The Tuscan Cookbook*. New York: Atheneum, 1982.

Plotkin, Fred. *Recipes from Paradise*. New York: Little, Brown, 1997.

Robuchon, Joel. *Cuisinez comme un grand chef,* vol. 3. Paris: TF1 Editions, 1999.

Roden, Claudia. *The Book of Jewish Food*. New York: Alfred A. Knopf, 1996.

Rubel, William. *The Magic of Fire*. San Francisco: Ten Speed Press, 2002.

Santich, Barbara. *The Original Mediterranean Cuisine*. Chicago: Chicago Review Press, 1996.

Scrambling, Regina. "When the Path to Serenity Wends Past the Stove." *New York Times,* 19 September, 2001.

Sherman, Chris."The Ancient Taste of Morocco." *St. Petersburg Times,* 17 April, 2002.

Sherman, Paul W. "Darwinian Gastronomy: Why We Use Spices." *BioScience,* June 1999.

Slater, Nigel. "Hot Off a Street Vendor's Brazier." *The Observer* (London), 14 November, 1999.

Sonrel, Andree. *Cuisinez mieux*. Paris: Edition Pierre Roger, 1935.

Toussant-Samat, Maguelonne. Translated by Anthea Bell. *History of Food*. Cambridge, Mass.: Blackwell, 1992.

Unsal, Ayfer. *Gaziantep Yemekeri Yeme Içme*. Istanbul: Ilctisim, 2002.

Van Over, Charles. *The Best Bread Ever*. New York: Broadway Books, 1997.

Willinger, Faith. *Red, White and Greens: The Way Italians Eat with Vegetables*. New York: Harper-Collins, 1996.

Wolfert, Paula. *Couscous and Other Good Food from Morocco*. New York: Harper & Row, 1973.

———. *Paula Wolfert's World of Food*. New York: Harper & Row, 1988.

Yee, Laura. "Days of Simmer." *Restaurants & Institutions,* 1 September, 1999.

Zana-Murat, Andree. *De mère en fille la cuisine Juive Tunisienne*. Paris: Albin Michel, 1998.

Zepos, Daphne. "Tangy Feta Cheese Is Suprisingly Versatile." *Fine Cooking,* August/September 2001.

INDEX

Index